Corporate Risk Management after the COVID-19 Crisis

Transformations in Banking, Finance and Regulation

Print ISSN: 2752-5821
Online ISSN: 2752-583X

Presently, the banking and finance sectors evolve within a globalized and highly uncertain environment. Each business and financial decision requires careful consideration of country-specific and international factors due to high levels of shock transmission and volatility spillovers. Furthermore, it would be remiss to omit the COVID-19 health crisis, which caused harmful effects to all areas of the real economy and made profound changes in the way our firms, economies, and markets used to function.

Many other already well-known aspects, including the repercussions of quantitative easing policies, disruptive technologies in finance (e.g., FinTech, Big Data, Data Analytics, Artificial Intelligence, and Blockchains), as well as innovative financing instruments for startups (e.g., ICOs and crowdfunding) are currently revolutionizing banking and finance and posing numerous challenges to regulatory bodies and policymakers. Climate change emergencies also put pressure on governments and firms worldwide to improve policy on governance, corporate social responsibility, and sustainability practices.

This book series "Transformations in Banking, Finance and Regulation" attempts to address these issues by focusing on transformative perspectives in banking and finance. Accordingly, it provides evidence-based guidance, recommendations, and pathways to assist businesses and policy decision-makers through an interdisciplinary and in-depth understanding of ongoing changes in the behavior of economic agents.

Published

Vol. 7 *Corporate Risk Management after the COVID-19 Crisis*
edited by Suman Lodh and Monomita Nandy

Vol. 6 *Islamic Accounting and Finance: A Handbook*
edited by Khaled Hussainey and Hidaya Al Lawati

Vol. 5 *FinTech Research and Applications: Challenges and Opportunities*
edited by Daisy Chou, Conall O'Sullivan and Vassilios G Papavassiliou

For the complete list of volumes in this series, please visit
www.worldscientific.com/series/tbfr

Transformations in Banking, Finance and Regulation
Volume 7

Corporate Risk Management after the COVID-19 Crisis

Editors

Suman Lodh
Kingston University London, UK

Monomita Nandy
Brunel University London, UK

World Scientific

NEW JERSEY • LONDON • SINGAPORE • BEIJING • SHANGHAI • HONG KONG • TAIPEI • CHENNAI • TOKYO

Published by

World Scientific Publishing Europe Ltd.
57 Shelton Street, Covent Garden, London WC2H 9HE
Head office: 5 Toh Tuck Link, Singapore 596224
USA office: 27 Warren Street, Suite 401-402, Hackensack, NJ 07601

Library of Congress Cataloging-in-Publication Data
Names: Nandy, Monomita, editor. | Lodh, Suman, editor.
Title: Corporate risk management after the COVID-19 crisis / editors, Suman Lodh, Kingston University London, UK, Monomita Nandy, Brunel University London, UK.
Description: New Jersey : World Scientific, [2024] | Series: Transformations in Banking, Finance and Regulation, 2752-5821 ; vol. 7 | Includes bibliographical references and index.
Identifiers: LCCN 2023016699 | ISBN 9781800614222 (hardcover) | ISBN 9781800614239 (ebook) | ISBN 9781800614246 (ebook other)
Subjects: LCSH: Risk management. | Crisis management. | Corporations--Management. | COVID-19 Pandemic, 2020---Economic aspects.
Classification: LCC HD61 .C6725 2024 | DDC 658.15/5--dc23/eng/20230413
LC record available at https://lccn.loc.gov/2023016699

British Library Cataloguing-in-Publication Data
A catalogue record for this book is available from the British Library.

For any available supplementary material, please visit
https://www.worldscientific.com/worldscibooks/10.1142/Q0419#t=suppl

Desk Editors: Aanand Jayaraman/Ana Ovey/Shi Ying Koe

Typeset by Stallion Press
Email: enquiries@stallionpress.com

https://doi.org/10.1142/9781800614239_fmatter

About the Editors

Suman Lodh, PhD, is an Associate Professor in Finance at Kingston University London, UK. His research interests are in the area of green finance and climate change, small and medium-sized enterprises, sustainability, corporate governance, earnings management, and banking. Suman worked on multiple externally funded projects including SME financing for biodiversity and nature-positive SME finance funded by the Natural Environmental Research Council (UKRI) and the Department for Business, Energy and Industrial Strategy, UK Government. Prior to joining at Kingston University, he served as the research lead and the chair of the research ethics committee for the Accounting and Finance Department at Middlesex University, London. He also serves as an associate editor of *Journal of Applied Accounting Research.* His articles were published in top international peer-reviewed academic journals (such as *International Review of Financial Analysis*, *Journal of Business Ethics*, *The International Journal of Accounting*, and *Corporate Governance: An International Review*) and the UK parliament. Suman is an accredited researcher of the Office for National Statistics, UK, and the Treasurer (Executive Trustee) of British Accounting and Finance Association, UK.

Monomita Nandy is a Professor in Accounting and Finance and Vice Dean International – CBASS, Brunel University London, UK. She has completed her PhDs from the University of Calcutta, India, and the University of Rome Torvergata, Italy. She worked as visiting research fellow at Lally Business School, New York, and Radboud

University, Holland. Before joining Brunel University, she taught at different universities in India and at Surrey University, UK, where she was awarded for her innovative and technology-led teaching. She is recognized internationally for her interdisciplinary research. Her research focuses on application of modern technology in sustainability issues and technological advancement in emerging issues in corporate finance, accounting, and banking. Her research works are published in high-impact international peer-reviewed journals. She is involved in editorial and review activities of some international journals, and regularly presents her research work at leading conferences in business and management. Her research evidence is valued by the UK Parliament, Sustainability Board in India, Small Business Charter in the UK, and the Chartered Institute of Taxation in England. Monomita conducts research on policy relevance and shares her research expertise by participating in the consultation initiated by the Financial Reporting Council (FRC), European Union (EU) Commission, and His Majesty's Revenue and Customs (HMRC) and her work draws attention from the Media. She is the co-chair of the South-East Group of the British Accounting and Finance Association. Her research attracts external funding, her university student–industry collaboration is appreciated by the London Chamber of Commerce and her research collaboration with local businesses is highly appreciated by the business and local authorities. Furthermore, her research generates a considerable amount of social aid that supports the sustainable growth of the economy with a long-term socio-economic impact.

https://doi.org/10.1142/9781800614239_fmatter

About the Contributors

Christopher Gan is a Professor in Accounting and Finance, Head of Department, Department of Financial and Business System, Faculty of Agribusiness and Commerce, Lincoln University, Christchurch, New Zealand. He is recognised internationally for research leadership in banking, microfinance, stock markets, and Asian financial economics. He serves on the editorial boards of several distinguished international journals and is the chief editor of the *International Review of Applied Economics.* He is the Minjiang Scholar, Distinguished Professor in the College of Economics and Finance at Fujian Agriculture and Forestry University, Fuzhou, China. He is also the Visiting Professor at the International Department, Chonnam National University, Gwangju, South Korea. He has won several awards for excellence in teaching, including the National Teaching Excellence Award in 2003. In 2017, he instigated and presently leads the Yunus Social Business Centre at Lincoln University. It is the first Yunus Social Business Centre in New Zealand.

Dolapo Lawrence, BTech, MSc, graduated from Middlesex University in 2021 with MSc Innovation Management and Entrepreneurship. In her dissertation, she examined the impact of COVID-19 and survival strategies among small and medium-sized enterprises in Nigeria. She received her first degree BTech in Accounting and Management from Ladoke Akintola University (LAUTECH), Nigeria, in 2011. Dolapo is presently working as the product manager in her family business in Nigeria, where she brings in new and different ideas for considerable growth and development.

Ewa Dalek-Trudnowska is a final year PhD candidate at Middlesex University London. Her research project has an interdisciplinary character and concerns the European Union legislation, artificial intelligence (AI) systems, and political economy. She holds LLM (Merit) in International Commercial Law (University of South Wales) and MA (Merit) in Archaeology (Warsaw University). As an archaeologist, she is interested in the technological development of societies. As a lawyer, she is also fascinated by the development of AI systems and the nature of future human–robot relations. Her research interest includes legislation applicable to artificial intelligence. She has experience in owning and managing a business, inter alia, as an owner and director of Mazovitz Archaeological Company, which employed up to 25 workers.

Ignatius Ekanem, PhD, MBA, SFHEA, is a Senior Lecturer at Middlesex University Business School, London, and a Visiting Professor at the Institute of Science and Technology, Yenagoa, Nigeria. He specialises in financial management of small and medium-sized enterprises (SMEs), small business development, and economic regeneration. He has published in reputable journals, including *The British Accounting Review, International Small Business Journal, Journal of Small Business and Enterprise Development, International Journal of Entrepreneurial Behaviour and Research, International Journal of Consumer Studies*, and *Social Science and Medicine.* He has written 2 books and 7 book chapters and is a co-author of over 20 official reports. His most recent books include, *Understanding Bankruptcy: Global Issues, Perspectives and Challenges*, Nova Science Publishers, New York; and *Writing a Business Plan: A Practical Guide*, Routledge, London. He has also written and presented many conference papers both in the UK and internationally. He has received Best Paper Awards from Barclays Bank for 'Best Paper on General Under-Represented Groups' — ISBE 2003 Conference; and from *International Small Business Journal* for 'Best Paper for Academic Rigour' — ISBE 2004 Conference. He holds an MBA from London South Bank University, and a PhD in Financial Management and PGCHE, both from Middlesex University, London. He is a Senior Fellow of the Higher Education Academy (SFHEA). Dr Ekanem can be contacted at i.ekanem@mdx.ac.uk.

Imad A. Moosa is currently a Professor of Economics at Kuwait University. He has held positions at the Royal Melbourne Institute of Technology, Monash University, La Trobe University, and The University of Sheffield. He has received formal training in model building, exchange rate forecasting, and risk management at the Claremont Economics Institute (United States), Wharton Econometrics (United States), and the Center for Monetary and Banking Studies (Switzerland). Before turning to academia in 1991, he worked as a financial analyst, financial journalist, and an investment banker for over 10 years. He was also an economist at the International Monetary Fund in Washington DC and acted as an advisor to the U.S. Treasury. Imad's work encompasses the areas of international finance, banking, risk management, macroeconomics, and applied econometrics. He has published extensively in these areas, producing more than 250 papers and 26 books. His latest books include *Contemporary Issues in the Post-Crisis Regulatory Landscape, Econometrics as a Con Art, The Economics of COVID-19,* and *Fintech: A Revolution or a Transitory Hype.*

Linh Tu Ho is a Lecturer in Finance, Faculty of Agribusiness and Commerce, Lincoln University, New Zealand. Her research focuses on investment, risk, and financial markets. Using the applied quantitative approach, Linh has expanded her research to risk management, sustainable investment, finance technology, and green finance. She has won a few awards, including the Sustainable Finance — INFINZ prize and semi-finalist of the InSPiR2eS Global PITCHING RESEARCH® Competition (IGPRC) in 2022. Linh has a publication record in peer-reviewed books and journals. She serves as a reviewer for several international journals such as *International Journal of Social Economics*, *Journal of Asian Business and Economic Studies*, *Environmental Systems and Decisions*, and *Economics and Finance in Indonesia*. She presented at several leading conferences, including the *Accounting and Finance Association of Australia and New Zealand Conference (AFAANZ)*, *International Congress on Modelling and Simulation (MODSIM)* in Australia, and *New Zealand Association of Economists Annual Conference (NZAE).*

Mazin A. M. Al Janabi is a Full Research-Professor of Finance & Banking and Financial Engineering. He is a research fellow at the Economic Research Forum (ERF). The ERF is a regional think tank committed to supporting high-quality economic research to contribute to sustainable development in the Middle East and North African (MENA) countries. Professor Al Janabi worked for many years as a Full Research-Professor of Finance & Banking and Financial Engineering at EGADE Business School, Tecnologico de Monterrey, Mexico, UAE University (UAEU) in Abu Dhabi, UAE, and at Al Akhawayn University in Ifrane (AUI), Morocco, among other academic institutions. He holds a PhD degree in Nuclear Engineering from the University of London, UK, and has more than 30 years of real-world experience in science and technology think tanks, engineering enterprises, financial markets, and academic institutions and in many different roles. He has worked for top international financial groups (e.g. ING-Barings and BBVA) where he held several senior management positions, such as Director of Global Market Risk Management, Head of Trading Risk Management, and Head of Derivative Products. Professor Al Janabi has strong interest in research and development within emerging economies and has several publications in international refereed journals, books, and chapters in books. Furthermore, his research and developments in quantitative finance have been formally classified in the academic literatures as the "*Al Janabi Model*" for Liquidity Risk Management (Liquidity-Adjusted Value-at-Risk, LVaR Model). Professor Al Janabi has published in top-tiered journals such as: *European Journal of Operational Research*, *Journal of Forecasting*, *International Review of Financial Analysis*, *Physica A: Statistical Mechanics and Its Applications*, *European Actuarial Journal*, *Annals of Operations Research*, *Complexity*, *International Journal of Finance & Economics*, *Applied Economics*, *Economic Modelling*, *Review of Financial Economics*, *Journal of Asset Management*, *Service Industries Journal*, *Journal of Modelling in Management*, *Studies in Economics and Finance*, *Emerging Markets Finance and Trade*, *Studies in Economics and Finance*, *Journal of Risk Finance*, *Journal of Banking Regulation*, *Annals of Nuclear Energy*, among others.

Neha Puri, PhD, is an Assistant Professor at Amity College of Commerce & Finance, Amity University, Uttar Pradesh, India. She has 14+ years of experience and has 4 research scholars currently under her guidance. Her research papers have appeared in Scopus, Web of Science, ABDC journals, UGC-listed journals, and other peer-reviewed journals. She has contributed chapters in IGI Global, Taylor & Francis, Apple Academic Press, Emerald, and Springer. She is also on the review board of reputed international journals. She is a reviewer/editorial board member in various national/international journals. She has presented nine technical papers at national and international conferences and won the best research paper award twice.

Vikas Garg, PhD, is Assistant Director of the Executive Programs Management Domain at Amity University, Uttar Pradesh, India. He has almost 20+ years of experience and has more than 10 PhD scholars currently under his guidance. He has published numerous research papers in various Scopus- and ABDC-indexed international and national journals. He serves as associate editor of the *Journal of Sustainable Finance and Investment* (indexed in the WoS and Scopus). He also serves as the book series editor for Taylor and Francis for three book series: *Technology Innovations: Strategies for Business Sustainability and Growth*; *Emerging Trends in Technology in Management and Commerce*; and *Electronic Commerce Management for Business*. He has been working with new innovative ideas in the field of patents and copyrights. He has been the lead organiser in conducting various international conferences, workshops, and case study competitions, including those affiliated with the Institute of Electrical and Electronics Engineers (IEEE). He has been conferred with many national and international awards for being the best academician, researcher, and employee.

https://doi.org/10.1142/9781800614239_fmatter

Contents

https://doi.org/10.1142/9781800614239_fmatter

Introduction: Problematising the Post-Pandemic Corporate Risk Management — Future Directions of Research

Monomita Nandy[*,‡] **and Suman Lodh**[†,§]

[*]*Brunel University London, London, UK*
[†]*Kingston University London, Surrey, UK*
[‡]*monomita.nandy@brunel.ac.uk*
[§]*s.lodh@kingston.ac.uk*

In my view, from a purely risk management perspective, COVID-19 will represent a shift towards more frequent risk identification and risk management.

Zoltán Szöllősi
Director of Deloitte Risk Advisory

Introduction

The COVID-19 (SARS-CoV-2) pandemic exposed the corporate sectors to a new set of uncertainties. Several unprecedented restrictions in the daily lives of people created an adverse impact on society, businesses, and the global economy. During the peak of the pandemic, there were many precautionary as well as mandatory measures taken such as travel ban, work from home, closing of schools, and national lockdowns to prevent the spread of the virus. However, the above initiatives of the policymakers to protect the public health also contributed to the challenges for the businesses of different sizes operated by and for the people. All business sectors tried every possible way to adjust with the new economic and financial environment to continue their business and services. The government and policymakers of almost all countries injected finance in the economic system to support the sectors to mitigate the challenges imposed by restrictions associated with the COVID-19 pandemic. However, the initiatives of public and private sectors to protect the economy fell short compared to the speed of the damage caused by the COVID-19. Rapid drying out of business liquidity questioned the solvency of the corporates and the financial market began to feel the stress in the economy. The international stock markets started showing signs of uncertainty (Contessi and De Pace, 2021) and investors observed a strong market risk contagion (Liang *et al.*, 2021). Even when the financial market became volatile, the corporate sectors tried to adopt new ways of operations to keep their supply chain operating and continued to invest their business and personal savings.

During the spread of COVID-19, several policy measures created a strain on the financial movement in the economy. Thus, governments of many economies introduced financial intervention to support the economy to recover from this crisis (Iyer and Simkins, 2022). For instance, the UK government announced a number of measures including *Eat Out to Help Out*, the job retention scheme, and the statutory sick pay.[1] The Coronavirus Job Retention Scheme (CJRS) or "the Furlough" scheme covered 80% of employee salaries up to a maximum of £2500 per month. By August 2021, the scheme successfully supported 1.3 million businesses and 11.6 million jobs in the UK.[2] Yue and Cowling (2021) mentioned that the CJRS estimated a total cost of around £60 billion. After initially ignoring the 4.6 million self-employed, the UK government announced the Self-Employment Income Support Scheme, which awarded grants of 70% of average monthly trading profits calculated from tax returns for

[1] According to IMF (2021), these steps involve foregone revenues equivalent of 16% of GDP of the country.

[2] https://www.ons.gov.uk/employmentandlabourmarket/peopleinwork/employmentandemployeetypes/articles/anoverviewofworkerswhowerefurloughedintheuk/october2021.

2018 and 2019. This scheme only applied to those self-employed who earned less than £50,000 in profit for the relevant period (Yue and Cowling, 2021). Similarly, on 15 March 2022, the Federal Reserve in the United States announced a 0% interest rate policy and an unlimited quantitative easing programme. Lopez and Spiegel (2021) showed that the US Paycheck Protection Program of Lending Facility (part of CARES Act) was successful in encouraging banks to support small businesses through the programme. Several measures were taken by the German government to protect businesses and start-ups affected by the COVID-19 crisis including taxation support, state-supported short-time work compensation schemes, improved measures to guarantee bank loans, special programs provided by Kreditanstalt für Wiederaufbau (PWC, 2020), and an emergency aid that offers one-off lump sum payments to self-employed facing substantial revenue declines (Block *et al.*, 2022). However, the rapid increase in COVID-19 cases overrode the support of the governments to protect jobs during the difficult time. In summary, the job loss resulted in less flow of money into the economy. Individuals in the society either lost their savings in protecting their businesses or spent money just to maintain the day-to-day living costs. There was a lack of interest in saving money in banks and many businesses failed to pay back their dues to the banks. In addition, the declining bank deposits resulted in limited availability of debt in the corporate sector. Furthermore, the use of cashless instruments increased during the pandemic (Jonker *et al.*, 2022) to avoid contracting the virus. However, at the same time, the demand for cash (physical money) during the pandemic also increased (Ashworth and Goodhart, 2021). As a result, a huge imbalance between demand and supply in the market was observed. The uncertainty in one market started transmitting to other markets, and the global financial market became vulnerable and remained fragile even after almost three years of the start of the COVID-19 crisis. The Wuhan outbreak was not only a health-related issue all over the world, it created a fresh channel of risk spillover from one sector to another and started playing an instrumental role in adversely affecting the international financial system (Guo *et al.*, 2021). Thus, the world economy started experiencing a new type of corporate risk generated from a crisis created by the COVID-19.

Because of the extensive impact of the COVID-19 crisis on corporate risk, it is important to know to what extent the corporate world recovered from this crisis. How did the corporate sectors from different regions of the world economy experience the crisis? If the response of the corporates to the crisis was different in different sectors and countries, was it because of the variation in their risk management strategies? As the COVID-19 crisis adversely affected all sectors of business, it is almost impossible to capture all the types of risks imposed by the crisis. In this book, we try to capture some of the risks generated from the COVID-19 crisis, which are still ongoing, and we try to share knowledge about the good practices around risk management by businesses of different sizes from various industries, which can lead to future possibilities of risk management in addressing risks of a similar nature.

In the following sections, we summarise what is corporate risk and what is its link with COVID-19 — how the risk can be managed effectively by businesses of different sizes, followed by the summary of the book chapters.

Risk and Effective Management Strategies

In general, a quantifiable probability of loss or reduced expected return is termed as risk (McNeil *et al.*, 2015). According to Kuritzkes and Schuermann (2006), a business risk is defined as a non-systematic risk in the context of valuation of assets. So, the types of business risks vary in accordance with their internal and external origin (Toma and Alexa, 2012). The risks in economic activities include business relationships with suppliers and customers who may pose a threat to them. According to the Basel and Solvency Risk Assessment Standards in Banks and Insurance Companies, a financial risk is any event or operation which may adversely affect the ability of the organisation to accomplish objectives or implement a strategy (Kuritzkes and Schuermann, 2006). Thus, identification and proper assessment of a possible risk are effective risk management tools. However, the effect of COVID-19 on the economy was unanticipated and unforeseen. So, the knowledge of the businesses and their stakeholders about risk management related to such uncertainty was not sufficient. The 2008 global financial crisis (GFC) triggered flight to quality as investors moved from choosing risky to safe assets (Adrian *et al.*, 2019). Gold and silver, which were the *safe havens* for investors during the GFC, became unstable assets during the COVID-19 pandemic. Even, the impact of the previous health crisis (e.g., Ebola, 2014–2016) remained confined to certain regions. The adverse effect of the pandemic and the associated economic vulnerability raised questions on the suitability of traditional risk management strategies followed by the corporate world. Is it the time to think and redesign a better interpretation of risk imposed by COVID-19 and develop a risk management strategy to be adopted during and after the pandemic? Should we consider both newspaper-based economic uncertainty and subjective uncertainty together to understand the macroeconomic impact of COVID-19, as proposed by Baker *et al.* (2020)? According to a report by McKinsey,[3] appropriate risk management can improve businesses' operations by digitising and applying advanced analytics to a variety of operations and can also optimise the organisation performance by "clarifying responsibilities, increasing accountability, and matching talent to jobs ... laying a necessary foundation for rationalising governance." Thus, without any doubt, a detailed discussion about COVID-19 risks on business operations and identifying a strategy for effective and resilient management of the risks are needed for sustainable business contribution towards the world economy.

Corporate Risks Sourced from COVID-19

A voluminous literature since the beginning of 2020 has focused on the impact of COVID-19 on businesses in accounting, finance, management, law, and economics to understand the risks and uncertainties associated with the pandemic (see Rinaldi, 2022). In addition, the long-term uncertainty of the pandemic introduces confusion for corporates and their stakeholders, including the investors. For instance, Brennan *et al.* (2022) document that COVID-19 has changed the language and rhythm of corporate reporting. Tompkins (2020) reports that the frequency of profit warning increased significantly in the first quarter of 2020. Analysing a panel of international banks, Hardy and Takats (2020) show that the global borrowing has

[3]https://www.mckinsey.com/capabilities/risk-and-resilience/our-insights/a-fast-track-risk-management-transformation-to-counter-the-covid-19-crisis#/.

been more prevalent among countries with stronger economic activity and lower financial vulnerability during the pandemic. Furthermore, studies show that the pandemic significantly affected the stability of financial markets (see Adekoya and Oliyide, 2021) and unconventional monetary policies are needed to ease the impacts (Bhar and Malliaris, 2021).

A stream of studies report that the impact of the pandemic is sector-specific. For example, Narayan *et al.* (2022) show that manufacturing, food, healthcare, and information technology sectors observed high positive returns. On the other hand, transportation, entertainment, and hospitality sectors suffered the most. Existing studies try to investigate the variations of the impact of the COVID-19 crisis on different sectors to suggest the factors that need to be considered in the risk management strategies. Moreover, other researchers explain how the businesses developed a link between risks generated from COVID-19 and their risk management strategies in explaining the anomalies in the financial market or change in the behaviour of their stakeholders. For instance, Ke (2022) identifies how the risk can be responsible for increasing cost of equity capital, while Armantier *et al.* (2022) find changes in consumer behaviour during the pandemic. Several other studies focus on various risks associated with COVID-19 and its impact on the behaviour of investors not only in the short term but also in the long run (Narayan *et al.*, 2020; Salisu *et al.*, 2021). Interestingly, on a positive note, He and Harris (2020) and Qiu *et al.* (2021) show that corporate sustainability reporting (CSR) should play an essential role in corporate risk management strategies in the post-pandemic period. There is a high possibility that embedding CSR in corporate risk management will be used by corporates as an effective instrument to communicate their contribution towards their stakeholders in the society. Such a positive attitude of the corporates for the society allows them to draw the attention of investors and generate funds to have a sustainable growth in the future. This is in line with Broadstock *et al.* (2021) who show that the corporate stakeholder engagement in the form of CSR can lower downside risks between companies and their external partners, customers, and financiers. Berger *et al.* (2021) show how relationship banking progressed over the course of the pandemic. In summary, there exists evidence in the existing literature about the risk management strategies adopted by the corporates to mitigate the corporate risk generated from COVID-19. It is an important responsibility of the academic community to share the good practices observed in existing research with the wider community and to encourage the research community to provide new evidence to mitigate the ongoing risk and develop an efficient risk management strategy for an agile world economy. The research about the impact of COVID-19 on the corporates and their stakeholders will continue over the years to come.

Corporate Supply Chain and Small and Medium-Sized Enterprises

The Small and Medium-sized Enterprises (SMEs), very often considered a social entrepreneurship, contribute significantly to corporate supply chain and towards the economic growth of a country. We observe a positive link between economic growth and SMEs' contribution, both in developing and developed countries. For instance, SMEs generate three-fifths[4] of the employment in the UK private sector. However, SMEs in every country suffer from certain challenges that become severe when the corporate world becomes vulnerable because of any crisis. Among the major challenges faced by SMEs is resource constraints, which is captured in the existing literature (e.g., Wenke *et al.*, 2021). The flow of resources in SMEs is heavily dependent on the efficient risk–return strategy of the corporates. During the COVID-19 crisis, when the big corporates failed to generate enough revenue, the drying liquidity affected the SMEs, specifically their supply chains. For example, approximately 80% of the UK's SMEs experienced a negative revenue impact and reduced cash flow during the COVID-19 pandemic (Bank of England, 2020; McKinsey & Company, 2020). Compared to larger companies, SMEs use less economies of scale and have less access to resources (Burgstaller and Wagner, 2015), which makes them the most vulnerable group during such crises. In a study on the US Producer Price Index (PPI) inflation, Santacreu and LaBelle (2022) show that both demand and supply shocks due to the supply chain disruptions played a key role in the

[4]https://www.fsb.org.uk/uk-small-business-statistics.html.

PPI between January and November 2021. A survey conducted by the Connected Commerce Council of more than 5016 European small and medium-sized businesses carried out in November–December 2020 found that practically all SMEs were affected (Digitally Driven, 2021). In addition, another survey conducted by National Bureau of Economic Research (NBER) of more than 5800 small businesses in the USA found that 43% of small firms were expected to be closed by December 2020 (Bartik *et al.*, 2020). The closure of thousands of SMEs becomes inevitable despite many organisations, such as US Small Business Administration and the UK Federation of Small Businesses, which provide loans to small businesses through banks, credit unions, and other financial institutions with the goal of keeping small businesses open and retaining employees on their payroll (Fairlie and Fossen, 2021). Furthermore, SMEs operating in the supply chain in sectors such as tourism, hospitality, entertainment, and air transportation were particularly hard hit with regard to their sales (ONS, 2020). It can be noted that, SMEs use their invested capital mainly for implementation of current operations and do not record sufficient cash flows in relation to the assumed plans. Thus, as the cash generation may not match the forecast, these companies face financial problems. To stabilise a steady growth in the world economy, it is important for the corporates to put enough weight on the growth of the SMEs, in their supply chain, while drawing the risk management strategies to develop a sustainable corporate growth model for the future.

Advanced Technology and Post-Pandemic Risk Management

The onset of COVID-19 and its associated uncertainty in economic activities generated too much information, which created a new set of challenges for the corporates. The more we started to know about the nature of the virus, the faster the process and practices of the traditional economic activities began to change. As a result, we observed ups and downs in the economic activities, as and when the effect of the virus remained at its peak, and the vaccine started rolling out, the proposals for lockdowns were scraped, and natural immunity became a norm. In other words, the corporate world started to learn the need for frequent risk identification and captured the same in their risk management strategies. Such a change in corporate risk management was reflected in the new trend of economic activities around the world. It is important to note that during the pandemic several new data relevant for corporate risk management were generated. However, the nature of these data was complex and so it was very hard for the corporates to do any risk forecasting in the short run with the existing forecasting tools. Few companies, performing better compared to their peers during the pandemic, managed to apply advanced technologies, like blockchain technology, deep learning artificial intelligence technology, and others to apply the machine learning algorithms to capture several COVID-19-related risks associated with their business operation in developing the risk management model. The wide range of advantages of big data analytical tools became a blessing for the corporates during the pandemic in their risk management framework. The ability to capture strongly correlated risk factors with higher precision in the corporate risk management allowed the economy to continue at a lower pace. Alongside the corporates, these advanced technologies also supported certain SMEs, who mainly managed to adopt the technology in the pre-pandemic period. For instance, Hansen and Bøgh (2021) show that artificial intelligence has transformed the nature and scope of entrepreneurial activity in SMEs. Similarly, evidence shows that SMEs that adopt digital technology aided by artificial intelligence managed to enhance their competitive advantage and productivity (Kumar *et al.*, 2022). In 2021, 40% of UK businesses, regardless of their size, planned to invest in artificial intelligence to help them adapt to and recover from the COVID-19 pandemic.[5] The COVID-19 pandemic and the ongoing effect of the same across the world made it very clear to the corporate world that they need to remain prepared in assessing much information at high speed with higher accuracy to develop their risk management strategies. Without the use of advanced technology, it is almost impossible to develop an efficient risk management framework. Thus, it is important to widely share the success stories of the corporates in using advanced technologies in their risk management.

---

[5]https://www.gov.uk/government/publications/ai-activity-in-uk-businesses/ai-activity-in-uk-businesses-executive-summary.

This helps to build confidence among their peers and stakeholders who are yet to adopt advanced technology in their sustainable growth model in the post-pandemic era.

Summary of Book Chapters

The six chapters in this book offer a wide-ranging view of risks associated with the COVID-19 in different countries, and the risk management strategies adopted by the corporates and their stakeholders.

In the first chapter, titled "COVID-19, the Growth of Fintech, and the Rise of Risk Management Challenges", the author argues for the adoption of disruptive advanced technology (fintech in this study) by the financial service sectors to support the operation of companies. The study discusses in detail about the success of the fintech industry in the pre-pandemic period. However, because of extensive volatility in the market, the pandemic increased challenges for the corporates in setting up a rigorous and robust risk management system to capture the possible risk in the adoption of disruptive technology. The findings suggest that the fintech industry failed to capture fraud and loose ends of the COVID-19 risks in their risk management during the pandemic.

The second chapter, "The Impact of the COVID-19 Pandemic and the European Union Artificial Intelligence Act on the Implementation of AI Systems in Europe", discusses the effectiveness and limitation of the European Union's Artificial Intelligence (AI) Act for risk management, in the context of the COVID-19 crisis. In this socio-legal study, the author focuses on the importance of regulatory compliance in technology-led corporate risk management frameworks. The study further examines if the EU Artificial Intelligence Act imposes a risk on companies that implement AI systems in their business operations in Europe. Furthermore, the author investigates the challenges and opportunities in implementing different types of AI risk management systems by corporates and their impact on the workforce during the COVID-19 crisis.

The third chapter is "Method Development Aspects of Liquidity Risk Modelling: Dynamic Algorithms for Reinforcement Machine Learning Under Crisis Market Perspectives". It focuses on liquidity risk modelling during a crisis. The discussion of this chapter starts with the assessment of Liquidity-Adjusted Value-at-Risk when a particular market is affected by a crisis. When most of the industries in a financial market are affected by a crisis, it is always a challenge for the investors to optimise their multi-asset portfolio return. Very often it is not possible to apply the conventional portfolio theory when the breadth and depth of the crisis are too deep. COVID-19 crisis imposes a similar challenge in portfolio risk management. The authors adopted the *Al Janabi* optimisation algorithms in explaining how the portfolio return can be optimised during a complex crisis. The study also argues that its proposed risk management model can be successfully applied in the big data ecosystem.

The fourth chapter of the book, titled "Corporate Governance in Banking Industry: A Case of Indian Banking Sector Pre and Post COVID-19", is based on the banking sector in India. The authors argue that in the absence of a stakeholder-focused governance mechanism, it is hard to withstand any adverse impact of any crisis. In this chapter, they discuss about the importance of the banking sector in the development and economic growth of an emerging economy. The main findings of the research show that banks which considered the risk associated with social responsibilities in their risk management in the pre-pandemic period performed better during the pandemic. The authors suggest that to deal with future uncertainties, banks must start paying more attention towards their non-financial stakeholders rather than the financial shareholders.

The fifth chapter is on "The Impact of COVID-19 Crisis on SMEs and Their Risk Management and Survival Strategies: Evidence from Nigeria". The authors argue that among the key stakeholders of the corporates are the small and medium-sized enterprises. In this chapter, the authors, examine the effect of COVID-19 on the small and medium-sized enterprises in the context of Nigeria and discuss their risk management strategies after the pandemic. By applying the Keynesian Theory of Business Cycle, the Social-Ecological Theory, and the Social-Cognitive Theory, the authors conceptualise the risk management approach to be adopted by the small and medium-sized enterprises after the pandemic.

The last chapter is titled "Artificial Intelligence, T-Shaped Teams, and Risk Management Post COVID-19 and Beyond". In this final chapter, the authors explore the opportunity to apply Artificial Intelligence (AI) and T-Shaped Teams in the context of corporate risk management. The study focuses on the companies which have already adopted Artificial Intelligence in their business operations. As the adoption of the advanced technology is heavily dependent on the interest and willingness of the employees of the corporates, the research examines the roles of the workforce, especially T-Shaped teams, in Artificial Intelligence adoption. Based on the findings of their research, the authors provide a guide for building T-Shaped Teams for risk management using Artificial Intelligence. The chapter concludes on a positive note by recommending that in future, to capture new risk, the corporates should build T-Shaped Teams and develop risk management strategies using Artificial Intelligence.

References

Adekoya, O.B. and Oliyide, J.A. (2021). How COVID-19 drives connectedness among commodity and financial markets: Evidence from TVP-VAR and causality-in-quantiles techniques. *Resources Policy*, 70, 101898.

Adrian, T., Crump, R.K. and Vogt, E. (2019). Nonlinearity and flight-to-safety in the risk-return trade-off for stocks and bonds. *The Journal of Finance*, 74(4), 1931–1973.

Armantier, O., Goldman, L., Koşar, G., Topa, G., Van der Klaauw, W. and Williams, J.C. (2022). What are consumers' inflation expectations telling us today? (No. 20220214). Federal Reserve Bank of New York.

Ashworth, J. and Goodhart, C. (2021). The great Covid cash surge-digitalisation hasn't dented cash's safe haven role. (CEPR Discussion Paper No. DP16618). Centre for Economic Policy Research.

Baker, S.R., Bloom, N., Davis, S.J. and Terry, S.J. (2020). Covid-induced economic uncertainty (No. w26983). National Bureau of Economic Research.

Bank of England (2020). Available at: https://www.bankofengland.co.uk/paper/2020/open-data-for-sme-finance. Accessed on 11 November 2022.

Bartik, A.W., Bertrand, M., Cullen, Z.B., Glaeser, E.L., Luca, M. and Stanton, C.T. (2020). How are small businesses adjusting to COVID-19? Early evidence from a survey (No. w26989). National Bureau of Economic Research.

Berger, A.N., Bouwman, C.H., Norden, L., Roman, R.A., Udell, G.F. and Wang, T. (2021). Is a friend in need a friend indeed? How relationship borrowers fare during the COVID-19 crisis? How relationship borrowers fare during the COVID-19 crisis (May 25, 2021). Kelley School of Business Research Paper (2021–2001).

Bhar, R. and Malliaris, A.G. (2021). Modeling US monetary policy during the global financial crisis and lessons for COVID-19. *Journal of Policy Modeling*, 43(1), 15–33.

Block, J.H., Fisch, C. and Hirschmann, M. (2022). The determinants of bootstrap financing in crises: evidence from entrepreneurial ventures in the COVID-19 pandemic. *Small Business Economics*, 58(2), 867–885.

Brennan, N.M., Edgar, V.C. and Power, S.B. (2022). COVID-19 profit warnings: Delivering bad news in a time of crisis. *The British Accounting Review*, 54(2), 101054.

Broadstock, D.C., Chan, K., Cheng, L.T. and Wang, X. (2021). The role of ESG performance during times of financial crisis: Evidence from COVID-19 in China. *Finance Research Letters*, 38, 101716.

Burgstaller, J. and Wagner, E. (2015). How do family ownership and founder management affect capital structure decisions and adjustment of SMEs? Evidence from a bank-based economy. *The Journal of Risk Finance*, 16(1), 73–101.

Contessi, S. and De Pace, P. (2021). The international spread of COVID-19 stock market collapses. *Finance Research Letters*, 42, 101894.

Digitally Driven (2021). European small businesses find a digital safety net during COVID-19. Report. Connected Commerce. Available at: https://digitallydriven.connectedcouncil.org/europe/. Accessed 15 May 2021.

Fairlie, R. and Fossen, F.M. (2022). The early impacts of the COVID-19 pandemic on business sales. *Small Business Economics*, Mar 31: 1–2.

Guo, Y., Li, P. and Li, A. (2021). Tail risk contagion between international financial markets during COVID-19 pandemic. *International Review of Financial Analysis*, 73, 101649.

Hansen, E.B. and Bøgh, S. (2021). Artificial intelligence and internet of things in small and medium-sized enterprises: A survey. *Journal of Manufacturing Systems*, 58, 362–372.

Hardy, B. and Takats, E. (2020). International banking amidst COVID-19: resilience and drivers. Available at SSRN 3746155.

He, H. and Harris, L. (2020). The impact of COVID-19 pandemic on corporate social responsibility and marketing philosophy. *Journal of Business Research*, 116, 176–182.

IMF (2021). *Fiscal Monitor: Database of Country Fiscal Measures in Response to Pandemic.* Washington: IMF.

Iyer, S.R. and Simkins, B.J. (2022). COVID-19 and the economy: Summary of research and future directions. *Finance Research Letters*, 102801.

Jonker, N., van der Cruijsen, C., Bijlsma, M. and Bolt, W. (2022). Pandemic payment patterns. *Journal of Banking and Finance*, 143, 106593.

Ke, Y. (2022). The impact of COVID-19 on firms' cost of equity capital: Early evidence from US public firms. *Finance Research Letters*, 46, 102242.

Kumar, M., Raut, R.D., Mangla, S.K., Ferraris, A. and Choubey, V.K. (2022). The adoption of artificial intelligence powered workforce management for effective revenue growth of micro, small, and medium scale enterprises (MSMEs). *Production Planning and Control*, 1–17.

Kuritzkes, A. and Schuermann, T. (2006). What we know, don't know and can't know about bank risk: A view from the trenches. In *The Known, the Unknown and the Unknowable in Financial Risk Management*, Diebold, F.X. and Herring, R.J., Eds. Princeton, NJ: Princeton University Press, 103–144.

Liang, C., Li, Y., Ma, F. and Wei, Y. (2021). Global equity market volatilities forecasting: a comparison of leverage effects, jumps, and overnight information. *International Review of Financial Analysis*, 75, 101750.

Lopez, J.A. and Spiegel, M.M. (2021, April). Small business lending under the PPP and PPPLF programs. Federal Reserve Bank of San Francisco.

McNeil, A.J., Frey, R. and Embrechts, P. (2015). *Quantitative Risk Management: Concepts, Techniques, and Tools*, revised edition. Princeton University Press.

McKinsey & Company. (2020). UK small and medium-size enterprises: Impact of the COVID-19 crisis. Available at https://www.mckinsey.com/industries/public-and-social-sector/our-insights/uk-small-and-medium-size-enterprises-impact-of-the-covid-19-crisis.

Narayan, P.K., Devpura, N. and Wang, H. (2020). Japanese currency and stock market — What happened during the COVID-19 pandemic? *Economic Analysis and Policy*, 68, 191–198.

Narayan, P.K., Gong, Q. and Ahmed, H.J.A. (2022). Is there a pattern in how COVID-19 has affected Australia's stock returns? *Applied Economics Letters*, 29(3), 179–182.

ONS (2020). Coronavirus and the impact on output in the UK economy. Available at: https://www.ons.gov.uk/economy/grossdomesticproductgdp/articles/coronavirusandtheimpactonoutputintheukeconomy/july2020.

PWC (2020). Finanzielle Unterstützung in der COVID-19 Krisenlage-Factsheet für Startups und KMUs (Financial support in the

COVID-19 crisis situation — Factsheet for start-ups and SMEs) Available at: https://www.pwc.de/de/startups/finanzielle-unterstuetzung-von-startups-und-kmu-in-der-covid-19-krisenlage.pdf. Accessed 11 November 2022.

Qiu, S.C., Jiang, J., Liu, X., Chen, M.H. and Yuan, X. (2021). Can corporate social responsibility protect firm value during the COVID-19 pandemic? *International Journal of Hospitality Management*, 93, 102759.

Rinaldi, L. (2022). Accounting and the COVID-19 pandemic two years on: Insights, gaps, and an agenda for future research. *Accounting Forum* (pp. 1–32). Routledge.

Santacreu, A.M. and LaBelle, J. (2022). Global supply chain disruptions and inflation during COVID-19. *Federal Reserve Bank of St. Louis Review.*

Salisu, A.A., Vo, X.V. and Lawal, A. (2021). Hedging oil price risk with gold during COVID-19 pandemic. *Resources Policy*, 70, 101897.

Toma, S.V. and Alexa, I.V. (2012). Different categories of business risk. *Annals of the University Dunarea de Jos of Galati: Fascicle: I, Economics & Applied Informatics*, 18(2).

Tompkins, K. (2020). COVID-19 has now triggered 215 profit warnings. CityA.M. Available at: https://www.cityam.com/covid-19-has-now-triggered-215-profit-warnings/. Accessed on 11 November 2022.

Wenke, K., Zapkau, F.B. and Schwens, C. (2021). Too small to do it all? A meta-analysis on the relative relationships of exploration, exploitation, and ambidexterity with SME performance. *Journal of Business Research*, 132, 653–665.

Yue, W. and Cowling, M. (2021). The COVID-19 lockdown in the United Kingdom and subjective well-being: Have the self-employed suffered more due to hours and income reductions? *International Small Business Journal*, 39(2), 93–108.

https://doi.org/10.1142/9781800614239_0001

Chapter 1

COVID-19, the Growth of Fintech, and the Rise of Risk Management Challenges

Imad A. Moosa

Department of Economics, Kuwait University, Kuwait City, Kuwait

imad.moosa@gmail.com

Abstract

The COVID-19 pandemic has had both positive and negative effects on the fintech industry. The negative effects can be seen in terms of increasing incidence of contractual disputes with customers, failure to meet payments, defaults, and delayed repayments. The positive effects can be seen through growth in the number and value of fintech transactions and the influx of new customers as the non-pharmaceutical interventions intended to stem the spread of the virus enhanced the tendency to use digital financial services. The effects of the pandemic, both positive and negative, have risk management and regulatory implications. The negative effects have forced some fintechs to change their business models and take protective measures to face changing conditions. The massive growth of the fintech industry, bolstered by the positive effects, is likely to boost the incidence of corporate failure and aggravate the risks posed to financial stability and consumers. The rise of fintech makes the financial system more vulnerable to increasing frequency and severity of operational loss events through a rising incidence of fraud and system failure.

1. Introduction

The COVID-19 pandemic has led to the emergence of new challenges in risk management and consequently financial regulation, which is an observation that has been made repeatedly in the literature (for example, Lee and Shin, 2018; Xia *et al.*, 2020; Tian and Han, 2021; Moosa, 2022; Najaf *et al.*, 2022). The pandemic has provided a big boost for the fintech industry, which (in a narrow sense) consists of new start-ups attempting to disrupt existing financial institutions by using novel technology to provide financial services. While the use of technology leads to efficiency and consumer satisfaction, it brings with it new kinds of risks to consumers and the fintech firms themselves. By boosting the fintech industry, the pandemic has led (indirectly) to the rise of new kinds of risks and consequently to big challenges for risk managers and financial regulators. On the other hand, the pandemic has affected the operations of fintechs negatively — for example, by leading to a higher incidence of default, which forced some firms to change their business models and take protective measures. The pandemic has had big positive effects and small negative effects on fintechs, both of which came with risk management considerations.

Measures taken by governments worldwide to contain or slow down the spread of the virus made it necessary to introduce restrictive non-pharmaceutical measures, such as lockdowns, curfews, and quarantines. Even without these measures, people became increasingly reluctant to go out shopping for fear of catching the virus. The alternative is to shop online and pay electronically, which is the essence of fintech. For the same reason, people became reluctant to go to banks to deposit, withdraw, or transfer money. And for the same reason, people became unable to use cash payments, even unwilling to do so, as rumours spread about the virus riding on cash to infect people. This is why the growth of fintech was spectacular in 2020 when activity was dwindling in 2019 (see Figure 3, which is based on data provided by Statista). The spectacular growth must have materialised because the positive effects of the pandemic on the fintech industry more than offset the negative effects.

The objective of this chapter is to identify the risk management challenges that face fintech companies and the relevance of the pandemic. The starting point is the definition of fintech, followed by identification of the functions of fintechs and a description of their operations, including the kind of technology they use to provide financial services. The effect of the pandemic on the growth of fintech is presented next, where it is shown how growth accelerated in 2020 as a result of the pandemic and what measures were taken to contain the virus. The risk management challenges facing fintechs and the regulatory implications are examined before the statement of some concluding remarks. The contribution of this chapter to the fintech literature is that it presents a narrative linking the growth of the fintech industry to the pandemic and the consequent risk management and regulatory challenges.

2. Definition of Fintech

The word "fintech", short for "financial technology", refers to the technology itself or to the industry consisting of firms using technology to provide financial services. Even though the use of technology in the provision of financial services can be traced back to the 18th century (with the invention of the telegraph) or even earlier, the term "fintech" has only become widely used in the past few years. The term was added to the *Merriam-Webster Dictionary* in 2018, but its origin can be traced back to the early 1990s with the establishment by Citicorp (the predecessor of Citigroup) of the "Financial Services Technology Consortium" for the purpose of facilitating technological cooperation. It was an attempt by Citicorp to alter the perception of being "out of touch with market preferences (Hochstein, 2015a, 2015b). This view is challenged by Schueffel (2016) who notes that the term was used in the early 1970s when Abraham Leon Bettinger, the vice president of Manufacturers Hanover Trust, described fintech as "an acronym which stands for financial technology, combining bank expertise with modern management science techniques and the computer" (Bettinger, 1972).

An indication of the growth of interest in fintech is the frequency of Google search for "fintech" and related terms, where figures on the frequency of search are available on Google Trends (https://trends.google.com/). Frequency is measured as an index taking the maximum value of 100 during a time period that can be specified in advance (in this case January 2004–February 2022).

For the purpose of comparison, data were collected on the frequency of Google search for "fintech" and related terms, including "financial technology", "digital finance", "digital financial services", and "fintech companies", as well as the question "what is fintech?". The data are plotted in Figure 1, showing exponential growth in the search for "fintech" starting in 2014. This kind of explosive growth cannot be seen in the search for "financial technology", even though "fintech" is short for "financial technology". It seems, however, that the term "fintech" has been replacing the term "financial technology". Similar patterns are observed in the search for "fintech companies" and the question "what is fintech?" The patterns of search for "digital finance" and "digital financial services" are similar, but the growth in the search for these terms has been slower than growth in the search for "fintech".

Some observers believe that fintech is inherently difficult to define because the industry changes rather quickly over time as more and more technology entrepreneurs enter the market. A widely held view is that a universally accepted definition of fintech is not available. For example, Varga (2017) argues that "a great variety of definitions of the concept exist in academic practice and business journals", which he attributes to the "fast evolution" of the industry. Zavolokina *et al.* (2016) note that "FinTech is a very broad phenomenon" and that "its meaning still remains ambiguous for most of the people". The absence of an industry-wide consensus on a single definition of fintech is attributed by Gray and Leibrock (2017) to the blurred boundaries between technology providers and financial services firms.

Numerous definitions of fintech have appeared in the academic literature and the media. Leong and Sung (2018) define "fintech" to include more than finance on the basis of a survey of what people refer to as fintech. Likewise, Schueffel (2016) proposes a definition that is based on "synthesis building on commonalities of the definitions that have been applied to Fintech in literature". The definition suggested by Schueffel (2016) is the following: "Fintech is a new financial industry that applies technology to improve financial activities".

Opinions differ on whether fintech encompasses only newly emerging technology-based financial companies, or if existing (traditional) financial institutions are part of the fintech industry, simply because they produce new technology-based services. There seems to be an

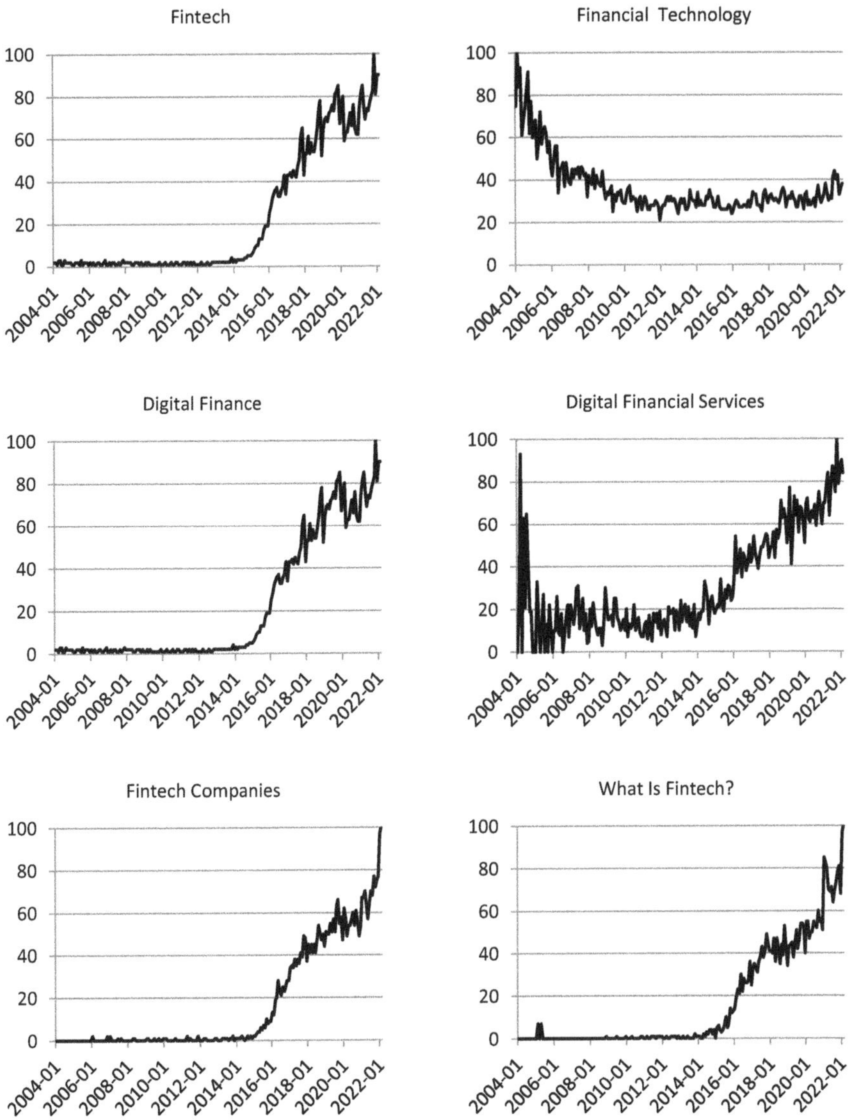

Figure 1. The frequency of fintech and related terms on Google search.

agreement that fintech refers to companies that develop financial services by relying on state-of-the-art technology. After reviewing several definitions, Varga (2017) proposes a definition that can be used to distinguish fintech from traditional, transforming, or already digitised financial institutions and to emphasise the importance of technology, service, and business model design and the regulatory environment with regard to fintech companies. The definition goes as follows: "Fintech refers to non- or not fully regulated ventures whose goal is to develop novel, technology-enabled financial services with a value-added design that will transform current financial practices".

The definition that Arner *et al.* (2015) introduce initially is that fintech refers to "the application of technology to finance", suggesting that this definition gives rise to three specific observations. The first observation is that fintech is not an inherently novel development for the financial services industry because the adoption of technology by the finance industry can be traced back to the 19th century. The second observation is that the financial services industry has been one of the prime purchasers of the products and services of information technology (IT) firms. As a matter of fact, the finance industry became the single largest purchaser of IT by the mid-1990s, a position that it has retained to this day. The third observation is that fintech is not confined to specific sectors (such as financing) or business models (such as peer-to-peer lending) — it rather covers the entire spectrum of services and products traditionally provided by the financial services industry.

Fintech may be defined by the outcomes it brings. Tikam (2020) identifies three outcomes, the first of which is disruption — that is, when technology is used to disrupt or transform financial services by creating new products and business models that fall outside the realm of traditional financial services (for example, peer-to-peer lending). The second outcome is technology-induced operational efficiency, when technology is used to improve performance or reduce the cost of providing financial services. The third outcome is improvement in customer experience, when technology is used to enhance customer service (for example, mobile banking). This means that a possible definition for fintech is that it involves the use of technology to disrupt or transform traditional financial services, enhance performance, and improve customer service.

Out of the tens of definitions found in the literature, no one definition is the best definition and no definition is completely right or wrong. Even different dictionaries contain different definitions.

In the *Oxford Dictionary*, fintech is defined as "computer programs and other technology used to support or enable banking and financial services". In *Dictionary.com*, it is defined in two different ways. The first is that it represents "digital technological innovations utilized by customers or institutions in the financial services industry". The second is that it is a "company that uses or develops such technologies". In *Collins Dictionary*, the following definition can be found: "digital technology used to support banking and financial services". It follows that the definition of fintech may refer to technology, products, or companies that are related in the following sense: the fintech industry consists of companies that use specific technology to come up with products that facilitate financial transactions.

A Google search for "definition of fintech" returns tens of definitions that refer to technology, industry, companies, and ideas. A technology-based definition is that fintech is technology that is utilised to help companies, business owners, and consumers better manage their financial operations, processes, and lives by utilising specialised software and algorithms that are used on computers and, increasingly, smartphones. A definition that refers to companies is that fintech encompasses companies that combine innovative business models and technology to enable, enhance, and disrupt financial services. An industry-based definition is that fintech is an emerging industry that uses technology to improve activities in finance. A definition based on ideas is the following: fintech encompasses ideas that provide solutions for customers unable to get loans from a traditional bank and consumers to shop online without using a credit card.

Some definitions have been adopted by international organisations. The World Economic Forum (WEF) defines fintech as "the use of technology and innovative business models in financial services" (World Economic Forum, 2015). The Basel Committee on Banking Supervision (BCBS) uses the working definition of the Financial Stability Board (FSB), which goes as follows: "technologically enabled financial innovation that could result in new business models, applications, processes, or products with an associated material effect on financial markets and institutions and the provision of financial services" (BCBS, 2018). The adoption of this definition is justified on the grounds that it is useful in the light of the current fluidity of fintech developments. The formal definition adopted by the International Monetary Fund (IMF) is spelt out by Taylor *et al.* (2019) as follows: fintech is "the advances in technology that have the potential to transform the provision of financial services spurring the development of new business models, applications, processes, and products". This is actually the definition used in the IMF–World Bank's Bali Fintech Agenda (BFA), which was launched in 2018 as a framework of high-level issues that countries should consider in their own domestic fintech policy discussions (see, for example, IMF, 2018).

It seems that so much fuss is made about the definition of fintech, which makes one wonder what value-added we may obtain from the quest for the "perfect definition", if ever there is such a thing. We might as well accept a simple definition such as "the use of technology to provide financial services and execute financial transactions".

It seems, therefore, that "fintech" is a rather loose concept that is used in different senses to mean different things. The first sense is that fintech refers to financial technology or the technology used by financial institutions. In another sense, fintech refers to the industry comprising all financial institutions using technology, which is the fintech industry in a broad sense. The industry in a narrow sense comprises the new firms (start-ups) using technology to provide financial services that are distinct from the services provided by tradition financial institutions. For the purpose of this chapter, fintech is taken to be the new firms utilising technology to provide financial services.

3. Functions and Operations

The word "functions" is used here to refer to the activities undertaken by fintech companies to produce digital financial services. Fintech encompasses a variety of financial activities and transactions, such as transferring money, depositing a cheque by using a mobile phone, bypassing a bank branch to apply for credit, raising money for a new business by using crowdfunding, and managing investments without the assistance of a real human being.

Theoretically, the provision of financial services by using technology can be examined by using the basic framework of how technology is included in the production function. This kind of analysis is proposed by Moosa (2022) where a production function, in which output

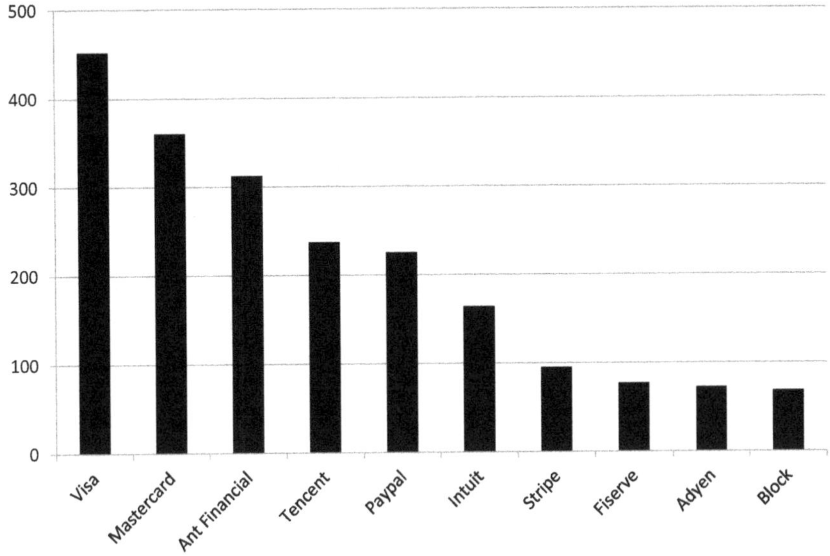

Figure 2. Top 10 fintech companies by market value.

is a function of labour, shifts upwards by the introduction of more sophisticated technology. Otherwise, an isoquant representing combinations of labour and capital that produces a given amount of output shifts downwards as a result of the introduction of more sophisticated technology. This framework can be used to demonstrate that the technology used to provide financial services is capital-deepening, in the sense that it boosts the productivity of capital more than that of labour. This is why fintech is believed to have an adverse effect on employment.

In a broad sense, the fintech industry (or ecosystem) consists of (i) fintech service providers; (ii) the technology used by fintech service providers to transform financial services; (iii) intermediaries using fintech to broker financial services; (iv) regulators; and (v) fintech enablers, providing support for the growth of the industry. Service providers are the fintech firms that provide financial services. By early 2022, the combined market value of the top 10 fintech service providers (the so-called fintech "unicorns") amounted to \$2.06 trillion. In Figure 2, we can see the top 10 fintech companies by market value.

Regulators play an important part in the fintech ecosystem by bringing trust and credibility to licensed firms and reassuring investors that their money is safe when dealing with fintech firms. Increasingly, regulators are playing an enabling role to drive the growth of fintech, on the grounds that fintech firms are conducive to safety by stimulating more competition. Fintech enablers take many shapes and forms, including accelerators, incubators, consultants, advisers, investors, and the media. Enablers facilitate or enhance an existing process or solution, motivated by the profit that can be realised by contributing to the development of the fintech industry. In a narrow sense, enablers are the technology platforms that rent out their core banking infrastructure to enhance financial apps and services.

The regulatory stance with respect to fintech may be based on the proposition that the characteristics of shadow banking are strikingly similar to those of fintech firms. The proponents of shadow banking argue against the regulation of shadow banking on the basis of the perceived characteristics of shadow financial institutions. Shadow banking, the proponents would argue, is superior to traditional banking, just as fintech start-ups are typically portrayed to be superior to traditional financial institutions. The argument that shadow banking is a "natural consequence of growth" is equally applicable to fintechs, because (like shadow banking) they provide much-needed, growth-triggered diversified set of financing modes and sources. Wallison's (2012) view that the regulation of shadow banking would "add costs that will impair economic growth" is equally applicable to fintech firms that provide cheaper financial services. The proposition that shadow banking is little understood is even more valid for fintech because the use of complex technology makes it difficult for the average person to understand how they operate. As in the case of shadow banking, the continued growth of fintech is indicative of its ability to provide "important financial intermediation functions that are distinct from those performed by banks and capital markets" as suggested by Claessens *et al.* (2012). Those who argue against the regulation of shadow banking suggest that regulation kills the innovation brought about by shadow banking, an argument that is even more valid for fintech because of the technological innovation adopted and used by fintech firms to provide financial services. And, as in the case of shadow banking, self-discipline can be used as a regulating mechanism that precludes the use of "costly regulation". This is the traditional argument that it makes sense to allow the inmates to run the asylum.

The similarity between shadow banking and fintech has been debated for some time. Gelis (2016) claims that fintech is often placed (by traditional banks) under the shadow banking umbrella characterised by opacity, excessive risk-taking, malpractice, negligence, and fraud. Ghosh (2020) suggests that shadow banks include fintech lenders, describing them as the "prime source of the spike in auto-debit failures". Seru (2019) refers to "the business model of fintech shadow banks" and to the "financial technology adopted by shadow banks". Bao and Huang (2020) refer to "the importance of shadow banking, especially through fintech lending" and to "the performance of traditional and shadow banking systems, and fintech lending specifically", implying that fintech lending is an activity of the shadow banking system. Buchak *et al.* (2018) refer to "fintech and non-fintech shadow banks".

On the other hand, Gelis (2016) uses two arguments to dispute the classification of fintech under shadow banking. The first is that neither the fintech ecosystem nor the fintech lending industry can be identified as shadow banking according to the FSB's definition of fintech. The second is that the regulation of peer-to-peer (P2P) lending should differ from the prudential rules applied to traditional banks, since activities, risk exposure, and the risks posed to the economy are different. It is true that P2P lending is different from the lending of traditional banks, but it involves more counterparty risk and it is perhaps more susceptible to fraud. The common characteristic shared by shadow banks and fintechs is "innovation", financial innovation as the product of shadow banks, and technological innovation as the product of fintechs.

If fintechs are indeed like shadow banks, one may infer the risks facing fintechs and the regulatory implications from the work on shadow banks. The Financial Stability Board (2017) has assessed the evolution of shadow banking activities and the adequacy of post-crisis policies designed to address these risks. The FSB makes three recommendations in this respect. The first is to enhance system-wide oversight of shadow banking and policy responses to address the identified risks by establishing a systematic process for assessing the financial stability risks posed by shadow banking. The second is to strengthen the monitoring of shadow banking activity and data collection. The third is to complete the remaining policy development at the international level and implement the agreed policy recommendations to reduce risks and arbitrage opportunities across jurisdictions and sectors. Perhaps these recommendations are valid for the fintech industry.

4. Technology as a Source of Risk

The technology used by fintech firms in the provision of financial services is not unique to the finance industry, which makes one wonder why it is referred to as "financial technology". For instance, artificial intelligence is used in the provision of financial services, but it is also used to make driverless cars and robots. Table 1 provides a description and lists the applications of the technology used for the provision of financial services.

The use of technology brings with it technology-related risks. The BCBS (2004) classifies the operational risk by source into people risk, process risk, and technology risk. An extensive use of novel technology brings with it direct exposure to technology risks, including new technology failure, technology-related operational errors, system failure, outdated hardware, computer viruses, and hacking. People risk and process risk intensify with the use of novel technology. Examples of people risk are misuse of important information, embezzlement, unauthorised fund transfers, and unauthorised trading. The same is true of process risk such as employee error, inadequate quality control, inadequate security, inadequate supervision, inadequate transaction completion, lack of proper due diligence, and the loss of critical information. Aguayo and Slusarczyk (2020) refer explicitly to the operational risk arising from the digitisation of banking services, including (among others) defects and failures, loss of data integrity, violation of a technical system, and cyber-attacks. They use the concept of "digital operational risk", which they attribute to

Table 1. The technology used by the finance industry.

Technology	Description	Applications in finance
Artificial intelligence	A technology that enables a machine to simulate human behaviour.	Customer support, detection of anomalies, credit card fraud, ultra-high-frequency trading, and numerous other applications.
Machine learning	A technology that is intended to allow machines to learn from data for the purpose of producing accurate output.	Risk management, portfolio management, algorithmic trading, high-frequency trading, fraud detection, loan and insurance underwriting, document analysis, trade settlements, and money-laundering prevention.
Big data	Huge datasets that cannot be processed effectively with traditional applications.	Illegal trading activity, high-frequency trading, pre-trade decisions, sentiment measurement, risk analytics, anti-money laundering, and fraud mitigation.
Quantum computing	Used in conjunction with artificial intelligence and machine learning to solve complex problems very quickly.	Detection of patterns in past data and predicting the behaviour of financial systems by using Monte Carlo simulations.
Internet of Things	Billions of physical devices that are connected to the internet for the purpose of collecting and sharing data.	Analysis of customer behaviour, offering personalised services, construction of customer profiles, and fraud detection. Insurance companies can use IoT to determine the insurance premium charged to a driver by monitoring actual driving patterns.

(*Continued*)

Table 1. (*Continued*)

Technology	Description	Applications in finance
Aggregators	An aggregator is any device that provides multiple services to other devices or users, either with its capabilities or by forwarding transmissions in a more concentrated and efficient way.	Provision of payment and settlement services. Processing aggregators allow merchants to accept credit cards and bank transfers without having to set up their merchant accounts.
Biometric identification	A technology used for identifying and authenticating individuals through unique biological characteristics.	Customer identification.
Regulation technology (Regtech)	Management of regulatory processes within the financial industry through technology, including monitoring, reporting, and compliance.	Provision of anti-fraud and risk management services for digital transactions, finding solutions for compliance with anti-money laundering and the enforcement of sanctions.
Blockchain technology	A system of recording information in a way that makes it difficult or impossible to change by hacking or cheating the system.	Streamlining payment processing, speeding up and securing transactions, minimising auditing complexity, making credit reports more accurate and transparent, reducing settlement time, and exchanging funds more quickly and securely. Applications in finance also include stock exchange transactions, asset ownership, document certification, tokenisation of assets, credit reference, derivatives (with smart contracts), and payment systems.

internal sources (defects or failures) and external sources (fraud risk, technological risk, and cyber risk).

5. The Effect of COVID-19

The COVID-19 pandemic has provided a boost to the fintech industry as lockdowns and social distancing have forced people to resort to digital financial services and e-commerce, a trend that is likely to continue in a post-COVID world. An indicator of the growth of fintech is the number of fintech start-ups, where a start-up is a company in the first stages of operations, founded by one or more entrepreneurs for the purpose of developing a product for which they believe there is demand. In Figure 3, we can see the number of fintech start-ups emerging during the period 2018–2022 in three geographical regions (the Americas; Europe, the Middle East, and Africa; and Asia-Pacific). We can see the big jump in 2020 and the continuation of the trend in 2021, which was a significant change from the flat pattern observed in 2019, before the advent of the pandemic. Figure 4 displays the percentage growth rates. For the whole world,

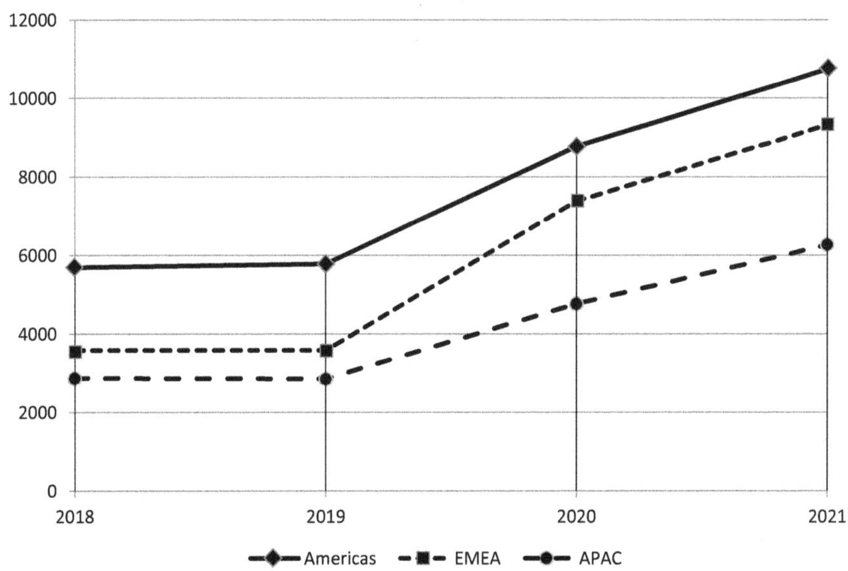

Figure 3. Number of fintech start-ups.

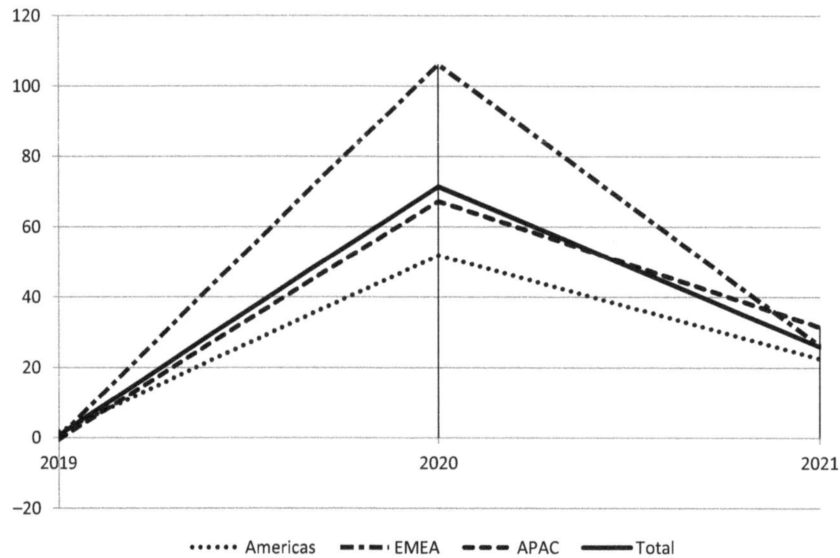

Figure 4. Growth rates of fintech start-ups.

the growth rate jumped from 0.7% in 2019 to over 71% in 2020. In 2019, the growth rate was even negative at −0.5% in the Asia-Pacific region, compared with 67% in 2020. According to the DeVere Group (2021), the use of fintech apps increased more than 61% between the start of the pandemic and April 2021.

In Figure 5, we can see changes in indicators of fintech activity in the first two quarters of 2020 compared with the same period in 2019. These indicators include transaction volume (or value), number of transactions, number of corporate customers, and number of new customers. These four indicators reflect a positive effect of the pandemic as fintechs experienced rapid growth in all of them, particularly the number of new customers. Four other indicators reflect the negative effects of the pandemic, including contractual disputes with customers, non-payments, default on outstanding loans, and arrears or late repayments. All of these indicators went up.

Several reasons can be suggested as to why the pandemic provided a boost for the adoption of fintech. It has led to an increase in the use of digital banking, driven by the ease of use and limited access to traditional banking services due to restrictions on movements and the shift to working from home. Furthermore, the pandemic has led

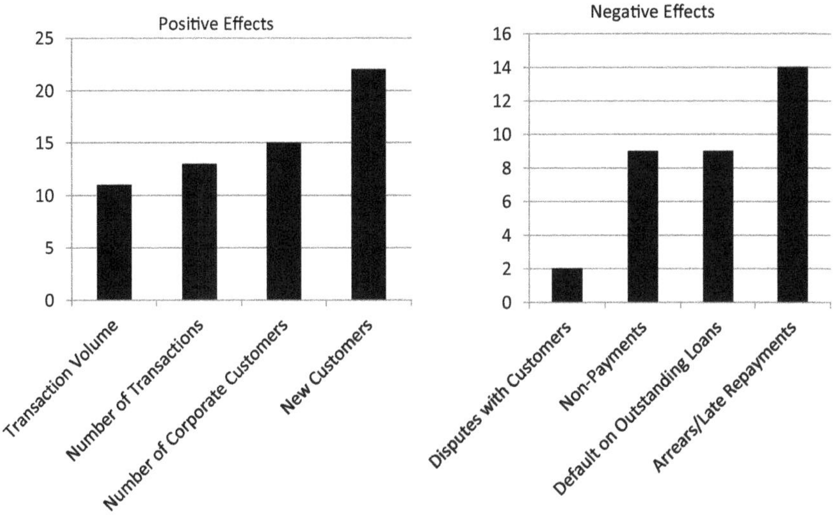

Figure 5. Changes in fintech activity indicators (first two quarters of 2020).

to an increase in the demand for essential goods and e-commerce activities, as consumers strived to minimise in-person contact. In response to the price hikes caused by disruptions in supply chains, consumers might have resorted to hoarding and stockpiling essential goods, using digital payments for acquiring these goods. The Paycheck Protection Program (PPP), introduced by the US government in response to the pandemic, was partially implemented by using fintech.

Agur *et al.* (2020) point out that digital financial services allow for social distancing and that the services provided by fintech take on added value in response to the COVID-19 crisis. However, they warn that "attempting to quickly scale up digital financial services in the short timeframe during which a crisis response needs to be formulated is not merely challenging but potentially also risky". Specifically, they warn of the risks to stability and integrity, suggesting a scaling up of the use of digital financial services in response to a crisis could lead to a worsening of operational constraints, cyber-attacks, fraud, money laundering, data loss, and privacy invasions.

Even after life returns to "normal", it is likely that some changes in behaviour as a result of the pandemic will persist, including the ways in which consumers do banking, pay bills, and conduct transactions. Walden and Foreman (2020) identify "five pandemic-sparked fintech trends worth keeping an eye on". The first is that the adoption of fintech among older populations has gone up. The second is shifting consumer perceptions of online banking towards greater adoption. The third trend is that low-cost remittance platforms are gaining traction, which is why they note that "an area that may change forever as a result of COVID-19 is remittances". Trend number four is that traditional banks and credit unions are striving to improve customer experience online. Last, but not least, the pandemic has led to the growth of online retail spending in a big way, which is likely to persist in a post-COVID world.

The effects of the pandemic on digital finance and fintech adoption are examined by Fu and Mishra (2022) who use mobile application data from a globally representative sample to find that the spread of the virus and related government lockdowns led to a sizeable increase in the rate of finance app downloads. Their results suggest that traditional incumbents saw the largest growth in their digital offerings during the initial period, but that "BigTech" companies and newer fintech providers ultimately outperformed them over time. The Australian Securities Exchange (ASX) (2021) found that the pandemic enhanced growth in the Australian fintech sector, in that fintechs raised record capital during the pandemic and more of them became profitable as the sector matured rapidly. The ASX also found that the market for fintechs became larger than ever as COVID boosted consumer interest in transactions online.

The pandemic created some risk management problems for fintechs. A joint study of the World Bank, World Economic Forum, and Cambridge Judge Business School (2020) revealed that fintech firms reported some operational and funding challenges during the pandemic. Two-thirds of firms surveyed said that they changed their business models by reducing fees, changing qualification criteria, and easing payment requirements. About 60% of the respondents launched new products and value-added services, such as offering information. About 40% of the surveyed firms indicated that they have either introduced or are in the process of introducing enhanced fraud or security measures as a response to business conditions under the pandemic. Other operational challenges reported by firms included more agent or partner downtime and rising unsuccessful transactions and access requests. Furthermore, fintech firms reported higher expenses for onboarding and data storage.

The effect of the pandemic on fintech varies by the kind of activity. In the context of payments, for example, it had a negative impact on point-of-sale (POS) payments due to the slow recovery in spending globally. However, P2P digital payments grew strongly while e-commerce payments witnessed a secular shift as consumers moved away from using cash and cards to digital alternatives such as online payment and internet banking. In the business of lending, the incidence of missing regular payments by consumers and businesses went up, which prompted companies in the lending business to minimise losses by using advanced credit-risk algorithms. In investment services, fintech firms in the retail brokerage business benefitted from market volatility and from the tendency of consumers to look for hybrid robo-advisors and deeply integrated platforms.

Table 2 provides a summary of selected studies dealing with COVID-19 in relation to fintech, some of which deal with fintech in general whereas others deal with specific functions of fintech. For example, Najaf *et al.* (2022) examine how the pandemic has changed the key determinants of P2P lending while Abdillah (2020) look at the efficiency of the Go-Pay service. More general studies include Fu and Mishra (2022), who investigate the effect of the pandemic on the rate of finance app downloads, and Le *et al.* (2021), who assess the intention to use fintech post-COVID 19. The paper by Gao (2022) examines the joint effect of the lockdowns and fintech on the establishment of new manufacturing firms, also showing that fintech is not intensively related to labour demand in the manufacturing sector.

6. The Challenges Facing Fintech

The rise of fintech during the pandemic brought with it the possibility of mass failure of these firms, with implications for financial stability and consumer protection. Five reasons for the failure of fintechs are identified by Boyd (2021): underfunding (which is the most common reason for failure), wrong choice of investment partners, compliance problems, fierce competition (ease of entry coupled with the difficulty of establishing a foothold), and economic downturn, which makes it

Table 2. Selected studies of the effects of COVID on fintech.

Authors	Journal	Methods	Findings/Recommendation
Najaf *et al.* (2022)	*Journal of Sustainable Finance & Investment*	Qualitative	COVID-19 has brought a drastic change in the key determinants of P2P lending.
Financial Stability Board (2022)	*FSB Report*	Qualitative	The pandemic has accelerated the trend towards digitalisation of retail financial services.
Fu and Mishra (2022)	*Journal of Financial Intermediation*	Quantitative	The spread of COVID-19 and lockdowns led to a sizeable increase in the rate of finance app downloads.
Al-Nnawayseh (2020)	*Journal of Open Innovation*	Quantitative	Perceived benefits and social norms significantly affect the intention to use fintech applications.
Abdillah (2020)	*Scientific Journal of Informatics*	Quantitative	The Go-Pay service is efficient but needs to improve its novelty. Additional knowledge for user experience using fintech applications.
Alber and Dabour (2020)	*International Journal of Economics and Finance*	Quantitative	Social distancing may affect digital payments.

Le (2021)	*Heliyon*	Quantitative	The intention to use fintech post-COVID 19 is enhanced by lockdown, trust, data security and privacy, and staff services.
Bao and Huang (2021)	*Journal of Financial and Quantitative Analysis*	Quantitative	Fintech companies are more likely to expand credit access to new and financially constrained borrowers after the start of the pandemic.
Le *et al.* (2021)	*Research in International Business and Finance*	Quantitative	Outbreak of COVID-19 exacerbated volatility transmission across asset classes, while subsequent decreases in new confirmed cases reduced the intensity of spillovers.
Gao (2022)	*Economic Analysis and Policy*	Quantitative	Lockdown policies and fintech have negative impacts on new firm creation in the manufacturing sector and longer pandemics induce more severe destruction of firm registrations. Fintech is not intensively related to labour demand in the manufacturing sector.

difficult to raise capital in a timely manner. Shevlin (2019) adds two more reasons. The first is thinking that a fintech start-up is the same as any other tech start-up, which implies failure to understand the psychology of financial affairs. The second is competing solely on cost by providing cheap services when banks and other traditional financial institutions have massive economies of scale. Bouvier (2016) makes the same point by referring to "thinking that competing on cost will win the day", which he identifies as a cause of failure. He also emphasises legal and regulatory factors, such as failure to understand regulatory rules and paying little attention to compliance.

The lack of funding, as a reason for the failure of fintech start-ups, is emphasised by Murthy *et al.* (2019) who attribute this problem to factors that discourage potential funders from engaging with fintechs. These factors include "too many models", "too little clarity", "a crowded space with many ideas", and "few metrics for success". Even if the underlying idea is good, it is difficult to assess the operational performance of early-stage fintechs, which makes it difficult for funders (such as prospective investors and established financial institutions) to determine whether a start-up has what it takes to bring its ideas to the market successfully. They also suggest that regulators struggle to regulate and supervise new kinds of fintech services in the absence of metrics that can be used to determine a firm's capabilities and risks.

Some reasons for the failure of fintechs, even before they start, have been identified as mistakes. Agrawal (2021) argues that "start-ups always kick off on a wave of optimism, often with the desire to change the world", but they soon "hit rough water", particularly when they want to change the world overnight. Fintech start-ups seem to overlook considerations such as uniqueness of the product (doing something better than anyone else), the existence of a market for the product, whether or not the product serves any meaningful purpose, the formulation of a marketing plan, and the continuity of demand.

All of these considerations and reasons for failure have been observed in reality. Boyd (2021) gives examples of real fintech firms that failed for one reason or another, including funding difficulties, fraud, inadequate demand, strategic factors, and takeovers. Wonga, established in 2006 to provide short-term online loans, is an interesting case because the reason for failure was that the company's

AI system lent money to people who could not afford to pay back (so much for making the right lending decisions by utilising AI). Wirecard, established in 1999 to provide payment processing and risk management services, failed as a result of fraud. ScaleFactor, established in 2013 to provide software for automating and streamlining back-office tasks, failed because the pandemic wiped out demand.

7. Fintech Risks from a Regulatory Perspective

The advent of fintech has brought with it increasing reliance on technology as well as closer interconnectedness and complexity. These, as well as economies of scale in IT applications, have led to the emergence of new risks for consumers, firms, and financial stability. Table 3 reports the findings of selected studies of risk management in the fintech industry. These studies deal with various kinds of risks to which fintechs are exposed, including cyber risk, financial risk, regulatory risk, and credit risk. Xia *et al.* (2020) propose a model that can be used to identify risk from the text posted on online loan investment platforms. It can be used to guide investors' investment and improve the management of financial technology platforms, while Tian *et al.* (2021) examine the binary classification algorithms used to detect fraud and predict risk. Ng and Kwok (2017) look at some aspects of the regulatory response to the rise of fintech, suggesting that financial regulators are in a position to harness comprehensive risk-based mechanisms to embrace exposures to cyber risk.

According to KPMG (2019), the risks posed by the advent of fintech can be classified according to who is exposed to these risks: (i) risks to consumers and investors, (ii) risks to financial services firms, and (iii) risks to financial stability. At least five kinds of risks to consumers are associated with fintech. The first is the lack of understanding, as a typical consumer is unlikely to have full knowledge of the underlying products. The second is the risk of mis-selling of products as technology may inadvertently (or intentionally) provide new means for misleading consumers, exposing them to fraudulent activities. The third is the risk of financial exclusion, as increasing digitisation may exclude the old, vulnerable, and those with computer illiteracy. The fourth pertains to data, as consumers are vulnerable to the loss of data, and they may not understand how and for

Table 3. Selected studies of risk management in fintech.

Authors	Journal	Methods (qualitative or quantitative)	Findings/Recommendation
Hedwige (2019)	*Journal of Risk Management in Financial Institutions*	Qualitative	Fintech can be disruptive both for banks and regulators.
Ng and Kwok (2017)	*Journal of Financial Regulation and Compliance*	Qualitative	By adopting a strategic approach that seizes opportunities associated with fintech, financial regulators harness comprehensive risk-based mechanisms to embrace exposures to cyber risks.
Tian *et al.* (2021)	*Information Discovery and Delivery*	Qualitative	Most of the research adopts binary classification algorithms to detect fraud and predict risk.
Lee and Shin (2018)	*Business Horizons*	Qualitative	Fintech start-ups have to deal with many types of risks, including financial risk and regulatory risk.
Gomber *et al.* (2018)	*Journal of Management Information Systems*	Qualitative	Going forward, assessing the innovations, disruptions, and transformations in the fintech revolution will need to be done on a repeated basis.
Gai *et al.* (2018)	*Journal of Network and Computer Applications*	Qualitative	Identifying fundamentals of forming active fintech solutions.
Das (2019)	*Financial Management*	Qualitative	The great strides made in computing technology, mathematics, statistics, psychology, econometrics, linguistics, cryptography, big data, and computer interfaces have combined to create an explosion of fintechs.

Jagtiani and Lemieux (2019)	*Financial Management*	Quantitative	Non-traditional data are increasingly used by fintech lenders.
Giglio (2021)	*Journal of Risk Management in Financial Institutions*	Qualitative	Identification of six Fintech business models implemented by fintech start-ups.
Giudici *et al.* (2019)	*Frontiers in Artificial Intelligence*	Quantitative	Credit risk accuracy of peer-to-peer platforms can be enhanced by leveraging the topological information embedded into similar networks, derived from borrowers' financial information.
Xia *et al.* (2020)	*Annals of Operations Research*	Quantitative	A model can be applied to identify the risks from the text posted on online loan investment platforms. It can be used to guide investors' investment and improve the management of financial technology platforms.
Wang *et al.* (2021)	*Research in International Business and Finance*	Quantitative	By using financial technology, commercial banks can improve their traditional business model by reducing bank operating costs, improving service efficiency, strengthening risk control capabilities, and creating enhanced customer-oriented business models.

what purpose their data are used. The fifth is reduced competition as markets get dominated by a small number of large firms because of economies of scale in technology and data handling.

Risks to firms arise because the development of fintech has led to intensification of competitive pressures, which means that most firms will struggle to survive. Then there is the risk of governance, as board members and senior management may not have sufficient understanding of fintech and related risks, which means that they may be unable to identify, measure, manage, and control the risks arising from intensive use of technology, which invariably affects operational resilience. Also problematical is the increasing use of outsourcing to third-party providers of technology and data. Fintech may prove to be yet another example of the familiar story of business developments running ahead of the ability of some firms to put in place the systems and controls necessary to manage the underlying risks.

Firms are exposed to the risk of data handling. While they are expected to meet existing data protection requirements, they also need to take a proactive approach to the possibility that regulators entertain the idea of a fundamental re-thinking of data privacy, security, and protection. The potential for misuse and concerns about data privacy and protection intensify as customer data become more valuable and sought after. Furthermore, data limitations may make it difficult for firms to validate outcomes, particularly when artificial intelligence is used to analyse datasets for the purpose of generating solutions.

Further risks pertain to compliance with anti-money laundering (AML) requirements. Some fintech applications raise difficult legal questions, particularly when cross-border operations extend across different national legal and regulatory frameworks. As far as business model viability is concerned, regulatory requirements may have an impact on a firm's strategy and business model because some business opportunities may be constrained by regulators (for example, restrictions on sales of some products to more vulnerable and less sophisticated consumers and retail investors). Firms may also need to adjust their products in response to regulatory requirements.

The fintech industry is still small relative to the size of the traditional financial system, and no new fintech firm is big enough to be too big to fail or qualify as a systemically important financial institution. At present, therefore, the risk posed by fintech to financial stability is fairly small. However, potential risks to financial stability may arise from a number of fintech-related developments, whose magnitude and precise nature may not be trackable accurately, owing to the unavailability of sufficient information. These developments pertain to concentration, alternative channels of financial intermediation, herd-like behaviour, the use of crypto assets, and system-wide vulnerabilities. As far as concentration is concerned, a high concentration of fintech firms as the dominant players in the market may lead to the rise of a systemically important entity. Alternative channels of financial intermediation pertain to non-bank providers of credit, payment systems, and other financial services, which may grow rapidly without proper regulation. Herd-like behaviour, which is a source of concern, may arise from the widespread use of similar machine learning and other techniques to guide lending and trading. Regulators are also concerned about system-wide vulnerabilities arising from the increasing levels of operational risk and cyber risk in the financial system.

The Basel Committee on Banking Supervision has identified a "wide variety of risks" associated with fintech, such that these risks "cut across various sectors and often blend both tactical and strategic risk elements", particularly with reference to the banking sector (BCBS, 2018). Strategic risk is the risk to the profitability of individual banks arising from a rapid unbundling of bank services to fintech firms. Potential losses could be incurred by existing financial institutions as a result of declining market share or profit margin if new entrants are able to use technology more efficiently to deliver less expensive services that meet customer expectations more effectively. Operational risk is seen as having two dimensions: a systemic dimension (the rise of fintech leads to more IT interdependence between incumbent financial institutions and fintech firms) and an idiosyncratic dimension (individual firms may find it difficult to manage and control operational risk as a result of increasing complexity of the system). Compliance risk arises because banks will need appropriate AML monitoring processes if they process transactions on behalf of the customers of fintech companies. Fintech brings with it outsourcing risk, the possibility that ambiguity could arise with respect to the responsibilities of various participants in the value chain when more parties are involved in the offering of a financial product. Naturally, new technologies and business models can lead to a rise in cyber risk, particularly in the absence of adequate controls. Last, but not least, the use of new technology and the emergence of new financial service providers can aggravate the volatility of existing bank funding sources, leading to a higher level of liquidity risk.

Regulators respond to the risks to which consumers and firms are exposed by adjusting the regulatory perimeter, which is used to determine which activities require authorisation and what level of protection consumers can expect for the financial products they purchase. Specific responses to risks to consumers include measures of consumer and data protection. Specific responses to the risks facing firms include governance, risk management, and operation resilience. As far as risks to financial stability are concerned, the response takes the form of data analysis and emerging regulatory interventions.

8. Concluding Remarks

Due to its significant impact and longevity, the COVID-19 crisis has revealed itself not as a short-term emergency but as a systemic crisis. The pandemic brought with it uncertainty that has affected the corporate decision-making process. It has led to global business interruption, pressure on the healthcare system, economic slump, supply shortages, cyber threats to remote work, psychological stress, job insecurity, family health concerns, public fears, rumours, and uncertainty about the future. More specific effects are that it has spurred the adoption of telehealth and e-commerce and made corporate operations more complex. These developments are bound to have implications for the corporate risk management process and financial regulation.

As far as the fintech industry is concerned, the COVID-19 pandemic has had both positive and negative effects. On the one hand, the pandemic has created significant economic hardships due to closure of businesses and layoffs. Therefore, the negative effects can be seen in terms of contractual disputes with customers, non-payments, defaults, and late repayments. On the other hand, the non-pharmaceutical measures adopted by governments to stem the spread of the virus enhanced the tendency to use digital financial services. The positive effect can be seen through rising number and value of transactions and growing number of customers. This positive effect led to the spectacular growth of the fintech industry in 2020 and 2021.

Both the negative and positive effects have risk management and regulatory implications. The negative effects forced some fintechs to change their business models and take protective measures. The positive effects have resulted in massive growth of the fintech industry, which would likely lead to an increase in the incidence of corporate failure, as well as aggravated risk to financial stability and consumers. Fintech boosts both the frequency and severity of operational loss events by enhancing the opportunity to commit fraud and the possibility of system failure.

This chapter presents a narrative linking the growth of fintech to the pandemic, which would aggravate the risks of fintech and the associated regulatory challenges. The regulatory authorities may not be capable of coping with the pace of new regulatory challenges, but this is not a matter to be ignored. Of utmost importance is the need to re-examine repeatedly the regulatory perimeter, which should be updated on a regular basis. Giving fintechs a free pass because they are "innovative" and "disruptors" would be a grave mistake. After all, fintech is more likely to be a transitory hype than a revolution.

References

Abdillah, L.A. (2020). FinTech e-commerce payment application user experience analysis during COVID-19 pandemic. *Scientific Journal of Informatics*, 7, 265–278.

Agrawal, A.J. (2021). 5 hidden mistakes that cause startups to fail before they even start. Available at: https://www.startupgrind.com/blog/5-reasons-why-your-startups-products-have-failed-from-the-beginning/.

Aguayo, F.Z. and Slusarczyk, B. (2020). Risks of banking services' digitalization: The practice of diversification and sustainable development goals. *Sustainability*, 12, 1–10.

Agur, I., Peria, S.M. and Rochon, C. (2020). Digital financial services and the pandemic: Opportunities and risks for emerging and developing economies. IMF Special Series on COVID-19, 1 July.

Alber, N. and Dabour, M. (2020). The dynamic relationship between FinTech and social distancing under COVID-19 pandemic: Digital payments evidence. *International Journal of Economics and Finance*, 12, 109–117.

Al-Nnawayseh, M.K. (2020). FinTech in COVID-19 and beyond: What factors are affecting customers' choice of FinTech applications? *Journal of Open Innovation*, 6, 153–167.

Arner, D.W., Barberis, J.N. and Buckley, R.P. (2015). The evolution of Fintech: A new post-crisis paradigm? https://core.ac.uk/download/pdf/38088713.pdf.

ASX (2021). Pandemic boosts growth in Australian Fintech Sector, 27 January. https://www2.asx.com.au/blog/listed-at-asx/pandemic-boosts-growth-in-australian-fintech-sector.

Bao, Z. and Huang, D. (2020). Shadow banking in a crisis: Evidence from FinTech during COVID-19. *Working Paper*. Available at: https://iceanet.org/wp-content/uploads/2021/11/Huang.pdf.

Bao, Z. and Huang, D. (2021). Shadow banking in a crisis: Evidence from Fintech during COVID-19. *Journal of Financial and Quantitative Analysis*, 56, 2320–2355.

BCBS (2004). *Basel II: International Convergence of Capital Measurement and Capital Standards: A Revised Framework*. Basel: Bank for International Settlements.

BCBS (2018). *Sound Practices Implications of Fintech Developments for Banks and Bank Supervisors*. Basel: Bank for International Settlements.

Bettinger, A. (1972). FINTECH: A series of 40 time shared models used at manufacturers Hanover trust company. *Interfaces*, 2, 62–63.

Bouvier, P. (2016). Ten reasons why Fintech firms fail. *Finyear*, 1 March, https://www.finyear.com/Ten-Reasons-why-Fintech-firms-fail_a35516.html.

Boyd, A. (2021). 10 Fintechs that failed (and why). *Finty*, 7 May, https://finty.com/us/research/fintech-failures/.

Buchak, G., Matvos, G., Piskorski, T. and Seru, A. (2018). Fintech, regulatory arbitrage, and the rise of shadow banks. *Journal of Financial Economics*, 130, 453–483.

Claessens, S., Pozsar, Z., Ratnovski, L. and Singh, M. (2012). Shadow banking: Economics and policy priorities. Available at: http://www.voxeu.org/article/shadow-banking-economics-and-policy-priorities.

Das, S.R. (2019). The future of Fintech. *Financial Management*, 48, 981–1007.

DeVere Group (2021). Fintech App usage up 61% year-on-year. Press Release, 28 April.

Financial Stability Board (2017). Assessment of shadow banking activities: Risks and the adequacy of post-crisis policy tools to address financial stability concerns, 3 July, Basel, Switzerland.

Financial Stability Board (2022). FinTech and market structure in the COVID-19 pandemic: Implications for financial stability, 21 March. Available at: https://www.fsb.org/2022/03/fintech-and-market-structure-in-the-covid-19-pandemic-implications-for-financial-stability/.

Fu, J. and Mishra, M. (2022). Fintech in the time of COVID-19: Technological adoption during crises. *Journal of Financial Intermediation*, 50, 1–30.

Gai, K., Qiua, M. and Sun, X. (2018). A survey on FinTech. *Journal of Network and Computer Applications*, 103, 262–273.

Gao, J. (2022). Has COVID-19 hindered small business activities? The role of Fintech. *Economic Analysis and Policy*, 74, 297–308.

Gelis, P. (2016). Why Fintech has absolutely nothing to do with shadow banking, 31 May. Available at: https://www.linkedin.com/pulse/why-fintech-has-absolutely-nothing-do-shadow-banking-philippe-gelis/.

Ghosh, S. (2020). Shadow banks, fintech companies lead in loan defaults. *Hindustan Times*, 17 November, https://www.hindustantimes.com/business-news/shadow-banks-fintech-companies-lead-in-loan-defaults/story-lqWROMMVba1VM46Nvb20LO.html.

Giglio, F. (2021). Fintech: A literature review. *European Research Studies Journal*, 24, 600–627.

Giudici, P., Hadji-Misheva, B. and Spelta, A. (2019). Network based scoring models to improve credit risk management in peer to peer lending platforms. *Frontiers in Artificial Intelligence*, 24 May. Available at: https://www.frontiersin.org/articles/10.3389/frai.2019.00003/full.

Gomber, P., Kauffman, R.J., Parker, C. and Weber, B.W. (2018). On the Fintech revolution: Interpreting the forces of innovation, disruption, and transformation in financial services. *Journal of Management Information Systems*, 35, 220–265.

Gray, A. and Leibrock, M. (2017). Fintech and financial stability exploring how technological innovations could impact. Available at: https://www.dtcc.com/-/media/Files/PDFs/Fintech-and-Financial-Stability.pdf

Hedwige, N. (2019). How disruptive are Fintech and digital for banks and regulators? *Journal of Risk Management in Financial Institutions*, 12, 217–222.

Hochstein, M. (2015a) Fintech (the word, that is) evolves, *American Banker*, 5 October, https://www.americanbanker.com/opinion/fintech-the-word-that-is-evolves.

Hochstein, M. (2015b) Friday flashback: Did Citi coin the term 'Fintech'? *American Banker*, 25 September, https://www.americanbanker.com/opinion/friday-flashback-did-citi-coin-the-term-fintech.

IMF (2018). The Bali Fintech agenda: A blueprint for successfully harnessing Fintech's opportunities. Press Release No. 18/388, 11 October

Jagtiani, J. and Lemieux, C. (2019). The roles of alternative data and machine learning in Fintech lending: Evidence from the Lendingclub consumer platform. *Financial Management*, 48, 1009–1029.

KPMG (2019). Regulation and supervision of Fintech: Ever-expanding expectations, March, https://assets.kpmg.com/content/dam/kpmg/xx/pdf/2019/03/regulation-and-supervision-of-fintech.pdf.

Le, L.T., Yarovaya, L. and Nasir, M.A. (2021). Did COVID-19 change spillover patterns between Fintech and other asset classes? *Research in International Business and Finance*, 58, doi: 10.1016/j.ribaf.2021.101441.

Le, M.T.H. (2021). Examining factors that boost intention and loyalty to use Fintech post-COVID-19 lockdown as a new normal behaviour. *Heliyon*, 7, e07821.

Lee, I. and Shin, Y.J. (2018). Fintech: Ecosystem, business models, investment decisions, and challenges. *Business Horizons*, 61, 35–46.

Leong, K. and Sung, A. (2018). FinTech (financial technology): What is it and how to use technologies to create business value in Fintech way. *International Journal of Innovation, Management and Technology*, 9, 74–78.

Moosa, I.A. (2022). *Fintech: A Revolution or a Transitory Hype*. Cheltenham: Edward Elgar.

Murthy, G., Fernandez-Vidal, M., Faz, X. and Barreto, R. (2019). Fintechs and financial inclusion, consultative group to assist the poor, May, https://www.cgap.org/sites/default/files/publications/2019_05_Focus_Note_Fintech_and_Financial_Inclusion_1_0.pdf.

Najaf, K., Subramaniam, R.K. and Atayah, O.F. (2022). Understanding the implications of Fintech peer-to-peer (P2P) lending during the COVID-19 pandemic. *Journal of Sustainable Finance and Investment*, 12, 87–102.

Ng, A.W. and Kwok, B.K.B. (2017). Emergence of Fintech and cybersecurity in a global financial centre: Strategic approach by a regulator. *Journal of Financial Regulation and Compliance*, 25, 422–434.

Schueffel, P. (2016). Taming the beast: A scientific definition of Fintech. *Journal of Innovation Management*, 4, 32–54.

Seru, A. (2019). Regulating banks in the era of Fintech shadow banks, 30 June. Available at: https://www.bis.org/events/agm2019/agm2019_speech_seru.pdf.

Shevlin, R. (2019). Why Fintech startups fail, *Forbes*, 29 July.

Taylor, C., Wilson, C., Holttinen, E. and Morozova, A. (2019). Institutional arrangements for Fintech regulation and supervision. *Fintech Notes*, No. 19/02.

Tian, X., He, J.S. and Han, M. (2021). Data-driven approaches in Fintech: A survey. *Information Discovery and Delivery*, 49, 123–135.

Tikam, J. (2020). Define Fintech, *Vedanvi*, 7 June, https://vedanvi.com/.

Varga, D. (2017). Fintech, the new era of financial services. *Budapest Management Review*, 48, 22–32.

Walden, S. and Foreman, D. (2020). 5 Fintech trends likely to stick around after the pandemic. *Forbes Advisor*, 28 September, https://www.forbes.com/advisor/author/swalden/.

Wallison, P.W. (2012). Does shadow banking require regulation? *American Enterprise Institute*, 14 June. Available at: http://www.aei.org/publication/does-shadow-banking-require-regulation/.

Wang, Y., Xiuping, S. and Zhang, Q. (2021). Can Fintech improve the efficiency of commercial banks? An analysis based on big data. *Research in International Business and Finance*, 55, January, Article 101338.

World Bank, World Economic Forum and Judge Business Scholl (2020). The global Covid-19 FinTech market rapid assessment study. Available at: https://www.jbs.cam.ac.uk/wp-content/uploads/2021/03/2020-ccaf-global-covid-fintech-market-rapid-assessment-study-v2.pdf.

World Economic Forum (2015). The future of FinTech a paradigm shift in small business finance. Available at: https://www.weforum.org/reports/future-fintech-paradigm-shift-small-business-finance.

Xia, H., Liu, J. and Zhang, Z.J. (2020). Identifying Fintech risk through machine learning: Analyzing the Q&A text of an online loan investment platform. *Annals of Operations Research* (Published online, 20 December), https://doi.org/10.1007/s10479-020-03842-y.

Zavolokina, L., Dolata, M. and Schwabe, G. (2016). FinTech — What's in a name? *Working Paper*, University of Zurich, Zurich, Switzerland.

https://doi.org/10.1142/9781800614239_0002

Chapter 2

The Impact of the COVID-19 Pandemic and the European Union Artificial Intelligence Act on the Implementation of AI Systems in Europe

Ewa Dalek-Trudnowska
Middlesex University London, The Burroughs, London, UK
ED602@live.mdx.ac.uk

Abstract

The COVID-19 pandemic accelerated the implementation of various types of Artificial Intelligence systems. That happened because the machines are not directly affected by the virus. This study concerns the European Union (EU). In Europe, the legislation systematically evolves and adjusts to quickly expanding technology in order to protect the EU residents and ensure the safe implementation of advanced technologies. The latest, and very innovative, is a proposed Regulation of the European Parliament and of the Council laying down harmonised rules on Artificial Intelligence, in short, the EU Artificial Intelligence (AI) Act. The EU AI Act applies to all industries. This is a socio-legal study that aims to analyse the impact of the European Union legislation on corporate risk management in relation to changes that result from the introduction of AI systems into business operations and the COVID-19 pandemic. This chapter focuses on regulatory compliance risk management and asks whether the EU Artificial Intelligence Act imposes a risk on companies that implement AI systems into their business operations in Europe. In addition, it investigates how the COVID-19 pandemic affected the implementation of different types of Artificial Intelligence systems as well as work and labour relations. Therefore, this study investigates the EU legislation related to AI systems.

1. Introduction

In the European Union (EU), the governing institutions closely monitor the industrial and technological development of Artificial Intelligence (AI) systems and their impact on the economy, public services, and society. As the changes in this area emerge, the European Union adjusts the legislative framework accordingly. The latest, and very innovative, is a proposal for a Regulation of the European Parliament and of the Council laying down harmonised rules on Artificial Intelligence, in short, the EU AI Act (European Parliament and the Council of the European Union, 2021). The Act applies to all industries. Therefore, this chapter gives an insight into the EU legislation on AI systems, which directly impacts how AI systems are implemented and operated by businesses in the Member States. The EU regulator intends to comprehensively regulate issues related to new technologies in order to create a sovereign, dynamically developing area in which residents feel legally secure and safe. This chapter addresses some of the issues related to the implementation of AI systems into business operations.

This chapter focuses on regulatory compliance risk management and asks whether the EU AI Act imposes a risk on companies that implement AI systems into their business operations in Europe. That is important because any changes in legislation "may account for legal risk if such regulatory changes affect the legality of certain transactions" (Culp, 2001, p. 440). Therefore, the EU AI Act may reduce the attractiveness of an investment in AI systems and slow down the company's development and competitiveness.

In addition, due to the COVID-19 pandemic, the governments of the Member States imposed a set of rules that had a direct effect on the way companies operate, such as social distancing. In relation to that, the pandemic caused major disturbances in companies' activities because it had a significant impact on labour relations

(Kaur and Kaur, 2021; Cortez and Forsythe, 2022), workers' working environments (Kasemy *et al.*, 2022), and the global supply chain (Anser *et al.*, 2021; Sajjad, 2021; Dubey *et al.*, 2022). Therefore, the companies had to adjust quickly to the new situation and requirements, and change the way they operate in order to continue their business operations.

This chapter investigates the phenomenon of the implementation of AI systems into business operations. The COVID-19 pandemic unexpectedly speeded up the process of implementation of different types of AI systems (Market Study Report, 2021) and shook the labour market (Su *et al.*, 2021; Tang *et al.*, 2022). That happened because the machines are not directly affected by the virus. Implementation of various AI systems concerns various sectors. For example, amid the COVID-19 crisis the first ward hospital run entirely by medical staff robots was opened (O'Meara, 2020). The robots delivered food, drinks, and drugs, monitored the vital signs of patients, and disinfected the ward area. Therefore, as the implementation of various AI systems into business operations progresses, the post-pandemic cost to achieve compliance with the EU AI Act may result in higher risk management-related activities, inter alia, leading to increased costs of running a business.

2. Literature Review

Human civilisation has entered the age of Artificial Intelligence systems, known as the Fourth Industrial Revolution, which at this stage of development cannot be stopped (Höller *et al.*, 2014; Wachter and Mittelstadt, 2019; Iansiti and Lakhani, 2020). AI systems are a subject of a global technological race. Many countries, among others the United States, China, and the European Union, heavily invest in technological development and are leaders in digitalisation. Simultaneously, many businesses are independently trying to develop AI systems that can perform tasks better and faster (Cave and ÓhÉigeartaigh, 2018; Schlesinger *et al.*, 2018). Each of these entities undertakes several activities aimed at improving systems-based AI.

There is no one agreed definition of AI systems because the term concerns different types of developed technologies, such as robots, autonomous cars, drones, or virtual assistants. However, one might see the strong similarities between them, and that is the ability to make a very quick decision or perform tasks faster and better than a human being (Acemoglu and Restrepo, 2019). Another common feature of AI systems refers to the ability to analyse and process a huge amount of data faster than any living person (Wu, 2021). Even AI systems that are now being evaluated outperform humans in terms of learning as well as gathering and analysing data (Moura *et al.*, 2019). In general, Artificial Intelligence might be described as "intelligent computer systems, that is, systems that exhibit the characteristic we associate with intelligence in human behaviour — understanding language, learning, reasoning, solving problems and so on" (Barr and Feigenbaum, 1982).

In Europe, the European Commission defines AI systems as: "systems that display intelligent behaviour by analysing their environment and taking actions — with some degree of autonomy — to achieve specific goals" (2018a). AI systems can be software or hardware-based and act in the virtual world (search engines, voice assistants, speech and face recognition systems) or be embedded in devices (autonomous cars, humanoid robots, drones). The European Commission gives ample examples of different types of AI systems (European Commission, 2018b): analytical intelligence, mechanical intelligence, intuitive intelligence, and empathic intelligence, capable of recognising the emotions of people (Huang and Rust, 2018). In addition, artificial consciousness is of particular interest to scientists and developers (Reggia, 2013; Miyazaki and Takeno, 2014; Tien-Jung, 2017).

There are three distinguished stages of Artificial Intelligence: Artificial Narrow Intelligence (ANI), Artificial General Intelligence (AGI), and Artificial Super Intelligence (ASI) (Kaplan and Haenlein, 2019). Apart from this typology of AI, often in the academic and professional literature the term process automation is mentioned, which refers to a feature of AI systems (Fernandez and Aman, 2018). The need for various types of AI systems is expanding. Although the phrases Artificial Intelligence and automation are frequently used interchangeably, there is a difference between them. That is because AI is designed to mimic human behaviour (Brandon *et al.*, 2020) while automation is pre-programmed software

(Goldberg, 2012). Generally, automation makes software or hardware perform the tasks automatically, without human intervention with a single purpose: to perform monotonous, repetitive work. Automation is mainly used in factories. For instance, robotic process automation enables "employees in a company to configure computer software or 'robots' to capture and interpret existing applications to process transactions, manipulate data, and communicate with other digital systems" (Fernandez and Aman, 2018). The main aim of process automation is to reduce the burden of repetitive and simple tasks on employees, but also reduce production costs and improve productivity. Currently, around 88% of businesses worldwide are planning to incorporate automation into their structures (Bulao, 2021).

Although the pandemic significantly accelerated the implementation of automation and other types of AI systems, this technology was already being introduced in many factories across the world. For instance, the Foxconn company that operates in China replaced 60,000 workers with automated robots (Graham, 2017). The company specialises in producing devices such as iPhones and iPads. In the same year, another factory in China replaced 90% of its workers with automated robots (Andrei, 2017). The Changing Precision Technology Company produces mobile phones. After the changes, the factory praised the productivity, which raised by 250%. Also, the defects dropped by 80% and the quality of the products was much better. The management of the company is planning a further reduction of employees to the final number of 20 workers (Andrei, 2017). A significant fraction of the industrial robots in Asia is installed in electronic factories.

In the European Union, the companies follow the Asian example. Although the process of implementing various AI systems into business operations is much slower, it progresses systematically. For example, in Germany the company Adidas opened what is called a 'SpeedFactory', operated by automated arms (Poltz, 2016). The factory employs only 160 workers and is equipped with 3D printers, computerised knitting, and robotic arms (Wiener, 2017). Gerd Manz, vice president of Adidas, said: "What we enable is speed. We can react to consumer needs within days" (De Leon Ovale, 2018). From an economical perspective, it helped the company shorten shipping delays and cut expenses. Therefore, the introduction of various

AI systems into business operations is progressing quickly. However, the extensive EU regulations may have a significant impact on this process.

3. Methods and Results

This is a socio-legal study that aims to analyse the impact of the European Union legislation on corporate risk management in relation to changes that result from the introduction of AI systems into business operations and the COVID-19 pandemic. This chapter focuses on regulatory compliance risk management and asks whether the EU AI Act imposes a risk on companies that implement AI systems into their business operations in Europe. In addition, it investigates how the COVID-19 pandemic affected the implementation of different types of AI systems as well as work and labour relations.

The differences in the speed of implementation of various AI systems between the US, Asian countries, and the EU are, inter alia, a result of the existing legislation. In the EU social market economy, the European Commission continuously develops the single market policies in order to regulate and promote "a highly competitive social market policy" to obtain the EU's potential "for growth in the service of human advancement" (2010). Another factor that influences the implementation of various AI systems in the EU is the level of investment in advanced technology. For comparison, in 2016 the US invested around €12.1 billion in Artificial Intelligence, while the EU invested only €3.2 billion (European Commission, 2020b). Therefore, in order to successfully compete with other countries in this field, the EU needs to significantly increase spending on various types of AI systems. Asia is the most important market for industrial robots, accounting for approximately two-thirds of the global supply. Especially China and Japan lead in the implementation of AI systems. In Europe, Germany is the main user of industrial machines (International Federation of Robotics, 2020). In 2020, the number of robotic units sold rose to nearly half a million (Bulao, 2021). Approximately 71% of all new robots were deployed in Asia, including China, which noted a 20% rise in robot installations, the highest rate ever recorded by a single country (International Federation of Robotics, 2021).

During the COVID-19 pandemic, there was a significant worldwide increase in the sale of service robots. The sale of five top applications that concern transportation, professional cleaning, medical devices, hospitality, and agriculture rose by 41% in the first year of the pandemic (International Federation of Robotics, 2021). The demand for service robots in transportation refers to delivery robots and autonomous mobile AI systems that operate indoors, for instance, in warehouses and factories. Professional cleaning robots, such as disinfection machines, were used as a response to sanitary and hygiene requirements during the pandemic and their sales rose by 92% in 2020 (International Federation of Robotics, 2021). Concerning AI systems used in healthcare, the increased demand mostly referred to robotic surgery devices and robots for rehabilitation. At this stage, it is worth noting that healthcare robots give rise to legal concerns about the data protection and privacy risks in human–robot interactions (Weng and Hirata, 2022).

During the COVID-19 outbreak, the process of implementation of various AI systems was the most visible in the retail sector. Before the virus outbreak, supermarkets had many cashiers and customer assistants on the store floors, however, a year later there were mostly self-checkout machines. This change is even clearer when looking at numbers. Prior to the pandemic, global AI retail market was valued at approximately $3 billion, but it is estimated that before 2027 it will reach nearly $24 billion (Market Study Report, 2021). The pandemic accelerated the implementation of different types of AI systems on an unprecedented scale. According to the study conducted by Facts and Factors (2021), in 2020 the global AI market was valued at $29.86 billion, but it will reach $299.64 billion by 2026. Similarly, the International Data Corporation estimates the global spending on AI systems to reach $110 billion in 2024 (2020).

The COVID-19 pandemic stimulated the growth of the commercial transactions conducted electronically on the internet. In Europe, many countries quickly adapted to the new situation caused by the lockdowns and switched to online commerce. For instance, the UK noticed 4.5 times higher online retail transactions in the first year of the pandemic (Figure 1). Therefore, in 2020 online retail constituted 24% of total retail sales in the country. For comparison, the total e-commerce sales in the six richest EU countries: the UK, Germany, Spain, France, Italy, and the Netherlands, was estimated to have

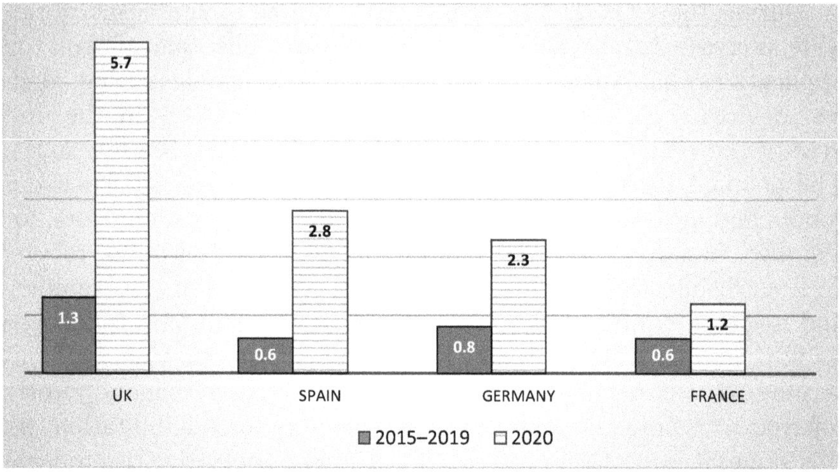

Figure 1. Growth of e-commerce as a share of total retail sales (%).

Source: Retailing by Euromonitor International 2021; own analysis.

grown by over 31.1% during this time (Centre for Retail Research, no date). In addition, it was predicted that in 2021 there will be more than 500 million e-commerce users in the European Union (*Ecommerce News*, 2021).

In the EU countries, the COVID-19 pandemic triggered an increase in online shopping among internet users. That was especially visible in Romania wherein in the first year of the pandemic online sales increased by 16% (Figure 2). However, companies across all Member States noted the significant interest of customers in online purchases. In 2019, 60% of the population aged between 16 and 74 in all European Union countries at least ordered products or used services online once for private use (Eurostat, 2020). Due to the pandemic, there was a significant increase in online shopping, and 73% of the European population with access to the internet shopped online in 2020 and 74%, in 2021. During the first year of the pandemic, especially younger generations aged between 16 and 54 showed particular interest in online shopping, they contributed to 78.5% of online shopping. In comparison, only 57% of people aged between 55 and 74 bought goods or services online in 2020 and 59%, in 2021 (Eurostat, 2022). However, there were significant differences between countries in relation to online customers' activities in 2020. Particular interest

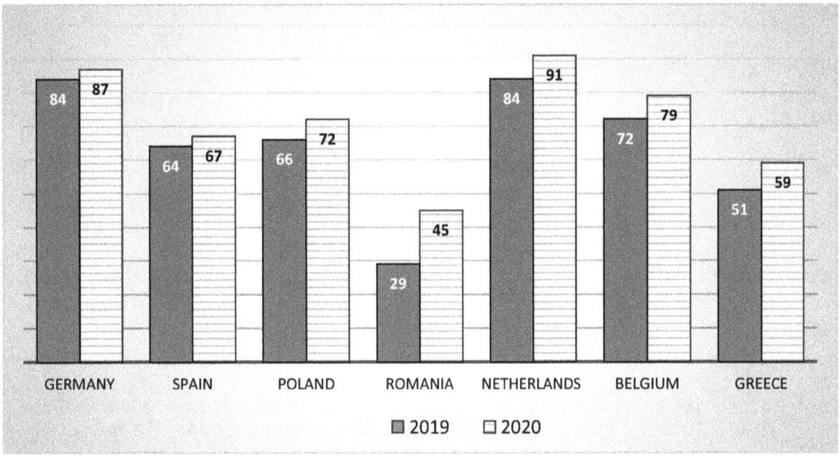

Figure 2. The change in online shopping trends in the biggest EU countries by number of citizens (%) in 2019 and 2020.

Source: Eurostat, 2020 and 2021b; own analysis.

of the population to order goods or services over the internet was shown by customers in the Netherlands, Germany, Denmark, Sweden, and Ireland (Eurostat, 2021b).

The COVID-19 pandemic and lockdowns imposed on the population resulted in another unexpected new phenomenon. To contain the pressure on healthcare services and slow down the spreading of the virus, people were told to stay indoors. As a result, those who were able could work remotely, others exercised the benefits of paid furloughs. These schemes introduced by governments helped to save the lives of many people. Comparing the situation before the start of the pandemic with the first lockdown in 2020, there was a sharp decrease in the total hours worked in the main job (Figure 3).

There was a significant drop in working hours in the second quarter of 2020 when the index fell to 87 points. It corresponds to a drop of 16 index points between the second quarter of 2019 and the second quarter of 2020. Considering, that the first wave of the pandemic was a surprise for the governments, businesses, and citizens, the EU responded relatively quickly to the challenge posed by the virus and moved smoothly to remote work. That scheme supported employment in some sectors, for instance, in manufacturing and education.

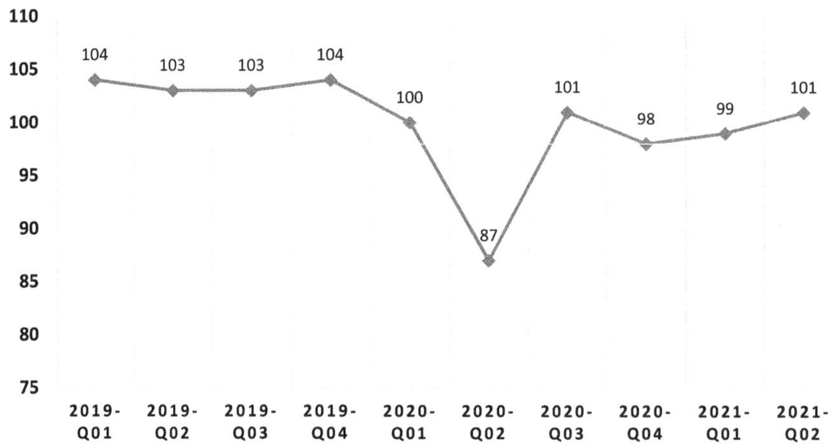

Figure 3. Total actual hours worked in the main job, quarterly (EU-27; people aged 20–64).

Source: Eurostat, 2021b; own analysis.

Based on the gained experience, the European countries prepared for another wave of the pandemic, and between the fourth quarter of 2019 and the fourth quarter of 2020 the EU-27 noted only a 6-index-points drop in the hours worked in the main job. The fall in the total hours worked took place because some jobs could not be done remotely and required the presence of the employee at the workplace (Figure 4). Jobs that do not require presence in the office or at the factory were performed remotely. The data proves that many jobs, for instance, sales or other customer services, could be carried out remotely. However, elementary occupations that consist mainly of routine tasks and require the use of hand and some physical effort could not be done remotely. Such occupations concern factory workers, plant and machine operators, and delivery drivers. For this reason, it seemed reasonable for the companies to switch from human workers to AI systems, such as automation or driverless vehicles. For instance, a self-driving vehicle delivered pizza to customers in the UK, in Milton Keynes. It's a town located 50 miles northwest of London. The delivery price was £1, and during the 2020 lockdown, the delivery was free for National Health Service (NHS) workers (Metz and Griffith, 2020).

The impact of the pandemic on the introduction of the AI systems and change in work structure was significant. Not only did

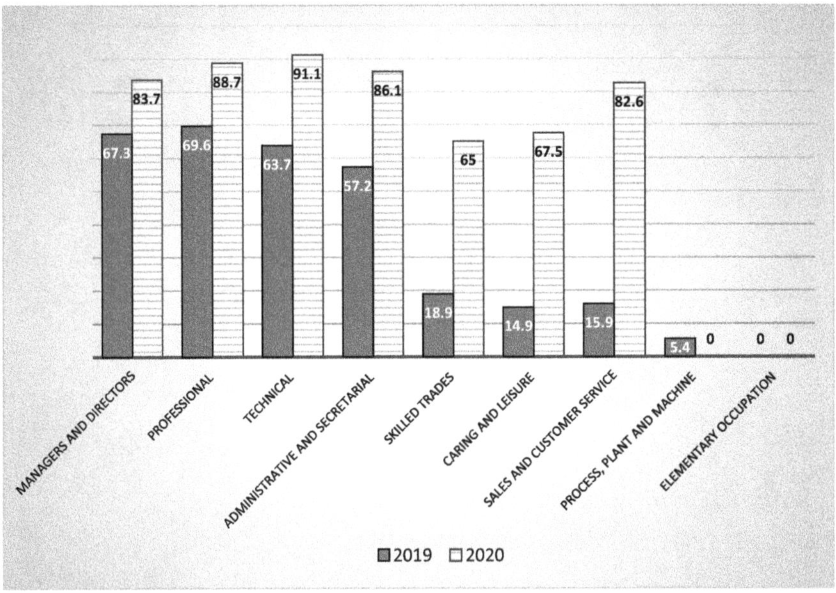

Figure 4. The proportion of employees doing any work at home due to COVID-19 by occupation (UK).

Source: UK Office for National Statistics, 2020; own analysis.

governments and businesses in the EU adjust quickly to the new reality but employees as well. The European Workforce Survey conducted in June 2020 showed that 62% of workers expect to work from home more often and expect increased flexibility in working arrangements (Moueddene *et al.*, 2021). Between 2019 and 2020, the percentage of employed people who work from home climbed dramatically, rising from 5.4% to 12.3% (Eurostat, 2021a). Many employees in Europe would like to continue working from home in the future (Figure 5).

The working from home scheme brings many benefits to businesses, employees, and the environment. For instance, by allowing the employees to work remotely, the company can save money because it does not need to provide office space, which usually is a big cost for any business. The office space is related to additional costs, such as electricity, water, heating, and internet. Remote work also saves employees time because they do not need to commute to the workplace and can contribute to their work–life balance.

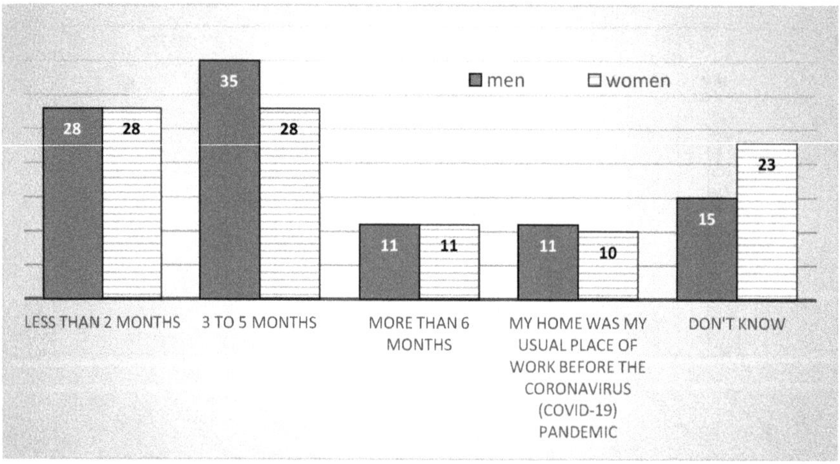

Figure 5. Future work-from-home plans by sex (UK).

Source: UK Office for National Statistics, 2021; own analysis.

In addition, it supports a smaller carbon footprint by helping to tackle climate change because fewer people commute to work and there are fewer vehicles on the roads, resulting in reduced greenhouse gas emissions. Therefore, many AI systems available, now and in the future, may greatly contribute to easier and better cooperation between governments, businesses, and people at large.

AI systems are already complex technology, however, and as noted by Ines de Matos Pinto, "AI and the consequences of its unregulated use can be easily understood by most since many have experienced how it has already permeated different areas of daily life" (De Matos Pinto, 2021, p. 620). In addition, scholars highlight that "governmental efforts to govern AI so as to maximise these benefits and minimise risks have only gained substantial traction in the past few years" (Huw *et al.*, 2021, p. 68). However, in Europe, the legislation systematically evolves and adjusts to quickly expanding technology in order to protect the EU residents and ensure the safe implementation of advanced technologies. Recently, the EU has proposed a harmonised regulation on AI systems — the EU AI Act mentioned earlier (European Parliament and the Council of the European Union, 2021). The specific objectives of the regulatory framework were laid down in the explanatory memorandum and highlighted the main points regarding AI systems: (i) that AI systems placed on the European market are safe and in accordance with the legislation on fundamental rights and the EU values, (ii) that there is legal clarity in order to encourage AI system investment and innovation, (iii) that it improves governance and effective enforcement of existing laws regarding rights of the EU citizens and AI systems' safety requirements, (iv) that it ensures the further development of the EU's Single Market for AI systems and prevents market fragmentation (European Parliament and the Council of the European Union, 2021, para 1.1).

The EU's Artificial Intelligence regulation aims to harmonise the rules on placing AI systems on the European market and makes the European Union a global leader in the development of safe, ethical, and trustworthy AI systems. The new legal instrument also focuses on building trust in advanced technologies by reducing the risks associated with AI systems and supporting investment and further development in this area. However, at the same time, it establishes bans on certain practices involving AI and defines certain conditions for high-risk AI systems that are meant to interact with people, such as transparency requirements. In addition, the scope of the regulation covers the post-market monitoring of AI systems and market supervision. Therefore, the main achievement of the EU Artificial Intelligence Act is that it prepares the ground for the forthcoming Artificial General Intelligence and establishes the legal base for future robot–human relations.

The proposal responds to the European Parliament's and European Council's requests for regulation concerning a well-functioning internal market for AI systems that are effectively addressed at the EU level and balance both, benefits and risks. In relation to that, in 2019, the European Council pointed out the significance of the development of AI systems in the light of the fully respected rights of the people and called for legislation that addresses the challenges raised by AI systems (Council of the European Union, 2019). A year later the European Commission published a White Paper on Artificial Intelligence highlighting that "a common European approach to AI is necessary to reach sufficient scale and avoid the fragmentation of the single market" (European Commission, 2020b). The Paper set out key elements for the regulatory framework for AI systems in Europe with special attention paid to technologies that pose a high risk. In addition, it included recommendations based on the Communication on Building Trust in Human-Centric AI (European

Commission, 2019a) and the Ethics Guidelines developed by the High-Level Expert Group on AI (High-Level Expert Group on Artificial Intelligence, 2019). According to the Guidelines, trustworthy AI should be lawful, ethical, and robust (European Commission, 2019b). However, in contradiction to the vision of the European Commission which concerned "ethical, secure and cutting-edge AI made in Europe" (European Commission, 2018a), the scope of the Guidelines extends to AI systems developed outside the EU and deployed or used in Europe. Although the recommendations presented by the High-Level Expert Group are not legally binding, some experts criticise their effectiveness (Veale, 2020).

In the European Union, there is a strong emphasis on citizens' social and human rights (Consolidated versions of the Treaty on European Union, 2016) and that has a direct and indirect effect on companies, for instance, when the companies try to implement new technologies into their business activities. In 2020, the Working Party on Fundamental Rights, Citizens Rights, and Free Movement of Persons prepared a draft Council Conclusion on the Charter of Fundamental Rights concerning the context of AI and digital change. The Conclusion concerns the problem of bias and unpredictability of some types of AI systems and the need to ensure that the technology is compatible with the fundamental rights of the EU citizens (Council of the European Union, 2021). In addition, the Council has called for an indication of which types of AI systems should be categorised as high-risk applications (European Council, 2020). In order to achieve that, the European Commission adopted a risk-based approach. The categorisation of AI systems was based on the assumption that the systems with a higher risk should be subject to broader and more restrictive requirements than the systems whose use is only associated with limited or low risk.

Therefore, based upon the EU AI Act, AI systems have been classified according to the level of risk they pose. The category 'an unacceptable risk' applies to systems that assess social credibility (social scoring) or solutions that use subliminal manipulation in order to influence people's behaviour (European Parliament and the Council of the European Union, 2021, Art 5). The AI systems that will fall into this category will be prohibited due to their contradiction with the fundamental rights and values of the EU. There are three exceptions to the prohibition of the use of real-time remote biometric identification systems: (i) to search for victims, for example, missing children, (ii) to prevent a threat to the life of a natural person or of a terrorist attack, (iii) to localise, detect, or prosecute a perpetrator or a suspect of a criminal offence. The detection and prosecution of the suspect of a criminal offence are codified in Article 2(2) of the Council Framework Decision 2002/584/JHA (2002). However, the wide range of exceptions to the prohibition of the use of real-time remote biometric identification systems has been already criticised by experts because it might present a risk of deep and disturbing intrusion into private lives (European Data Protection Supervisor, 2021).

The category of 'high-risk' applications concerns these AI systems that can significantly interfere with humans' lives and create a high risk to their health and safety. Article 6 of the Artificial Intelligence Act categorises AI systems as a 'high-risk' when the product is covered by the Union harmonisation legislation and listed in Annex II and referred to in Annex III of the Act. Based upon Article 28 of the Act, such systems will be subject to several strict obligations directed at manufacturers, distributors, importers, authorised representatives, and users. Examples of high-risk AI systems include remote real-time biometric identification of natural persons, systems used for recruiting or credit scoring, and systems used for making decisions, task allocation, and monitoring performance in work-related contractual relationships.

In addition, the EU AI Act imposes a set of obligations on importers and distributors who will be required to assess the AI system and demonstrate that it complies with the provisions of the regulation. For instance, in the case of the use of remote biometric identification and public infrastructure networks, the AI system will be assessed by a third party. The compliance of the AI systems with the legislation will be confirmed by a certificate issued by the notified body and will be valid for a maximum of five years. In addition, upon Article 60 of the Act, high-risk AI systems will be subject to entry in a special EU database. The EU database concerning high-risk AI systems refers to Article 6(2), which is registered in accordance with Article 51 of the Act. Based upon Article 52, the 'low-risk or minimal risk' category of AI applies to systems designed to interact with natural persons and will be subject to transparency requirements and information obligations. In that way, the users will know that they are interacting with an agent and not a human. However, as AI systems already interact with natural persons, there have been voices saying that in the EU more regulations are needed to secure occupational health and safety in the changing work environment (Jarota, 2021). Moreover, some experts highlight that the EU AI Act "pays too little attention to risks related to human autonomy, cybersecurity, market dominance and price manipulation" (Niet *et al.*, 2021, p. 4).

Key importance for the assessment of the scope of application has the definition of AI systems adopted in the regulation because it determines the scope of the upcoming legal framework for Artificial Intelligence. Article 3(1) of the EU regulation defines AI systems as "software that is developed with one or more of the techniques and approaches listed in Annex I and can, for a given set of human-defined objectives, generate outputs such as content, predictions, recommendations, or decisions influencing the environment they interact with." The definition of Artificial Intelligence adopted in the Act is very broad, which thus determines the wide scope of application. In addition, as noted by Bev Townsend, providers of AI systems are obliged to design bots and robots in a way that "natural persons are informed that they are interacting with AI systems" (2021, p. 5). However, in accordance with Article 52(1) of the Act, this obligation does not apply to AI systems authorised by law to prevent, detect, and prosecute criminal offences unless such systems are made accessible to the public in order to report a crime. In addition, the Act addresses the "issues through specific transparency and human oversight obligations" (Fink, 2021, p. 2).

Annex I to the regulation specifies the techniques and approaches of AI technologies, which constitute the basis for qualifying the given system into an adequate category. The European Commission is empowered to make changes to Annex I's list of techniques and approaches in order to keep it up to date with the market and technological developments in this area.

In regard to the developers that place AI systems on the market, whether for payment or free of charge, the Artificial Intelligence Act determines two types of providers. Upon Article 3(2) the term provider refers to a natural or legal person, public authority, agency, or another body that develops AI systems. In turn, the notion of a small-scale provider applies to a micro or small enterprise (Commission Recommendation concerning the definition of micro, small, and medium-sized enterprises, 2003) and is covered by Article 3(3) of the Act.

As a rule, the national market authorities will supervise the implementation of the new provisions. In addition, a new body will be established — the European Artificial Intelligence Board — responsible for the implementation of regulations and the development of standards in the field of AI systems. In addition, as per Article 56 Section 2(b) of the Act, the Board will coordinate "emerging issues across the internal market with regard to matters covered" by the EU AI Act.

The companies that do not comply with the Regulation will face the consequences. Article 71 of the Act establishes penalty systems for non-compliance with its provisions and the established standards. In this regard, Article 71 established three categories of fines (i) up to 30,000,000 EUR or, if the offender is a company, up to 6% of its total worldwide annual turnover for the preceding financial year, (ii) up to 20,000,000 EUR or, if the offender is a company, up to 4% of its total worldwide annual turnover for the preceding financial year, and (iii) up to 10,000,000 EUR or, if the offender is a company, up to 2% of its total worldwide annual turnover for the preceding financial year. In all cases, the higher amount is applied for the provision of incorrect, incomplete, or misleading information provided to the notified body and the national competent authority in response to their request.

The EU AI Act has a vertical direct effect, which means that individuals can invoke a provision concerning the country. The doctrine of vertical direct effect is a device that protects the rights of the EU citizens and applies in situations where EU law was not properly implemented into national legislation.

The Regulation enters into force on the twentieth day after publication in the *Official Journal of the European Union.* However, there will be a time needed between the legal instrument legally existing, and the date when the legal rights and obligations can be effectively exercised due to the complexity of regulated domains included in the EU AI Act. Therefore, the Regulation will enter into force on the twentieth day of its publication in the *Official Journal of the*

European Union but will apply 24 months after coming into force. However, as per Article 71 the penalty system shall apply 12 months following its publication in the *Official Journal*. In practice, the earliest the final text of the Act might be adopted by the EU Parliament and the Council is between the end of 2022 and the beginning of 2023, with the following period of 24 months to fully apply.

The scope of the EU AI Act aims to regulate the way the technologies are manufactured, distributed, and used. It has been recognised as a single basis approach that "really combines multiple risk assessments into a relatively complex overall process for managing AI risk" (Mahler, 2021, p. 254). However, some experts believe that there is still "significant room for improvement" (Hacker, 2021, p. 302). Although, as noted by Corrado Druetta, no single piece of legislation can regulate all aspects related to AI systems. Therefore, "AI regulation must be embedded in several instruments, which have to share common ethical principles and clear objectives in order to be consistent and effective" (Druetta, 2021, p. 9). Notwithstanding, the proposed Act is the most restrictive regulation on AI systems across the world and it has already received extensive attention from other countries, for example, "it is firmly on Australia's agenda" (Svantesson, 2021, p. 5). In addition, since the publication of the EU AI Act, other countries, such as the US and the UK, showed an interest in regulating AI systems (The White House, 2021; UK HM Government, 2021; US Federal Register, 2021).

In relation to business operations, the proposed EU legislation caused some concerns about its impact on the automation industry and the economy. For instance, the International Federation for Robotics expressed its view that the regulation "may hamper innovation" and "certainty for investment" (International Federation of Robotics, 2021). A report conducted by Benjamin Mueller suggests that the European Artificial Intelligence Act might not only limit the development and use of the technology but also impose additional costs on businesses operating in Europe. According to the provided data, the Act will result in reduced investment in AI systems by nearly 20% and it will cost the EU economy €10.9 billion per year by 2025 (Mueller, 2021). Concerning businesses, the implementation of the EU AI Act might result in a 40% profit reduction for companies operating in Europe (Mueller, 2021).

Although, as noted by Katerina Yordanova, "the strong human rights guarantees built into the process hinder their experimental nature and decrease their attractiveness, which is primarily based on the lifting of certain legal restrictions" (2022, p. 8). Therefore, regulating technologies might be a positive step towards balancing comprehensive human rights with innovation. The EU regulates many aspects related to the implementation, operation, and use of AI systems. In addition, the AI systems are regulated by the Resolution on intellectual property rights (European Parliament resolution (2020/2015(INL)), 2021), the Resolution on civil liability for AI systems (European Parliament resolution (2020/2014(INL)), 2021)), the Resolution on a framework of ethical aspects of Artificial Intelligence, robotics, and related technologies (European Parliament resolution (2020/2012(INL)), 2021), and the General Data Protection Regulation for personal data (European Parliament and the Council of European Union Regulation (EU) (2016/679), 2016). The EU legislation regulates all aspects of a company's activities. The complex legislation related to AI systems in the EU might affect international companies not used to very strict regulations on the protection of rights. For example, Amazon tests fully autonomous drones called Prime Air to deliver packages to customers. The non-human pilot transportation system is supposed to provide rapid parcel deliveries in 30 minutes or less after ordering. The company highlights the safety and efficiency of the service. However, to work autonomously the system needs to collect a huge amount of customer data that can affect the privacy of the EU residents, and therefore violate the General Data Protection Regulation.

The EU legislation extensively regulates how companies can operate in Europe and it has a direct effect on business operations. For instance, Amazon company already faces problems because it did not comply with the EU legislation concerning the non-public business data of third-party sellers (European Commission, 2020a). Restrictive regulations applying to AI systems and a careful approach towards AI systems are temporarily slowing down European transformation and adaptation to the quickly developing technologies. According to the European Investment Bank (2021) Report, compared to other countries Europe invests less in research and development (as a proportion of GDP) than other countries. As a result, the European companies grow slowly and are behind US and Asian firms, especially in the digital sector. For instance, there is no European company among the 20 largest tech businesses, and there are only 8 European companies on the list of 100 largest tech companies by market cap (Companies Market Cap, no date). According to the data, by 2020 37% of the European companies had not adopted any digital technologies (European Investment Bank, 2021). However, some sceptical opinions pointed out that "the AI Regulation is neither a panacea which will automatically guarantee Europe's leadership in AI nor a draconian legislative over-reach that will stifle innovative potential across the continent" (Lilkov, 2021, p. 172).

Nevertheless, although the extensive regulations concerning AI systems in Europe did not receive enthusiastic support from businesses, they are needed because one of the most important issues for companies to efficiently operate is the applicable Value-Added Tax (VAT). Therefore, companies operating within the 27 EU Member States must take proper measures to comply with the mandatory legislation in the country to which they sell their products or provide services. Article 3(2) of the EU AI Act defines the term provider as "a natural or legal person, public authority, agency or other body that develops an AI system or that has an AI system developed with a view to placing it on the market or putting it into service under its own name or trademark, whether for payment or free of charge". The definition has a wide scope and the notion of 'other body' might in the future apply to Artificial Intelligence.

Different regulatory frameworks between European countries related to AI systems would complicate trade, for example, in the cross-border e-commerce sector. Therefore, the AI Act creates a clear, stable, and predictable business environment for companies operating in the EU. While the legislation might not seem convenient for corporations now, it is transparent, and from the long-term perspective, companies will know what to expect and how to prepare to operate in Europe. Accordingly, the EU AI Act introduces unified regulations for all Member States and will result in simpler business operations across European countries. In addition, the Act has the potential to set international standards in relation to its risk-based approach.

4. Conclusion

This chapter analysed the impact of the European Union legislation on corporate risk management in relation to changes that result from the introduction of AI systems into business operations and the COVID-19 pandemic. This chapter focused on regulatory compliance risk management and asked whether the EU Artificial Intelligence Act imposes a risk on companies that implement AI systems into their business operations in Europe. In addition, it investigated how the COVID-19 pandemic affected the implementation of different types of AI systems as well as work and labour relations.

The lockdowns imposed on the population due to the COVID-19 pandemic resulted in a phenomenon. To take off the pressure from healthcare services and slow down the spreading of the virus, people were told to stay indoors. Those who could, worked remotely. However, elementary occupations that consist mainly of routine tasks and physical effort could not be done remotely. Such occupations concerned factory workers, plant and machine operators, and delivery drivers. As a result, to continue their activities many companies switched from human workers to AI systems, for example, automation or other types of AI systems, because the virus does not affect machines. Therefore, the impact of the COVID-19 pandemic on the implementation of Artificial Intelligence systems was significant because it unprecedently speeded up the process of implementing new technologies. The pandemic forced businesses to adjust quickly to this new situation and implement different types of technologies faster than they previously planned. That resulted in significant changes in the work structure with fewer human employees and more machines.

In the European Union, governing institutions closely monitor the industrial and technological development of AI systems and their impact on the economy and society and adjust legislation accordingly. The latest EU Artificial Intelligence Act caused some concerns about its impact on businesses and the economy because it regulates the way the technologies are manufactured, distributed, and used in all Member States. Companies operating within the 27 EU Member States must take proper measures to comply with the mandatory legislation in the country to which they sell their products or provide services. Upon the EU AI Act, AI systems have been classified according to the level of risk they pose. The category 'an unacceptable risk' applies to systems that assess social credibility (social scoring) or solutions that use subliminal manipulation in order to influence people's behaviour. The AI systems that fall into this category are prohibited in the EU due to their contradiction with the fundamental rights and values of Europe. Therefore, although the EU AI Act simplifies trade between the Member States, it does impose a corporate risk related to regulatory compliance. For instance, the EU AI Act imposes a set of obligations on importers and distributors who will be required to assess the AI system and demonstrate that it complies with the provisions of the regulation. For instance, in the case of the use of remote biometric identification and public infrastructure networks, the AI system will be assessed by a third party. The compliance of the AI systems with the legislation will be confirmed by a certificate issued by the notified body but will be valid up to five years.

The restrictive EU AI Act reduces the attractiveness of an investment in advanced technology and, as a result, may slow down a company's development and competitiveness. This is especially important in the light of the COVID-19 pandemic because companies had to adjust quickly to new restrictions and change the way they operate in order to continue their business operations. The pandemic speeded up the process of implementation of various AI systems. Therefore, the cost to achieve compliance may result in increased costs of running a business. The EU AI Act might not only limit the development and use of technology but also impose additional costs on businesses operating in Europe. Thus, compliance with the Act might result in a high reduction in profits.

References

Acemoglu, D. and Restrepo, P. (2019). Automation and new tasks: How technology displaces and reinstates labor. *The Journal of Economic Perspectives*, 33(2), 3–30. Available at: http://doi:10.1257/jep.33.2.3.

Andrei, M. (2017). Chinese factory replaces 90% of human workers with robots. Production rises by 250%, defects drop by 80%. Available at: https://www.zmescience.com/other/economics/china-factory-robots-03022017/. Accessed 15 February 2022.

Anser, M.K. *et al.* (2021). Does COVID-19 pandemic disrupt sustainable supply chain process? Covering some new global facts. *Environmental Science and Pollution Research International*, 28(42), 59792–59804. Available at: http://doi:10.1007/s11356-021-14817-2.

Barr, A., Cohen, P.R. and Feigenbaum, E.A. (1982). *The Handbook of Artificial Intelligence*, Vol. 2. Boston, MA: Addison Wesley.

Brandon, N. *et al.* (2020). Simulating exposure-related behaviors using agent-based models embedded with needs-based artificial intelligence. *Journal of Exposure Science & Environmental Epidemiology*, 30(1), 184–193. Available at: http://doi:10.1038/s41370-018-0052-y.

Bulao, J. (2021). 27+ astonishing robotics industry statistics you should know in 2021. Available at: https://techjury.net/blog/robotics-industry-statistics/#gref. Accessed 3 March 2022.

Cave, S. and ÓhÉigeartaigh, S. (2018). An AI race for strategic advantage: Rhetoric and risks. *Proceedings of the 2018 AAAI/ACM Conference on AI, Ethics, and Society, 17 December 2018*, 36–40.

Centre for Retail Research (no date). UK, Europe & N. America 2021... The pandemic curse. Available at: https://www.retailresearch.org/online-retail.html. Accessed 10 March 2022.

Commission Recommendation concerning the definition of micro, small and medium-sized enterprises (2003). *Official Journal* L 124, 36–41.

Companies Market Cap (no date). *Largest tech companies by market cap.* Available at: https://companiesmarketcap.com/tech/largest-tech-companies-by-market-cap/. Accessed 10 February 2022.

Consolidated versions of the Treaty on European Union (2016). *Official Journal* C 202, 7 June, 1–388.

Cortes, G.M. and Forsythe, E. (2022). Heterogeneous labor market impacts of the COVID-19 pandemic. *Industrial & Labor Relations Review* [Preprint]. Available at: http://doi:10.1177/00197939221076856.

Council Framework Decision 2002/584/JHA on the European arrest warrant and the surrender procedures between Member States (2002). *Official Journal* L 190, 1–20.

Council of the European Union (2019). Artificial Intelligence b) Conclusions on the coordinated plan on Artificial Intelligence — Adoption. Available at: https://data.consilium.europa.eu/doc/document/ST-6177-2019-INIT/en/pdf. Accessed 11 February 2022.

Council of the European Union (2021). The charter of fundamental rights in the context of artificial intelligence and digital change. Available at: https://www.consilium.europa.eu/media/46496/st11481-en20.pdf. Accessed 11 February 2022.

Culp, C.L. (2001). *The Risk Management Process Business Strategy and Tactics.* New York: John Wiley.

De Leon Ovale, M.C. (2018). Adidas speedfactory to improve manufacturing process. Available at: https://thebossmagazine.com/adidas-speedfactory/. Accessed 15 February 2022.

De Matos Pinto, I. (2021). The draft AI Act: A success story of strengthening parliament's right of legislative initiative. *ERA Forum*, 22(4), 619–641.

Druetta, C. (2021). AI in the making: Is EU artificial intelligence regulatory framework a good move for European manufacturing? Available at: https://www.lexology.com/pro/insideview/ai-in-the-making-is-eu-artificial-intelligence-regulatory-framework-a-good-move-for-european-manufacturing. Accessed 15 February 2022.

Dubey, R. *et al.* (2022). How frugal innovation shape global sustainable supply chains during the pandemic crisis: Lessons from the COVID-19. *Supply Chain Management*, 27(2), 295–311. Available at: http://doi:10.1108/SCM-02-2021-0071.

Ecommerce News (2021). Over 500 million ecommerce users in Europe in 2021. Available at: https://ecommercenews.eu/over-500-million-ecommerce-users-in-europe-in-2021/. Accessed 10 March 2022.

European Commission (2010). Communication from the Commission to the European Council, the Council, the Economic and Social Committee and the Committee of the Regions towards a Single Market Act for a highly competitive social market economy 50 proposals for improving our work, business and exchanges with one another, COM (2010) 608 final.

European Commission (2018a). Communication from the Commission to the European Parliament, the European Council, the Council, the European Economic and Social Committee and the Committee of the Regions; Coordinated Plan on Artificial Intelligence, COM (2018) 795 final.

European Commission (2018b). European Commission's High Level Expert Group on Artificial Intelligence, A definition of AI: Main capabilities and scientific disciplines. Available at: https://ec.europa.eu/futurium/en/system/ files/ged/ai_hleg_definition_of_ai_18_december_1.pdf. Accessed 17 February 2022.

European Commission (2019a). Communication from the Commission to the European Parliament, the Council, the European Economic and Social Committee and the Committee of the Regions Building Trust in Human-Centre Artificial Intelligence, COM(2019) 168 final.

European Commission (2019b). Ethics guidelines for trustworthy AI. Available at: https://digital-strategy.ec.europa.eu/en/library/ethics-guidelines-trustworthy-ai. Accessed 15 February 2022.

European Commission (2020a). Antitrust: Commission sends Statement of Objections to Amazon for the use of non-public independent seller data and opens investigation into its e-commerce business practices. Available at: https://ec.europa.eu/commission/presscorner/detail/en/ip_20_2077. Accessed 11 February 2022.

European Commission (2020b). White paper on artificial intelligence — A European approach to excellence and trust, COM (2020) 65 final.

European Council (2020). Special meeting of the European Council (1 and 2 October 2020) — Conclusions. Available at: https://www.consilium.europa.eu/media/45910/021020-euco-final-conclusions.pdf. Accessed 11 February 2022.

European Data Protection Supervisor (2021). Artificial Intelligence Act: A welcome initiative, but bun on remote biometric identification in public space is necessary. Available at: https://edps.europa.eu/press-publications/press-news/press-releases/2021/artificial-intelligence-act-welcomed-initiative_en. Accessed 22 March 2022.

European Investment Bank (2021). EIB Investment Report 2020/2021: Building a smart and green Europe in the Covid-19 era. Available at: https://www.eib.org/en/publications/investment-report-2020. Accessed 11 February 2022.

European Parliament and the Council of the European Union (2021). Proposal for a Regulation of the European Parliament and the Council laying down harmonised rules on Artificial Intelligence (Artificial Intelligence Act) and amending certain Union legislation Acts, COM/2021/206 final.

European Parliament and the Council of European Union Regulation (EU) 2016/679 on the protection of natural persons with regard to the processing of personal data (2016). *Official Journal L* 119, 1–88.

European Parliament resolution on a framework of ethical aspects of artificial intelligence, robotics and related technologies (2020/2012(INL)) (2021). *Official Journal C* 404, 63–106.

European Parliament resolution on intellectual property rights for the development of artificial intelligence technologies (2020/2015(INL)) (2021). *Official Journal C* 404, 129–135.

European Parliament resolution on civil liability regime for artificial intelligence (2020/2014(INL)) (2021). *Official Journal C* 404, 107–128.

Eurostat (2020). Digital economy and society statistics — households and individuals. Available at: https://ec.europa.eu/eurostat/statistics-explained/index.php?title=Digital_economy_and_society_statistics_-_households_and_individuals. Accessed 25 March 2022.

Eurostat (2021a). Employment — Annual statistics. Available at: https://ec.europa.eu/eurostat/statistics-explained/index.php?title=Employment_-_annual_statistics. Accessed 10 March 2022.

Eurostat (2021b). Your key to European statistics. Available at: https://ec.europa.eu/eurostat/web/products-eurostat-news/-/ddn-20210217-1. Accessed 10 March 2022.

Eurostat (2022). E-commerce statistics for individuals. Available at: https://ec.europa.eu/eurostat/statistics-explained/index.php?title=E-commerce_statistics_for_individuals. Accessed 10 March 2022.

Facts & Factors (2021). Artificial intelligence market by component (hardware, software, & services), by technology (deep learning, machine learning, natural language processing & machine vision), by deployment (cloud-based & on-premises), by end-verticals (healthcare, retail, BSFI, automotive, advertising and media, manufacturing, agricultural & others), and by regions — Global industry perspective, Covid-19 impact analysis, market valuation, business strategies, comprehensive study. Latest Trends & Forecasts, 2021–2026. Available at: https://www.fnfresearch.com/artificial-intelligence-market. Accessed 10 March 2022.

Fernandez, D. and Aman, A. (2018). Impacts of robotic process automation on global accounting services. *Asian Journal of Accounting and Governance*, 9, 123–131.

Fink, M. (2021). The EU Artificial Intelligence Act and access to justice, *EU Law Live*, 1–4.

Goldberg, K. (2012). What is automation? *IEEE Transactions on Automation Science and Engineering*, 9(1), 1–2. Available at: http://doi:10.1109/TASE.2011.2178910.

Graham, J. (2017). Trump may bring home Apple, but he can't lick robots, *Investor's Business Daily*, 17 March. Available at: https://www.proquest.com/docview/1878300519?parentSessionId=w%2FnauGdVMaxx4uhUBvz8sJ1GhslzlEwQ1vUxnBVKF2s%3D&accountid=12441. Accessed 17 February 2022.

Hacker, P. (2021). A legal framework for AI training data-from first principles to the Artificial Intelligence Act. *Law, Innovation and Technology*, 13, 257–301.

High-Level Expert Group on Artificial Intelligence set up by the European Commission (2019). Ethics guidelines for trustworthy AI. Available at: https://www.aepd.es/sites/default/files/2019-09/ai-definition.pdf. Accessed 30 March 2022.

Höller, J. *et al.* (2014). *From Machine-to-Machine to the Internet of Things: Introduction to a New Age of Intelligence.* Academic Press: Oxford.

Huang, M.-H. and Rust, R.T. (2018). Artificial intelligence in service. *Journal of Service Research*, 21, 155–172.

Huw, R. *et al.* (2021). Achieving a 'good AI society': Comparing the aims and progress of the EU and the US. *Science and Engineering Ethics*, 27, 68–69.

Iansiti, M. and Lakhani, K.R. (2020). *Competing in the Age of AI: Strategy and Leadership When Algorithms and Networks Run the World.* Boston, MA: Harvard Business Review Press.

International Data Corporation (2020). Worldwide spending on artificial intelligence is expected to double in four years, reaching $110 billion in 2024 according to new IDC spending guide. Available at: https://www.idc.com/getdoc.jsp?containerId=prUS46794720. Accessed 10 March 2022.

International Federation of Robotics (2020). *Welcome to the IFR Press Conference 24th September 2020 Frankfurt.* Available at: https://ifr.org/downloads/press2018/Presentation_WR_2020.pdf. Accessed 10 February 2022.

International Federation of Robotics (2021). World robotics 2021 — Service robots report released. Available at: https://ifr.org/ifr-press-releases/news/service-robots-hit-double-digit-growth-worldwide?utm_source=CleverReach&utm_medium=email&utm_campaign=NL+4%2F21&utm_content=Mailing_13230761. Accessed 3 March 2022.

Jarota, M. (2021). Artificial intelligence and robotisation in the EU—Should we change OHS law? *Journal of Occupational Medicine and Toxicology*, 16, 18–19.

Kaplan, A. and Haenlein, M. (2019). Siri, Siri, in my hand: Who's the fairest in the land? On the interpretations, illustrations, and implications of artificial intelligence. *Business Horizons*, 62(1), 15–25.

Kasemy, Z.A. *et al.* (2022). Technostress creators and outcomes among Egyptian medical staff and students: A multicenter cross-sectional study of remote working environment during COVID-19 pandemic. *Frontiers in Public Health*, 10, 796321–796321. Available at: http://doi:10.3389/fpubh.2022.796321.

Kaur, N. and Kaur, A. (2021). Capitalist agriculture, COVID-19 and agrarian labour relations in Punjab, India, *Journal of Agrarian Change*, 21(3), 638–650. Available at: http://doi:10.1111/joac.12428.

Lilkov, D. (2021). Regulating Artificial Intelligence in the EU: A risky game. *European View*, 20, 166–174.

Mahler, T. (2021). Between risk management and proportionality: The risk-based approach in the EU's Artificial Intelligence Act. In *Nordic Yearbook of Law and Informatics*, pp. 254–267. https://papers.ssrn.com/sol3/papers.cfm?abstract_id=4001444. Accessed 25 March 2022.

Market Study Report (2021). Global artificial intelligence (AI) in retail market size study, by offering (solution, services), by function (operation-focused, customer-focusing), by global artificial intelligence (AI) in retail (customer-focusing), by technology (computer vision, machine learning, natural language processing (LNP)) and regional forecasts 2020–2027. Available at: https://www.fortunebusinessinsights.com/artificial-intelligence-ai-in-retail-market-101968. Accessed 15 February 2022.

Metz, C. and Griffith, E. (2020). Lockdown hasn't stopped Milton Keynes' delivery robots. Available at: https://www.independent.co.uk/tech/delivery-robot-milton-keynes-coronavirus-a9537121.html. Accessed 17 February 2022.

Miyazaki, K. and Takeno, J. (2014). The necessity of a secondary system in machine consciousness, *Procedia Computer Science*, 41, 15–22.

Moueddene, K. *et al.* (2021). Policies for the post-pandemic world of work. Understanding the priorities of the European workforce. Available at: https://www2.deloitte.com/lu/en/pages/human-capital/articles/european-workforce-priorities-post-pandemic.html. Accessed 10 March 2022.

Moura, O.P., Novais, P. and Reis, L.P. (2019). *Progress in Artificial Intelligence 19th EPIA Conference on Artificial Intelligence, EPIA 2019, Vila Real, Portugal, September 3–6, 2019, Proceedings, Part II.* Cham: Springer International Publishing. Available at: http://doi:10.1007/978-3-030-30244-3.

Mueller, B. (2021). How much will the Artificial Intelligence Act cost Europe? Available at: https://www2.datainnovation.org/2021-aia-costs.pdf. Accessed 27 March 2022.

Niet, I., van Est, R. and Veraart, F. (2021). Governing AI in electricity systems: Reflections on the EU Artificial Intelligence Bill. *Frontiers in Artificial Intelligence*, 4, 690237.

O'Meara, S. (2020). Meet the engineer behind China's first robot-run coronavirus ward. *Nature*, 582, S53.

Poltz, J. (2016). Adidas to return mass shoe production to Germany in 2017. Available at: https://www.reuters.com/article/us-adidas-manufacturing/adidas-to-return-mass-shoe-production-to-germany-in-2017-idUSKCN0YG0X6. Accessed 15 February 2022.

Reggia, J.A. (2013). The rise of the machine consciousness: Studying consciousness with computational models. *Neural Network*, 44, 112–131.

Sajjad, A. (2021). The COVID-19 pandemic, social sustainability and global supply chain resilience: A review, *Corporate Governance (Bradford)*, 21(6), 1142–1154. Available at: http://doi:10.1108/CG-12-2020-0554.

Schlesinger, A., O'Hara, K. and Taylor, A. (2018). Let's talk about race: Identity, chatbots, and AI. In *Proceedings of the 2018 CHI Conference on Human Factors in Computing Systems, 21 April 2018*, pp. 1–14.

Su, C.-W., *et al.* (2021). COVID-19 pandemic and unemployment dynamics in European economies, *Economic Research—Ekonomska Istraživanja.* Available at: http://doi:10.1080/1331677X.2021.19 12627.

Svantesson, D. (2021). The European Union Artificial Intelligence Act: Potential implications for Australia, *Alternative Law Journal*, 47(1), 4–9.

Tang, S. *et al.* (2022). Change in unemployment by social vulnerability among United States counties with rapid increases in COVID-19 incidence-July 1–October 31, 2020. *PLoS One*, 17(4), e0265888–e0265888. Available at: http://doi:10.1371/journal.pone.02 65888.

The White House (2021). ICYMI: WIRED (opinion): Americans need a bill of rights for an AI-powered world. Available at: https://www.whitehouse.gov/ostp/news-updates/2021/10/22/icy mi-wired-opinion-americans-need-a-bill-of-rights-for-an-ai-powered-world/. Accessed 15 February 2022.

Tien-Jung, H. (2017). Imitating the brain with neurocomputer a "new" way towards artificial general intelligence. *International Journal of Automation and Computing*, 14(5), 520–531.

Townsend, B. (2021). Decoding the proposed European Union Artificial Intelligence Act. *American Society of International Law*, 25(20), 1–7.

UK HM Government (2021). National AI strategy, Command Paper 525. Available at: https://assets.publishing.service.gov.uk/government/uploads/system/uploads/attachment_data/file/1020402/National_AI_Strategy_-_PDF_version.pdf. Accessed 29 March 2022.

US Federal Register (2021). vol. 86 no. 80, 31 March 2021, FR Doc. 2021–06577 Filed 3-30-21.

Veale, M.A. (2020). Critical take on the policy recommendations of the EU high-level expert group on artificial intelligence. *European Journal of Risk Regulation*, 11(1), 1–10.

Wachter, S. and Mittelstadt, B. (2019). A right to reasonable inferences: Re-thinking data protection law in the age of big data and AI. *Columbia Business Law Review*, 2, 494.

Weng, Y. H. and Hirata, Y. (2022). Design-centered HRI governance for healthcare robots. *Journal of Healthcare Engineering*, 2022.

Wiener, A. (2017). Inside Adidas's robot powered, on demand sneaker factory. Available at: https://www.wired.com/story/inside-speedfac tory-adidas-robot-powered-sneaker-factory/. Accessed 15 February 2022.

Wu, Y. (2021). Cloud-edge orchestration for the internet of things: Architecture and AI-powered data processing. *IEEE Internet of Things Journal*, 8(16), 12792–12805. Available at: http://doi:10.1109/JIOT.2020.3014845.

Yordanova, K. (2022). The EU AI Act — Balancing human rights and innovation through regulatory sandboxes and standatization. Available at: https://www.competitionpolicyinternational.com/the-eu-ai-act-balancing-human-rights-and-innovation-through-regulatory-sandboxes-and-standardization/. Accessed 17 February 2022.

https://doi.org/10.1142/9781800614239_0003

Chapter 3

Method Development Aspects of Liquidity Risk Modelling: Dynamic Algorithms for Reinforcement Machine Learning Under Crisis Market Perspectives

Mazin A. M. Al Janabi

Full Research Professor of Finance & Banking and Financial Engineering, Merida, Yucatan, Mexico
mazinaljanabi@gmail.com

Abstract

This chapter reviews the methodological development phases of Al Janabi's (2012) optimisation algorithms for the assessment of Liquidity-Adjusted Value-at-Risk (LVaR) technique under crisis market outlooks. This chapter examines the different facets for the development of robust risk modelling techniques that attempt to address the problem of market/liquidity risk of multi-assets portfolios. The proposed theoretical foundations and optimisation algorithms have uncovered that better investable portfolios can be attained than using the conventional Markowitz (1952) portfolio theory. The modelling algorithms and optimisation techniques discussed in this chapter can aid in evolving risk and portfolio management practices, particularly in light of the consequences of the 2007–2009 financial crisis. In addition, the recommended risk management modelling techniques and optimisation algorithms can have key applications in reinforcement machine learning, expert systems, smart financial functions, Internet of Things (IoT), and financial technology (fintech) in big data ecosystems.

1. Introduction

Modern portfolio management faces new demands and challenges in light of the 2007–2009 global financial crunch. In response to the sub-prime crisis, market regulators are requiring more advanced modelling methods and algorithms as well as improved risk monitoring and modelling along with detailed and sophisticated risk management reports (Al Janabi, 2022, 2021b, 2021c).

Portfolio managers and other financial institutions are continuously exploring new methodologies and optimisation techniques to conduct comprehensive asset allocations for a number of scenarios across all asset classes (Al Janabi, 2022, 2021b, 2021c). The 2007–2009 global financial meltdown has prompted further industry calls for improved portfolio optimisation algorithms as well as modern risk monitoring and modelling techniques. To that end, reinforcement machine learning technologies present fresh opportunities to address these challenges, as there is an increasing effect of reinforcement machine learning techniques in portfolio optimisation and risk management applications, with many practical solutions already implemented and many more being explored (Al Janabi, 2022, 2021b, 2021c).

To that end, the main contribution of this chapter to the fields of financial engineering and reinforcement machine learning is to examine an optimisation algorithm to improve the asset allocation process of multi-assets portfolios by combining Liquidity-Adjusted Value-at-Risk (LVaR, henceforth) with a multivariate dependence modelling technique. In contrast to all existing published literatures pertaining to the application of reinforcement machine learning (e.g. Ban *et al.*, 2018; Kalayci *et al.*, 2019; Paiva *et al.*, 2019) to risk analysis and optimisation of portfolios, our proposed risk-engine and optimisation algorithm differs in important ways from previous, however related, research.

As such, our proposed approach is a robust enhancement of the traditional Markowitz (1952) mean–variance (MV) approach where the variance risk measure is replaced by multivariate LVaR optimisation algorithms that integrate the impacts of liquidity risk on portfolio selection.[1] As such, the novel modelling algorithms incorporate the microstructure effects of liquidity risk and shocks, as an additional key constraint, on the optimisation process of the risk-engine's objective function. The task is achieved by minimising the LVaR, while requiring a minimum expected return subject to imposing several financially meaningful operational constraints under event (adverse) market circumstances. As such, the focus in this work is on the forecast of risk measure, rather than on expected returns for two reasons: first, several studies have analysed the forecasts of expected returns in the context of MV optimisation (see, for instance, Best and Grauer, 1991). The common opinion is that expected returns are not easy to forecast, and that the optimisation process is very sensitive to these variations. Second, there exists a general notion that LVaR, in a wide sense, is simpler to assess than expected returns from historical data (Al Janabi, 2013, 2014). To that end, a comparison between the classical Markowitz (1952) MV efficient portfolios and investable LVaR portfolios is obtained by simulating different expected returns under event market conditions. Lastly, we show the usefulness of our optimisation algorithm for portfolio selection by considering selected diversified portfolios of commodity markets. We then carry out an empirical test by comparing daily LVaR measures and investable portfolios with the conventional Markowitz (1952) MV efficient portfolios technique. Finally, the empirical testing results are interesting in terms of theory as well as practical applications and provide an incentive for further research in the areas of LVaR optimisation algorithms, asset allocation, and selection of commodity portfolios. Moreover, the obtained asset allocation and optimised investable portfolios are widely applicable to any commodity portfolio management end-user, providing potential applications to practitioners and research ideas to academics.

Machine learning techniques have expanded from the study of pattern recognition and computational learning theory in artificial intelligence (Kalayci *et al.*, 2019). As such, machine learning algorithms

[1]The robust modelling technique and nonlinear quadratic optimisation algorithms implemented in this chapter are based on the Al Janabi model (Al Janabi, 2008; Madoroba and Kruger, 2014).

can explore the operating stages of a predictive model, from a training set of input observations and multiple-variables, in order to make decisions communicated as outputs, instead of strictly sticking to static programme commands. Furthermore, reinforcement machine learning, recognised as one of the technologies with important implications for portfolio optimisation and risk management, can permit the construction of more precise risk–return modelling algorithms by recognising complex, multidimensional, non-normal, and nonlinear patterns within large datasets across all asset classes. In portfolio optimisation and assets allocation context, only the best set of optimum solutions are selected to generate the next set of even better optimum outcomes. This optimisation process is repeated iteratively to converge on what eventually will yield the optimal set of portfolios with the highest expected returns and minimum risk profiles.[2]

The forecasting of financial risks has greatly evolved in the last three decades, from a modest indicator of market value, through more multifaceted internal models such as scenario-analysis to contemporary stress-testing and Value-at-Risk (VaR, henceforth) techniques. Present-day internal regulations for financial markets and institutions formulate some of the market risk management requirements in terms of percentiles of loss distributions; and, as such, VaR is fundamentally an upper percentile of the loss distribution function (Al Janabi, 2019).

Indeed, methodologies for the assessment of market risk have been well established and standardised in the academic as well as the financial market world. On the other hand, liquidity risk has gained less devotion from researchers, possibly because it is less substantial in developed countries where most of the market risk methodologies and techniques were devised (Al Janabi, 2013). Nevertheless, the recent rapid expansion of emerging markets' trading activities as well as the recurring turbulence in those markets, in the wake of the outcomes of the most recent financial crunch, has driven liquidity risk and its application to the portfolio optimisation enigma to the

[2]For some of the latest literature on reinforcement machine learning and expert systems in finance for modern portfolio optimisation and management, we refer the readers to Kalayci *et al.* (2019), Ban *et al.* (2018), Al Janabi (2019), and Paiva *et al.* (2019).

vanguard of market risk research and development (Al Janabi, 2013, 2019).

Against this backdrop and to address the above shortcomings, this chapter examines robust techniques for the optimisation of financial trading portfolios and for forecasting and assessing liquidity risk within a multivariate technique (that was expanded by Al Janabi (2012, 2014)).[3] Given the fact that literatures on modern portfolio management have been relatively inconclusive and provide mixed results, the aim of this chapter is to examine realistic optimisation algorithms that can produce better multi-assets allocation under event (crisis) market circumstances and construct realistic structured portfolios, subject to applying meaningful operational and financial constraints, predominantly in light of the shocks of the 2007–2009 financial crunch.

From this perspective, our theoretical risk techniques and practical applications have important implications for portfolio selection and asset management, mostly in light of the aftershocks of the 2007–2009 financial crisis. In short, the advantages of the theoretical and practical fundamentals of LVaR and its application to optimisation algorithms for portfolio selection include the following:

(1) The proposed optimisation algorithms can aid in advancing portfolio selection and management in financial markets by assessing investable portfolios subject to meaningful operational and financial constraints.

[3] In his research papers, Al Janabi (2012, 2014) has investigated and applied similar optimisation algorithms for commodity and stock markets. While his general optimisation elements and parameters are adapted herein, this chapter builds on Al Janabi's (2012, 2014) research papers and differs in the sense that it includes detailed optimisation algorithm approaches for portfolio selection and research design that can be accessible to market practitioners, particularly commodity and stock market asset management entities. The method validation process and research design include all the operational stages for risk–return estimation and portfolio optimisation that can be used for programming and reinforcement machine learning objectives. In addition, this chapter also includes in-depth analysis, discussion, and justification of LVaR as a portfolio selection technique as well as further considerations and recommendations for practical applications for asset management.

(2) Better investable portfolios can be achieved compared to the classical Markowitz (1952) mean–variance portfolio selection approach.
(3) The proposed modelling scheme and optimisation algorithms can be implemented by portfolio managers and risk managers for the valuation of proper asset allocations of diverse portfolios under adverse and event market outlooks.
(4) The robust risk-algorithms and portfolio optimisation techniques can aid in solving some real-world dilemmas under stressed and adverse market conditions, such as, the effect of liquidity when it dries up in financial and commodity markets, the impact of correlation factors when there is a switching in their signs, and the integration of the influence of nonlinear and non-normal distribution of assets' returns in portfolio optimisation and management.
(5) In addition, the recommended risk management modelling techniques and optimisation algorithms can have key applications in reinforcement machine learning, expert systems, smart financial functions, Internet of Things (IoT), and financial technology (fintech) in big data ecosystems.

The chapter proceeds as follows. The next section outlines the methods' details and examines the theoretical foundations and modelling parameters for portfolio selection using LVaR optimisation algorithms. This is followed by a full discussion of the optimisation algorithm for portfolio selection, as well as research design for portfolio management and validation of the optimisation method. This section also discusses the various parameters required for the optimisation engine and the construction of efficient and coherent portfolios for long and short-sales trading positions, and includes a graphical flowchart, which shows a concise outline of the risk-engine's operational stages and their interrelationships. This flowchart highlights the required input parameters for portfolio optimisation and selection and can aid in defining the processes for computer programming and reinforcement machine learning. The final section includes concluding remarks along with possible practical applications for portfolio selection and asset management.

2. Method Details

2.1. *Theoretical foundations and risk modelling algorithms*

Value-at-Risk (VaR) can be computed using a closed-form parametric method that is based on the Al Janabi model (Al Janabi, 2008; Madoroba and Kruger, 2014). To that end, to determine the VaR of multiple-assets portfolios, the volatility of each risk factor is extracted from a pre-defined historical observation period and can be estimated using generalized autoregressive conditional heteroskedasticity in mean, GARCH-M model, under the assumptions of adverse market settings. The potential effect of each component of the portfolio on the overall portfolio value is then worked out. These effects are then aggregated across the whole multiple-assets portfolio using the correlations parameters between the risk factors to give the overall VaR value of the portfolio with a given confidence level.

Set against this background, for a single trading position the absolute VaR can be defined in monetary terms as follows (Al Janabi, 2012, 2013, 2014, 2021a):

$$\text{VaR}_i = |(\mu_i - \alpha^*\sigma_i)(\text{Asset}_i^* Fx_i)| \tag{1}$$

where μ_i is the expected return of asset i, α is the confidence level (or in other words, the standard normal variant at confidence level α), and σ_i is the conditional volatility of the return of the security that constitutes the single position and can be estimated using a GARCH-M model. While the term Asset_i indicates the mark-to-market monetary value of asset i, Fx_i denotes the unit foreign exchange rate of asset i. If the expected return of the asset, μ_i, is very small or close to zero, then equation (1) can be reduced to[4]

$$\text{VaR}_i = |\alpha^*\sigma_i^*\text{Asset}_i^* Fx_i| \tag{2}$$

[4]If the purpose of the risk analysis is to investigate diverse commodities' dependences and related risk management measures, then Asset_i should be the mark-to-market prices of the individual commodities.

Indeed, equation (2) includes some simplifying assumptions, yet researchers and practitioners in the financial markets for the estimation of VaR for a single trading position routinely use it.

Trading risk in the presence of multiple risk factors is determined by the combined effect of individual risks. The extent of the total risk is determined not only by the magnitudes of the individual risks but also by their correlations. Portfolio effects are crucial in risk management not only for large diversified portfolios but also for individual instruments that depend on several risk factors. For multiple assets or a portfolio of assets, VaR is a function of each individual security's risk and the correlation factor $[\rho_{i,j}]$ between the returns on the individual securities as follows:

$$\text{VaR}_P = \sqrt{\sum_{i=1}^{n}\sum_{j=1}^{n} \text{VaR}_i\ \text{VaR}_j\ \rho_{i,j}} = \sqrt{[\text{VaR}]^T[\rho][\text{VaR}]} \qquad (3)$$

This formula is a general one for the calculation of VaR for any portfolio regardless of the number of securities. It should be noted that the second term of the above formula is rewritten in terms of matrix-algebra — a useful form to avoid mathematical complexity, as more and more securities are added. This approach can simplify the programming process and permits easy incorporation of short-sales positions in the market risk management process. This means, in order to calculate VaR (of a portfolio of any number of securities), we need to create first a transpose vector $[\text{VaR}]^T$ of individual VaR positions — an $(1xn)$ vector, and hence the superscript "T" indicates transpose of the vector:

$$[\text{VaR}]^T = [\text{VaR}_1 \quad \text{VaR}_2 \quad \ldots\ldots \quad \text{VaR}_n] \qquad (3a)$$

Second, a vector [VaR] of individual VaR positions — explicitly n rows and one column $(nx1)$ vector, such as

$$[\text{VaR}] = \begin{bmatrix} \text{VaR}_1 \\ \text{VaR}_2 \\ \cdots \\ \text{VaR}_n \end{bmatrix} \qquad (3b)$$

Finally, a matrix $[\rho]$ of all correlation factors (ρ) – an (nxn) matrix in the following form:

$$[\rho] = \begin{bmatrix} 1 & \rho_{1,2} & \rho_{1,3} & \cdots\cdots & \rho_{1,n} \\ \rho_{2,1} & 1 & \rho_{2,3} & \cdots\cdots & \rho_{2,n} \\ \rho_{3,1} & \rho_{3,2} & 1 & \cdots\cdots & \rho_{3,n} \\ \cdots\cdots & \cdots\cdots & \cdots\cdots & \cdots\cdots & \cdots\cdots \\ \rho_{n,1} & \rho_{n,2} & \rho_{n,3} & \cdots\cdots & 1 \end{bmatrix} \tag{3c}$$

2.2. *Integrating liquidity risk into LVaR algorithms using the Al Janabi model*

In fact, if returns are independent and they can have any elliptical multivariate distribution, then it is possible to convert the VaR horizon parameter from daily to any t-day horizon. The variance of a t-day return should be t times the variance of a 1-day return or $\sigma^2 = f(t)$. Thus, in terms of standard deviation (or volatility), $\sigma = f(\sqrt{t})$, and the daily or overnight VaR number [VaR (1-day)], it is possible to determine the liquidity adjusted VaR (LVaR) for any t-day horizon as follows (Al Janabi, 2013, 2021a):

$$\text{LVaR}(t - \text{day}) = \text{VaR}(1 - \text{day})\sqrt{t} \tag{4}$$

The above formula was proposed and used by *J.P. Morgan* in their earlier RiskMetrics^{TM} method (Morgan Guaranty Trust Company, 1994). This methodology implicitly assumes that liquidation occurs in one block sale at the end of the holding period and that there is one holding period for all assets, regardless of their inherent trading liquidity structure. Unfortunately, the latter approach does not consider real-life trading situations, where traders can liquidate (or rebalance) small portions of their trading portfolios on a daily basis. The assumption of a given holding period for orderly liquidation inevitably implies that assets' liquidation occurs during the holding period. Accordingly, scaling the holding period to account for orderly liquidation can be justified if one allows the assets to be liquidated throughout the holding period (Al Janabi, 2013, 2014, 2021a).

In what follows, we discuss a re-engineered approach for calculating a closed-form parametric LVaR with explicit treatment of liquidity trading risk and coherent assessment of investable portfolios.

The key methodological contribution is a different liquidity-scaling-factor than the traditional root-t multiplier. The proposed model and liquidity-scaling-factor is more realistic and less conservative than the conventional root-t multiplier. In essence, the suggested multiplier (add-on) is a function of a predetermined liquidity threshold(s) defined as the maximum position, which can be unwound without disturbing market prices during one trading day. The essence of the model relies on the assumption of a stochastic stationary process and some rules of thumb, which can be of crucial value for more accurate overall trading risk assessment during market stress (crisis) periods when liquidity dries up in consequence of a financial crisis (Al Janabi, 2013, 2014, 2021a). In addition, the re-engineered model is quite simple to implement even by very large financial institutions with multiple assets and risk factors. To that end, a practical framework of a methodology (within a simplified mathematical approach) is proposed in what follows, with the purpose of incorporating and calculating illiquid assets' horizon LVaR, detailed along these lines[5].

The market risk of an illiquid asset trading position is larger than the risk of an otherwise identical liquid position. This is because unwinding the illiquid position takes longer than unwinding the liquid position, and, as a result, the illiquid position is more exposed to the volatility of the market for a longer period of time. In this approach, an asset trading position will be thought of as illiquid if its size surpasses a certain liquidity threshold. The threshold (which is determined by traders for different assets and/or financial markets) is defined as the maximum position which can be unwound, without disrupting market prices, in normal market conditions, and during one trading day. Consequently, the size of the asset trading position relative to the threshold plays an important role in determining the

[5]The mathematical approach and modelling algorithms presented herein are largely drawn from Al Janabi's (2012, 2013, 2014, 2021a) research papers, and are based on the Al Janabi model for liquidity risk management in multiple-assets portfolios (Al Janabi, 2008; Madoroba and Kruger, 2014). For other relevant literature on liquidity risk, internal risk models, and portfolio selection, one can refer as well to Arreola-Hernandez and Al Janabi (2020), Al Janabi (2021a, 2021b, 2021c), Asadi and Al Janabi (2020), Arreola-Hernandez *et al.* (2017), Arreola-Hernandez *et al.* (2015), Grillini *et al.* (2019), Al Janabi *et al.* (2017), and Al Janabi *et al.* (2019), among others.

number of days that are required to close the entire position. This effect can be translated into a liquidity increment (or an additional liquidity risk factor) that can be incorporated into VaR analysis. If for instance, the par value of an asset position is \$20,000 and the liquidity threshold is \$5,000, then it will take four days to sell out the entire trading position. Therefore, the initial position will be exposed to market variation for 1 day, and the rest of the position (that is \$15,000) is subject to market variation for an additional three days. If it is assumed that daily changes of market values follow a stationary stochastic process, the risk exposure due to illiquidity effects is given by the following illustration, detailed as follows (Al Janabi, 2013, 2014, 2021a).

In order to take into account the full illiquidity of assets (that is, the required unwinding period to liquidate an asset), we define the following:

t = number of liquidation days (t-days to liquidate the entire asset fully);
σ^2_{adj} = variance of the illiquid asset trading position; and
σ_{adj} = liquidity risk factor or standard deviation of the illiquid asset trading position.

The proposed approach assumes that the trading position is closed out linearly over t-days and hence it uses the logical assumption that the losses due to illiquid trading positions over t-days are the sum of losses over the individual trading days. Moreover, we can assume with reasonable accuracy that asset returns and losses due to illiquid trading positions are independent and identically distributed (*iid*) and serially uncorrelated day-to-day along the liquidation horizon. Further, we can also assume that the variance of losses due to liquidity risk over t-days is the sum of the variance (σ_i^2, for all $i = 1, 2, \ldots, t$) of losses on the individual days, thus:

$$\sigma^2_{\text{adj}} = \left(\sigma_1^2 + \sigma_2^2 + \sigma_3^2 + \cdots + \sigma_{t-2}^2 + \sigma_{t-1}^2 + \sigma_t^2\right) \tag{5}$$

In fact, the square root-t approach (equation [4]) is a simplified special case of equation (5) under the assumption that the daily variances of losses throughout the holding period are all the same as the first day variance, σ_1^2, thus $\sigma^2_{\text{adj}} = \left(\sigma_1^2 + \sigma_1^2 + \sigma_1^2 + \cdots + \sigma_1^2\right) = t\sigma_1^2$. As discussed above, the square root-t equation overestimates asset liquidity risk since it does not consider that traders can liquidate small portions of their trading portfolios on a daily basis and then the whole trading position can be sold completely on the last trading day. However, this would be an overstatement of VaR; and the true VaR has to be between the 1-day position VaR and 1-day position VaR$\sqrt{t}$. Indeed, in real financial market operations, liquidation occurs during the holding period and thus scaling the holding period to account for orderly liquidation can be justified if one allows the assets to be liquidated throughout the holding period. As such, for this special linear liquidation case and under the assumption that the variance of losses of the first trading day decreases linearly each day (as a function of t), we can derive from equation (5) the following:

$$\sigma_{\text{adj}}^2 = \left(\left(\frac{t}{t}\right)^2 \sigma_1^2 + \left(\frac{t-1}{t}\right)^2 \sigma_1^2 + \left(\frac{t-2}{t}\right)^2 \sigma_1^2 + \cdots + \left(\frac{3}{t}\right)^2 \sigma_1^2 + \left(\frac{2}{t}\right)^2 \sigma_1^2 + \left(\frac{1}{t}\right)^2 \sigma_1^2\right) \tag{6}$$

In this manner, if the asset position is liquidated in equal parts at the end of each trading day, the trader faces a 1-day holding period on the entire position, a 2-day holding period on a fraction $(t-1)/t$ of the position, a 3-day holding period on a fraction $(t-2)/t$ of the position, and so forth. Evidently, the additional liquidity risk factor depends only on the number of days needed to sell an illiquid trading position linearly. In the general case of t-days, the variance of the liquidity risk factor is given by the following mathematical functional expression of t:

$$\sigma_{\text{adj}}^2 = \sigma_1^2 \left(\left(\frac{t}{t}\right)^2 + \left(\frac{t-1}{t}\right)^2 + \left(\frac{t-2}{t}\right)^2 + \cdots + \left(\frac{3}{t}\right)^2 + \left(\frac{2}{t}\right)^2 + \left(\frac{1}{t}\right)^2\right) \tag{7}$$

To calculate the sum of the squares, it is convenient to use a short-cut approach. From mathematical finite series, the following relationship can be obtained:

$$(t)^2+(t-1)^2+(t-2)^2+\cdots+(3)^2+(2)^2+(1)^2 = \frac{t(t+1)(2t+1)}{6} \quad (8)$$

Hence, after substituting equation (8) into equation (7), the following can be achieved:

$$\sigma^2_{\text{adj}} = \sigma^2_1 \left[\frac{1}{t^2}\{(t)^2+(t-1)^2+(t-2)^2+\cdots+(3)^2+(2)^2+(1)^2\}\right]$$

$$\text{or} \quad \sigma^2_{\text{adj}} = \sigma^2_1 \left(\frac{(2t+1)(t+1)}{6t}\right) \quad (9)$$

Accordingly, from equation (9) the liquidity risk factor can be expressed in terms of volatility (or standard deviation) as

$$\sigma_{\text{adj}} = \sigma_1 \left\{\sqrt{\frac{1}{t^2}\left[(t)^2+(t-1)^2+(t-2)^2+\cdots+(3)^2+(2)^2+(1)^2\right]}\right\}$$

$$\text{or} \quad \sigma_{\text{adj}} = \sigma_1 \left\{\sqrt{\frac{(2t+1)\,(t+1)}{6t}}\right\} \quad (10)$$

The final result of equation (10) is of course a function of time and not the square root of time as employed by some financial market participants based on the *RiskMetrics*^{TM} methodologies. The above framework can also be used to calculate LVaR for any time horizon. Likewise, in order to perform the calculation of LVaR under illiquid market conditions, it is possible to use the liquidity factor of equation (10) along with the definition of LVaR in equation (4) and define the following liquidity-adjusted VaR risk factor[6]:

$$\text{LVaR}_{\text{adj}} = \text{VaR}\sqrt{\frac{(2t+1)(t+1)}{6t}} \quad (11)$$

[6]It is important to note that equation (11) can be used to calculate LVaR for any time horizon subject to the constraint that the overall LVaR figure should not exceed at any setting the nominal exposure, in other words, the total trading volume.

where VaR = Value-at-Risk under liquid market conditions and; LVaR_{adj} = Value-at-Risk under illiquid market conditions. The latter equation indicates that $\text{LVaR}_{\text{adj}} > \text{VaR}$, and for the special case when the number of days to liquidate the entire assets is one trading day, then $\text{LVaR}_{\text{adj}} = \text{VaR}$. Consequently, the difference between $\text{LVaR}_{\text{adj}} - \text{VaR}$ should be equal to the residual market risk due to the illiquidity of any asset under illiquid market conditions. Actually, the number of liquidation days (t) necessary to liquidate the entire assets fully is related to the choice of the liquidity threshold; however, the size of this threshold is likely to change under stressed/crisis market conditions. Indeed, the choice of the liquidation horizon can be estimated from the total trading position size and the daily trading volume that can be unwound into the market without significantly disrupting asset market prices; and in actual practices, it is generally estimated as the absolute value of the following equality (Al Janabi, 2013, 2014, 2021a):

$$t = |\text{Total trading position size of Asset}_i / \text{Daily trading volume of Asset}_i|, \; s.t. \quad t \geq 1.0 \tag{12}$$

In effect, the daily trading volume of assets can be regarded as the average daily volume over some period of time, generally a month, or the volume that can be unwound in a severe crisis period. The trading volume in a crisis period can be roughly approximated as the average daily trading volume less a number of standard deviations. Although this alternative approach is quite simple, it is still relatively objective. Moreover, it is reasonably easy to gather the required data to perform the necessary liquidation scenarios (Al Janabi, 2013, 2014, 2021a).

In essence, the above liquidity scaling factor (or multiplier) is more realistic and less conservative than the conventional root-t multiplier and can aid financial entities in allocating reasonable and liquidity-market-driven regulatory and economic-capital requirements. Furthermore, the above mathematical formulas can be applied for the calculation of LVaR for every asset trading position and for the entire portfolio of assets. In order to calculate the LVaR for the full trading portfolio under illiquid market conditions ($\text{LVaR}_{P_{\text{adj}}}$), the above mathematical formulation can be extended, with the aid of equation (3), into a matrix-algebra form to yield the following

(Al Janabi, 2013, 2014, 2021a):

$$\begin{aligned} \text{LVaR}_{P_{\text{adj}}} &= \sqrt{\sum_{i=1}^{n}\sum_{j=1}^{n} LVaR_{i_{\text{adj}}}\text{LVaR}_{j_{\text{adj}}}\rho_{i,j}} \\ &= \sqrt{[\text{LVaR}_{\text{adj}}]^{T}\,[\rho]\,[\text{LVaR}_{\text{adj}}]} \end{aligned} \tag{13}$$

The elements of the vectors of equation (13), i.e. $\text{LVaR}_{i\text{adj}}$, for each trading asset can now be computed with the aid of equations (1), (2), and (11) in the following manner:

$$\text{LVaR}_{i\text{adj}} = |(\mu_i - \alpha^* \sigma_i)\text{Asset}_i^*\ Fx_i \sqrt{\frac{(2t_i+1)(t_i+1)}{6t_i}}| \tag{14}$$

On the other hand, in the special case when μ_i is small or close to zero, we can have

$$\text{LVaR}_{i\text{adj}} = |\alpha^* \sigma_i^* \text{Asset}_i^*\ Fx_i \sqrt{\frac{(2t_i+1)(t_i+1)}{6t_i}}| \tag{14a}$$

Now, we can define the ultimate two vectors $[\text{LVaR}_{\text{adj}}]^{T}$ and $[\text{LVaR}_{\text{adj}}]$ as follows:

$$[\text{LVaR}_{\text{adj}}]^{T} = \begin{bmatrix}\text{LVaR}_{1_{\text{adj}}} & \text{LVaR}_{2_{\text{adj}}} & \cdots & \text{LVaR}_{n_{\text{adj}}}\end{bmatrix} \tag{15}$$

$$[\text{LVaR}_{\text{adj}}] = \begin{bmatrix}\text{LVaR}_{1_{\text{adj}}} \\ \text{LVaR}_{2_{\text{adj}}} \\ \cdots \\ \text{LVaR}_{n_{\text{adj}}}\end{bmatrix} \tag{16}$$

The above mathematical structure (in the form of two vectors and a matrix, $[\text{LVaR}_{\text{adj}}]^{T}$, $[\text{LVaR}_{\text{adj}}]$, and $[\rho]$) can facilitate the programming process so that the portfolio manager can specify different liquidation days for the whole portfolio and/or for each individual trading security according to the necessary number of days to liquidate the entire multiple-assets fully.

3. Method Validation

3.1. *Scenario optimisation framework for structured portfolios*

To examine the relationship between assets' expected returns and volatility, we can implement a conditional volatility approach to determine the risk parameters that are needed for the LVaR's engine and thereafter for the estimation of assets' daily market liquidity risk exposure and investable portfolios' requirements. Indeed, the time-varying pattern of assets' volatility has been widely recognised and modelled as a conditional variance within the GARCH framework, as originally developed by Engle (1982, 1995). Engle (1982) introduced a likelihood ratio to test ARCH effects and a maximum likelihood method to estimate the parameters in the ARCH model. This approach was generalised by Bollerslev (1986) and Engle and Kroner (1995). The following generalised autoregressive conditional heteroskedasticity in mean, GARCH-M (1, 1) model, is used for the estimation of expected return and conditional volatility for each of the time-series variables (Al Janabi, 2013, 2014, 2021a) as follows:

$$R_{it} = a_i + b_i\sigma_{it} + \varepsilon_{it} \tag{17}$$

$$\sigma_{it}^2 = c_i + \beta_{i1}\sigma_{it-1}^2 + \beta_{i2}\varepsilon_{it-1}^2 \tag{18}$$

where R_{it} is the continuous compounding return of time series i, σ_{it} is the conditional standard deviation as a measure of volatility, and ε_{it} is the error term return for time series i. The denotations a_i, b_i, c_i, β_{i1}, and β_{i2} represent parameters to be estimated. The parameters representing variance are assumed to undertake a positive value.

Furthermore, three matrices of correlations can possibly be used for the assessment of LVaR, namely $\rho = 1$, 0, and empirical correlations. The objectives here are to establish the necessary quantitative infrastructures for advanced risk management analysis. Indeed, the assembled correlation matrices are essential parameters along with conditional volatility vectors for the calculations of LVaR, stress-testing, and LVaR of optimal and investable portfolios. As a result, these matrices and vectors can be integrated into the LVaR's engine to estimate optimal and investable portfolios under the notion of different unwinding horizons (closeout periods) and for various combinations of long/short-sales assets allocation (that is, by disallowing both long-only positions and borrowing constraints).

3.2. *Constraints and parameters for scenario optimisation using LVaR modelling algorithms*

In this chapter, we examine the methodological development facets of a model for optimising portfolio risk–return with LVaR constraints using realistic operational and financial scenarios. Essentially, our proposed approach is a robust enhancement of the classic Markowitz (1952) mean–variance approach, where the original risk measure, variance, is replaced by LVaR algorithms. The task is attained here by minimising LVaR, while requiring a minimum expected return subject to imposing several financially meaningful operational constraints under adverse market circumstances. Thus, by considering different expected returns, we can generate an optimal LVaR frontier under adverse crisis outlooks. Alternatively, we can also maximise expected returns while not allowing for large risks. For the purpose of this study, the optimisation problem can be formulated as follows (Al Janabi, 2013, 2014, 2021a).

It is possible to compute from equation (13) the minimum portfolio LVaR by solving for the following quadratic programming objective function:

$$\begin{aligned}\text{Minimise : } \mathrm{LVaR}_{P_{\text{adj}}} &= \sqrt{\sum_{i=1}^{n}\sum_{j=1}^{n} \mathrm{LVaR}_{i_{\text{adj}}}\mathrm{LVaR}_{j_{\text{adj}}}\rho_{i,j}} \\ &= \sqrt{[\mathrm{LVaR}_{\text{adj}}]^{T}\,[\rho]\,[\mathrm{LVaR}_{\text{adj}}]} \qquad (19)\end{aligned}$$

The above objective risk-function can be minimised subject to the following operational and financial budget constraints as specified by the portfolio manager:

$$\sum_{i=1}^{n} R_i x_i = R_P; \quad l_i \leq x_i \leq u_i \quad i = 1, 2, \ldots, n \qquad (20)$$

$$\sum_{i=1}^{n} x_i = 1.0; \quad l_i \leq x_i \leq u_i \quad i = 1, 2, \ldots, n \qquad (21)$$

$$\sum_{i=1}^{n} V_i = V_P \quad i = 1, 2, \ldots, n \tag{22}$$

$$[\text{LHF}] \geq 1.0; \quad \forall_i \quad i = 1, 2, \ldots, n \tag{23}$$

Here, R_P and V_P denote the target portfolio mean expected return and total portfolio volume, respectively, and x_i, the weight or percentage asset allocation for each asset. The values l_i and $u_i, i = 1, 2, \ldots, n$, denote the lower and upper constraints for the portfolio weights x_i. If we choose $l_i = 0$, $i = 1, 2, \ldots, n$, then we have the situation where no short-sales are allowed. Moreover, [LHF] indicates an $(nx1)$ vector of the individual liquidity horizon of each asset for all $i = 1, 2, \ldots, n$, where LHF_i is defined, with the aid of equation (11), for each trading asset in the following way (Al Janabi, 2013, 2014, 2021a):

$$\text{LHF}_i = \sqrt{\frac{(2t_i + 1)(t_i + 1)}{6t_i}} \geq 1.0; \quad \forall_i \quad i = 1, 2, \ldots, n \tag{24}$$

Now, the portfolio manager can specify different liquidity horizon and correlation factors and calculate the necessary LVaR to sustain the trading operation of the financial entity without subjecting the entity to insolvency matters. The rationality behind imposing the above constraints is to comply with current regulations (e.g. Basel III capital accord) which enforce capital requirements on investment companies, proportional to their LVaR and economic-capital, besides other operational limits (for instance, volume trading limits).[7]

Set against this background and to maximise its utility as a portfolio selection and management method, we have constructed

[7]The risk-engine and its objective function can be modified to take into consideration the effects of nonlinearity and non-normality of assets returns on assets allocation by implementing Kendall's tau algorithm as a measure of nonlinear dependence or any other copula-based models to replace the linear correlation factors. Likewise, it can easily be adapted to resolve the issue of non-normality of assets returns using Cornish–Fisher expansion (as a measure of non-normality) or any other relevant non-normality modelling techniques (Al Janabi, 2021a).

the portfolio management tool such that the proposed risk-engine and robust scenario optimisation algorithms can be used for computer programming and reinforcement machine learning objectives. The operational procedure, of the method validation process, is set according to the following stages (Al Janabi, 2021b).

3.2.1. *Stage (1) of the risk-engine and algorithms for portfolio optimisation and selection*

In this first stage, we make an attempt to define a nonlinear dynamic risk-function (i.e. objective function) of a multivariable. For this purpose, the nonlinear dynamic risk-function can be defined as a vector of the following: (1) Monetary investment in each asset-class; (2) Closeout periods (or unwinding periods) of each asset-class and the overall closeout periods of investable portfolios; (3) Overall trading volume of investible portfolios; (4) Constrained asset allocation proportions according to contemporary financial market regulations and subject to the imposition of rational and meaningful operational and financial boundaries; (5) Downside risk constraints so that additional risk resulting from any non-normality and illiquid assets may be used to estimate the characteristics of investable portfolios. This enables a much more generalised framework to be developed, with the distributional assumption most appropriate to the type of financial assets to be employed, and which can be of crucial value for more accurate market risk assessment during market stress periods and particularly when liquidity dries up; (6) Correlation coefficients among all asset classes; (7) Expected returns of investable portfolios; (8) Confidence level of estimated parameters under different scenarios and market settings; (9) Portfolio managers' choices of a combination of long/short-sales trading asset positions (Al Janabi, 2021a, 2021b).

3.2.2. *Stage (2) of the risk-engine and algorithms for portfolio optimisation and selection*

In the second stage, we define the corresponding robust scenario optimisation algorithm, which is based on quadratic programming techniques, subject to applying meaningful financial and operational constraints. Furthermore, in the development of portfolio investment policy there are many types of constraints that can be considered an integral part of the optimisation process. These constraints are drawn from rational financial investment considerations and can be used in various applications to bound percentiles of loss distributions; and they can include constraints on the asset classes that are allowable as well as concentration limits on investments. Moreover, in making the asset allocation decision, consideration must be given to any risk-based capital requirements. For this objective, the scenario optimisation algorithms can be defined as a minimisation algorithmic process of the dynamic objective risk-function, as follows (Al Janabi, 2021a, 2021b):

(1) The minimisation process is attained here by minimising the objective risk-function while requiring minimum expected returns subject to imposing several rational and meaningful financial and operational constraints;
(2) As a minimum, the bounding limits may include the following:
    (a) The target investable portfolio's expected return;
    (b) Total volume of the investable portfolio;
    (c) Monetary asset-allocation of each asset class;
    (d) Portfolio managers' choices of long-only positions or a combination of long/short-sales trading positions; and
    (e) Closeout or unwinding liquidity horizons of each asset class.

3.2.3. *Stage (3) of the risk-engine and algorithms for portfolio optimisation and selection*

In this final phase, we validate and compare the output results of investable portfolios obtained in Stage (2) with the requirements of investable portfolios defined in Stage (1). To that end, we attempt to rerun the optimisation-engine until a new convergence to meaningful investable portfolios is attained. At this stage, new investable portfolios with meaningful asset allocation structures, which satisfy the boundary conditions defined in Stage (2), are achieved accordingly (Al Janabi, 2021a, 2021b).

The following graphical flowchart shows a concise outline of the three operational stages and their interrelationships for computer programming and reinforcement machine learning objectives.

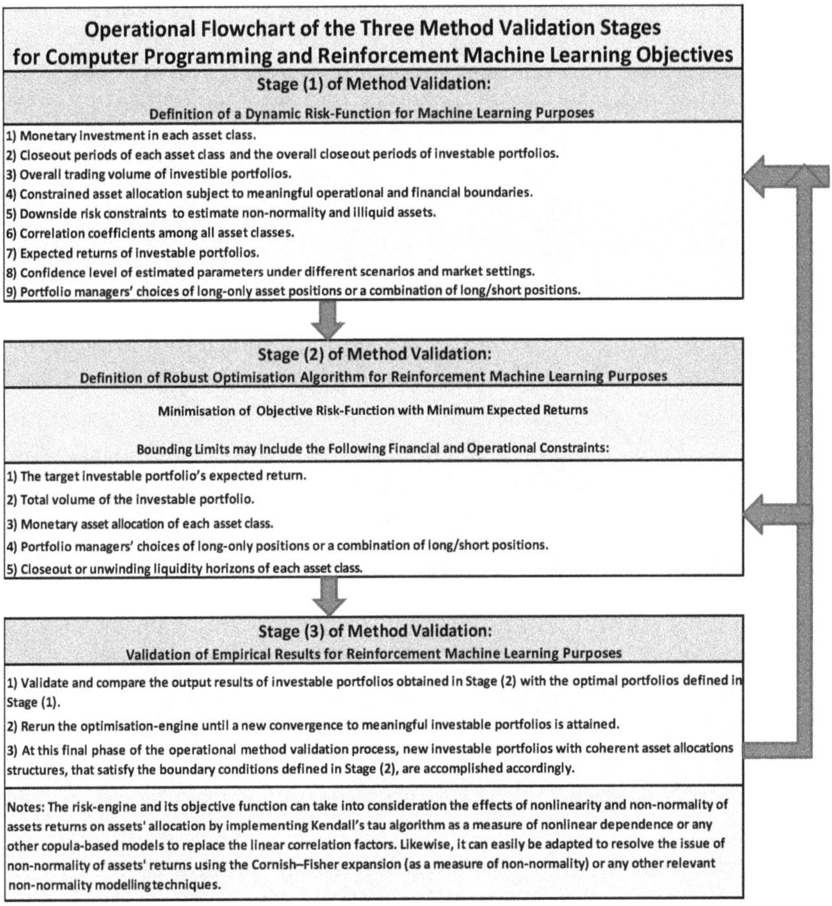

3.3. *Optimisation of efficient and investable (coherent) commodity portfolios — Case study of long- and short-sales asset allocation*

Against this backdrop, one example where the application of the method development aspects of LVaR is useful is in its implementation for portfolio and asset management services. As such, the above-developed methodology is applied to a diverse portfolio of 25 commodities, including energy, metal, agricultural, and other miscellaneous commodities (Al Janabi, 2012).[8]

As such, Figures 1 and 2 provide evidence of the empirical LVaR efficient frontier (under normal and stressed/crisis market settings) defined using a 97.5% confidence level. In this case, the optimal portfolio selection is performed by relaxing the short-sale constraint, for the different commodity assets. On the other hand, efficient portfolios cannot always be attained (e.g. short-sales without realistic lower boundaries on x_i) in the day-to-day real-world portfolio management operations and, hence, portfolio managers should establish proactive "coherent investable portfolios" under more realistic and restricted budget constraints (Al Janabi, 2012).

In this first case study, the weights are allowed to take negative or positive values. However, since arbitrarily high or low percentages have no financial sense, we decided to introduce lower and upper boundaries for the weights and in accordance with reasonable trading practices. Accordingly, it is interesting to note here that the four-benchmark portfolios (investable (coherent) portfolios [1], [2], [3], and [4]) are not positioned near the efficient frontier as indicated in Figures 1 and 2, respectively. This is because real-world considerations make it unlikely that a trading portfolio will behave exactly as theory predicts (Al Janabi, 2012). Imperfections such as restriction on the asset allocation of long and short trading positions, total trading volume, and liquidation closeout (or unwinding) horizons make it unlikely to create an efficient trading portfolio. Thus, this analysis and the implemented LVaR algorithm permit one to determine the asymmetric aspect of risk and, as such, it is a substantial improvement on the classical Markowitz (1952) mean–variance approach (Al Janabi, 2012).

Figure 1 demonstrates the empirical LVaR efficient frontier and "coherent investable portfolios" under normal market scenarios by relaxing short-sale constraints.

[8]For further details on the applied time-series dataset and empirical testing, we refer the readers to Al Janabi's (2012) research paper. Furthermore, all figures presented in this section and quantitative analyses of empirical results are drawn from Al Janabi's (2012) paper.

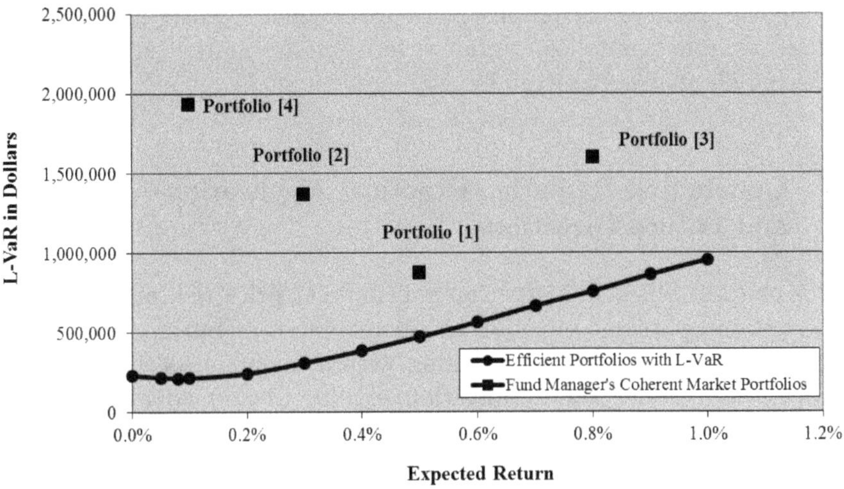

Figure 1. Efficient and coherent portfolios under normal market conditions (case of long and short trading positions).

Source: Al Janabi's (2012) research paper.

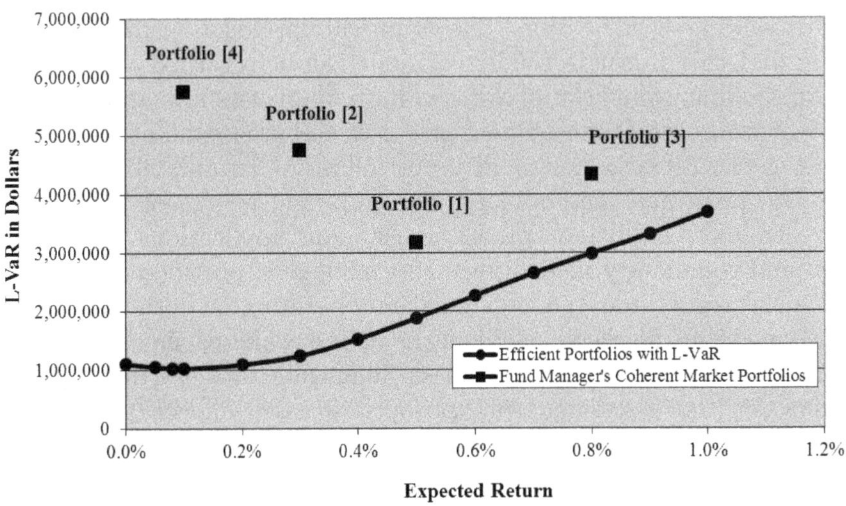

Figure 2. Efficient and coherent portfolios under severe market conditions (case of long and short trading positions).

Source: Al Janabi's (2012) research paper.

Figure 2 shows the empirical LVaR efficient frontier and "coherent investable portfolios" under severe (crisis) market scenarios by relaxing short-sale constraints.

4. Concluding Remarks, Practical Applications, and Future Directions

This chapter fills a fundamental gap in asset price risk management and optimal portfolio selection literatures by contributing a thorough reflection on trading risk modelling with a dynamic asset allocation process and under the supposition of illiquid and adverse market settings. Moreover, in this chapter, the author examines a portfolio selection model and an optimisation algorithm that allocates commodity assets by minimising the LVaR objective function subject to applying credible operational and financial constraints based on fundamental asset management considerations. The results show that the obtained investable portfolios lie off the efficient frontier for multiple-asset commodity portfolios that include both long- and short-sales asset allocation. The empirical optimisation results indicate that this alternate LVaR technique can be regarded as a robust portfolio management tool and can have many uses and applications in real-world asset management practices and predominantly for fund managers with large commodity portfolios (Al Janabi, 2012).

The presented methodology and empirical results of this chapter can have important practical uses and applications for financial and commodity institutions, risk managers, portfolio managers, financial regulators, and policymakers operating in both developed and emerging markets, particularly in the wake of the 2007–2009 financial crisis. For instance, risk managers and portfolio managers for the assessment of appropriate asset allocations of different structured investable portfolios can use the proposed modelling technique and simulation algorithms. In fact, the proposed optimisation algorithms have the potential of producing realistic risk–return profiles and may improve real-world understanding of embedded risks and asymmetric microstructure patterns and could potentially create better investable portfolios for portfolio managers in developing economies. Finally, the modelling framework can be constructive for financial service industries and commodity markets in developed and emerging economies, particularly in reinforcing rational economic-capital allocation in light of the aftermaths of the 2007–2009 sub-prime financial crisis (Al Janabi, 2012, 2013, 2014).

In a nutshell, the advantages of the LVaR techniques for risk and portfolio management practices include the following:

- The developed algorithms can aid in advancing portfolio management in financial and commodity markets by testing for investable portfolios subject to meaningful financial constraints.
- Investable portfolios cannot be achieved via Markowitz's (1952) classical portfolio approach as the empirical results indicate that investable portfolios lie off the efficient frontier.
- The optimisation algorithm has uncovered that risk managers and portfolio managers can obtain better investable portfolios, which are financially and operationally meaningful, than traditional Markowitz's mean–variance approach. Our robust risk algorithms indicated that portfolio managers can obtain financially meaningful Investable (Coherent) portfolios and demonstrated interesting market-microstructure patterns (e.g. the impact of closeout periods, overall trading volume, expected returns, etc., on the optimisation algorithm process) which cannot be attained by using the classical Markowitz mean–variance approach.
- Risk managers and portfolio managers responsible for allocating assets of meaningful investable portfolios under stressed and crisis market outlooks can use the proposed LVaR modelling techniques and optimisation algorithms.
- The modelling algorithms and optimisation techniques discussed in this chapter can aid in evolving risk management practices, primarily in the wake of the effects of the 2007–2009 financial meltdown.
- The robust risk algorithms and portfolio optimisation techniques can aid in solving some real-world dilemmas under stressed and adverse market conditions, such as: (1) The effect of liquidity when it dries up in financial and commodity markets; (2) The impact of correlation factors when there is a switching in their signs; and (3) The integration of the influence of nonlinear and non-normal distribution of assets' returns in portfolio optimisation and management.

- In addition, the recommended risk management modelling techniques and optimisation algorithms can have fundamental applications in reinforcement machine learning, expert systems, smart financial functions, Internet of Things (IoT), and financial technology (fintech) in big data ecosystems.

To summarise, while our applied liquidity model and investment portfolio analytics enable a better understanding of the role played by those liquidity trading risk components as well as a more exact measurement of their effect, some unresolved challenges remain. We expect that more research on liquidity risk will be done, and that a wide approach for assessing market liquidity risk will be devised based on the framework described in this study. Future study should concentrate on the following topics and/or paths of inquiry:

- We did not examine the dynamic interaction between portfolio trading activities and bid–ask price spread variations, even though our implemented liquidity risk factor model captures the time-volatility components of liquidity trading risk, which is just one part of trading liquidity risk (Al Janabi, 2021c). The dynamics of market effect might be tackled using time-series analysis and the broader methodological approach presented in Al Janabi's (2011) research study.
- Because the values of many assets are linked through futures and options contracts, implied volatility predictions can be used in LVaR calculations. Researchers and practitioners have argued that using implied volatility assessments in constructing VaR measures is better than using other techniques since implied volatility is the appropriate market's projection of volatility (Al Janabi, 2021c).
- One possible extension of this research would be to combine Extreme Value Theory (EVT) with the LVaR-GARCH-M (1,1) modelling approach to account for the effects of extreme events on risk–return analysis and multiple asset allocation in investible portfolios (Al Janabi, 2021c).
- Furthermore, our modelling algorithms may incorporate non-linear asset dependency utilising Kendall's tau-based modelling methodology (or any other copula-based methods) and can be easily fine-tuned to handle the concept of non-normality of asset returns using the Cornish–Fisher technique. As a result, combining

EVT with copula-based and Cornish–Fisher expansion may be an interesting possibility (Al Janabi, 2021b).

- Changing correlation parameters with a quantile correlation and/or combining the LVaR risk-engine and its objective function with the Entropy function and Wavelet-based Value-at-Risk approaches are also intriguing to examine (Al Janabi, 2021b).
- We may consider employing Hawkes processes to apply the LVaR modelling approach to portfolio management and risk management. Indeed, Hawkes processes modelling in finance is a new growing field with several potential applications for financial markets and institutions. All of these new fields of research show that Hawkes processes offer significant benefits in approximating and understanding difficult and complex market and financial events (Al Janabi, 2021b).

Compliance with Ethical Standards

Conflict of interest

The author declares no conflict of interest in this chapter.

Funding

This research study did not receive any funding from any entity or organisation.

References

Al Janabi, M.A.M. (2008). Integrating liquidity risk factor into a parametric value at risk method. *Journal of Trading*, summer issue, 76–87.

Al Janabi, M.A.M. (2011). A generalized theoretical modeling approach for the assessment of economic capital under asset market liquidity risk constraints. *The Service Industries Journal*, 31(13 & 14), 2193–2221.

Al Janabi, M.A.M. (2012). Optimal commodity asset allocation with a coherent market risk modeling. *Review of Financial Economics*, 21(3), 131–140.

Al Janabi, M.A.M. (2013). Optimal and coherent economic-capital structures: Evidence from long and short-sales trading positions under illiquid market perspectives. *Annals of Operations Research*, 205(1), 109–139.

Al Janabi, M.A.M. (2014). Optimal and investable portfolios: An empirical analysis with scenario optimization algorithms under crisis market prospects. *Economic Modelling*, 40, 369–381.

Al Janabi, M.A.M. (2019). Theoretical and practical foundations of liquidity-adjusted value-at-risk (LVaR): Optimization algorithms for portfolios selection and management. In *Expert Systems: Smart Financial Applications in Big Data Environments*, N. Metawa, M. Elhoseny, A. E. Hassanien and M. K. Hassan (Eds.). London, UK: Routledge; Taylor & Francis Group.

Al Janabi, M.A.M. (2021a). Is optimum always optimal? A revisit of the mean–variance method under nonlinear measures of dependence and non-normal liquidity constraints. *Journal of Forecasting*, 40(3), 387–415.

Al Janabi, M.A.M. (2021b). Multivariate portfolio optimization under illiquid market prospects: A review of theoretical algorithms and practical techniques for liquidity risk management. *Journal of Modelling in Management*, 17(3), 864–895.

Al Janabi, M.A.M. (2021c). Optimization algorithms and investment portfolio analytics with machine learning techniques under time-varying liquidity constraints. *Journal of Modelling in Management*. https://doi.org/10.1108/JM2-10-2020-0259.

Al Janabi, M.A.M. (2022). A novel modeling technique for the forecasting of multiple-asset trading volumes: Innovative initial-value-problem differential equation algorithms for reinforcement machine learning. *Complexity, S.I. Complexity Arising in Financial Modelling and its Applications*, 2022. Article ID 4965556. https://doi.org/10.1155/2022/4965556.

Al Janabi, M.A.M., Arreola-Hernandez, J.A., Berger, T. and Nguyen, D.K. (2017). Multivariate dependence and portfolio optimization algorithms under illiquid market scenarios. *European Journal of Operational Research*, 259(3), 1121–1131.

Al Janabi, M.A.M., Ferrer, R., and Shahzad, S.J.H. (2019). Liquidity-adjusted value-at-risk optimization of a multi-asset portfolio using a vine copula approach. *Physica A: Statistical Mechanics and Its Applications*, 536, 122579.

Arreola-Hernandez, J. and Al Janabi, M.A.M. (2020). Forecasting of dependence, market and investment risks of a global index portfolio. *Journal of Forecasting*, 39(3), 512–532.

Arreola-Hernandez, J., Hammoudeh, S., Khuong, N.D., Al Janabi, M.A.M., and Reboredo, J.C. (2017). Global financial crisis and dependence risk analysis of sector portfolios: a vine copula approach. *Applied Economics*, 49(25), 2409–2427.

Arreola-Hernandez, J., Al Janabi, M.A.M., Hammoudeh, S. and Nguyen, D.K. (2015). Time lag dependence, cross-correlation and risk analysis of U.S. energy and non-energy stock portfolios. *Journal of Asset Management*, 16(7), 467–483.

Asadi, S. and Al Janabi, M.A.M. (2020). Measuring market and credit risk under solvency II: Evaluation of the standard technique versus internal models for stock and bond markets. *European Actuarial Journal*. https://doi.org/10.1007/s13385-020-00235-0.

Ban, G.Y., El Karoui, N. and Lim, A.E.B. (2018). Machine learning and portfolio optimization. *Management Science*, 64, 1136–1154.

Best, M.J. and Grauer, R.R. (1991). On the sensitivity of mean-variance-efficient portfolios to changes in asset means: Some analytical and computational results. *Review of Financial Studies*, 4, 315–342.

Bollerslev, T. (1986). Generalized autoregressive conditional heteroskedasticity. *Journal of Econometrics*, 31(1), 307–327.

Engle, R.F. (1982). Autoregressive conditional heteroskedasticity. *Econometrica*, 50(1), 987–1008.

Engle, R.F. (1995). *ARCH Selected Readings, Advanced Texts in Econometrics*. Oxford: Oxford University Press.

Engle, R.F. and Kroner K. (1995). Multivariate simultaneous generalized ARCH. *Econometric Theory*, 11(1), 122–150.

Grillini, S., Sharma, A., Ozkan, A. and Al Janabi, M.A.M. (2019). Pricing of time-varying illiquidity within the Eurozone: Evidence using a Markov switching liquidity-adjusted capital asset pricing model. *International Review of Financial Analysis*, 64, 145–158.

Kalayci, C.B., Ertenlice, O., Akbay, M.A. (2019). A comprehensive review of deterministic models and applications for mean-variance portfolio optimization. *Expert Systems with Applications*, 125, 345–368.

Madoroba, S.B.W., Kruger, J.W. (2014), Liquidity effects on value-at-risk limits: Construction of a new VaR model.*Journal of Risk Model Validation*, 8(4), 19–46.

Markowitz, H. (1952). Portfolio selection. *Journal of Finance*, 7(1), 77–91.

Morgan Guaranty Trust Company (1994). *RiskMetrics-Technical Document*. New York: Morgan Guaranty Trust Company, Global Research.

Paiva, F.D., Cardoso, R.T.N., Hanaoka, G.P. and Duarte, W.M. (2019). Decision-making for financial trading: A fusion approach of machine learning and portfolio selection. *Expert Systems with Applications*, 115, 635–655.

https://doi.org/10.1142/9781800614239_0004

Chapter 4

Corporate Governance in Banking Industry: A Case of Indian Banking Sector Pre and Post COVID-19

Neha Puri* **and Vikas Garg**†
Amity University, Uttar Pradesh, India
**npuri@amity.edu*
†vgarg@gn.amity.edu

Abstract

For the banking industry and the economy to function correctly, corporate governance is required. Banks are critical to the economy because they facilitate the passage of funds from savers and depositors to activities that support business and contribute to economic growth. Banks' safety and soundness are vital to financial stability, and their business practices are thus critical to economic health. Governance faults within large banks playing a significant role in the financial system can propagate problems throughout the banking sector and the economy. Corporate governance should act as a major goal for the long-term protection of stakeholders' interests in accordance with the public interest. Shareholders' interests would be subsidiary to depositors' interests among stakeholders, particularly in retail banks. As a result, corporate governance ensures cooperative relevance and performance, and entails integrating members, management, and employees to policy, strategy, and decision-making processes. The present study focuses on the comparison between the expenditure incurred on corporate social responsibility pre- and post-COVID-19 crisis by banks in India, the initiatives and plans implemented so far, and the principles of Corporate Governance adopted by the banks in India. Banks, and the corporate governance of banks and other financial institutions, are unique. This is supported by empirical evidence, much of which was acquired after the financial crisis. Banks with traditional, shareholder-oriented corporate governance performed worse than banks with less shareholder-prone boards and less shareholder power. In the present study, the contribution of 15 banks, including public and private sector banks, of their average net profit towards CSR prescribed expenditure and CSR spent pre- and post-COVID-19 crisis is deliberated upon. Moreover, the study reflects the initiatives taken by both public and private sector banks to uplift society and extend their support during challenging days.

1. Introduction

The onset of the year 2020 witnessed the rapid spread of COVID-19 that hugely impacted society, business, and economy globally. According to WHO, 5.7 million demises have occurred due to the virus worldwide, with more than 386 million cases as of 2 February 2022. The worldwide spread of the virus has created several disruptions in businesses, stock markets, and the overall economy with countries resorting to complete lockdowns to combat an increasing number of cases. The restrictions carried out by the countries led to economic contraction, decreasing global GDP per capita by 5.3% in 2020 (Ferreira *et al.*, 2021).

The pandemic created an unprecedented disturbance in the global business and industry and posed several challenges. To overcome such challenges, Mishra *et al.* (2021) suggested focussing on improved infrastructure and better technology to ensure transparency in the supply chain in the global context. They emphasised the importance of constructing a predictive model that can help to prepare businesses to face such pandemics in the future based on the experiences gained in the current situation.

In the present circumstances, the focus has changed to corporate governance and its influence on company performance. Hsu and Liao (2021) analysed the impact of COVID-19 on the stock markets and the role of corporate governance in crisis times. In the context of stock markets, US returns data have depicted that the number of confirmed cases and deaths due to COVID-19 is positively related to the volatility in the returns and volume of trade. The study emphasised the importance of excellent corporate governance in reducing the negative impact on volume and stock returns. Companies examine several corporate governance variables, including CEO duality, family ownership, block ownership, independent directors, ownership concentration, board diversity, foreign investors, institutional ownership, and risk management committees. Companies' corporate governance procedures can influence their strength during times of crisis.

The analysis by Jebran and Chen (2021) has illustrated that the effective corporate governance mechanisms during the COVID-19 crisis were institutional ownership, block ownership, independent risk management committees, family ownership, and board independence. Gelter and Puaschunder (2020) have indicated three categories of corporate governance during the crisis that occurred due to COVID-19. The first category exerts that the companies need to be more resilient to the occurrence of unpredictable events or crises and be long-term oriented. The second category includes more focus on nationalism in corporate governance to protect the national interest with more foreign ownership and interconnected supply chains. The third emphasises the enlargement of the scope of corporate governance to include curbing inequality and climate change risk, which has already been at the centre of attention in recent years. While examining the effect of COVID-19 on corporate governance in Malaysia. Khatib and Nour (2021) reported that the board size did not matter in the time of crisis and board diversity significantly enhanced the firms' performance during the crisis.

The crisis created by the COVID-19 virus offered an opportunity to conduct research on corporate governance structure's impact on decision-making, success, and survival. The research in this area can help to understand whether the current governance mechanisms are sufficient to face a crisis like this pandemic. Such crises are bound to trigger long-term structural changes in policymaking, implementation, and corporate governance mechanisms (Zattoni and Pugliese, 2021).

May and Mackin (2020) have recommended some policy changes to overcome the challenges posed by the crisis. In relation to corporate governance, they have suggested that the structural changes that the companies should implement are to allocate funds in enterprise-level profit-sharing trusts. Further, the trusts should consist of a significant percentage of each company's stock and be held perpetually for the employees.

2. Empirical and Theoretical Background

The corporate governance system is a worldwide phenomenon that is impacted by differences in legal, structural, cultural, and ownership aspects. As a result, no one theory can be applied to all nations. Several theories may be more suitable to some countries as compared to others, and may be applicable at different times depending on the circumstances of the countries. Several theories express the relationship between different stakeholders of the company and their activities, namely, agency theory, stewardship theory, resource dependency theory, stakeholder theory, legitimacy theory, and social contract theory. The basic premise for the agency theory is that ownership and control are separate. Stewardship theory states that the executives and managers work for the shareholders, manage the company, and make profits for them. Stakeholders' theory suggests that the executives of the company have to take into account the interest of all the stakeholders, including employees and suppliers. The resource dependency theory emphasises the role of the directors in providing access to the resources that are needed by the company. The legitimacy theory and social contract theory both state that there is a contract between the business and society.

Corporate governance mechanisms in the banking sector differ from other sectors because they come from an under-regulated industry (Adams and Mehran, 2003). During the pandemic, the role of governance attributes had been highlighted. Ltifi and Hichri (2021) have examined the effects of governance of financial institutions on the consumers' attitudes and behaviour as well as knowledge of social responsibility during the COVID-19 pandemic in the banking sector and tested the moderating role of brand identification in the sector. The findings depict that there is a positive influence of good corporate governance on knowledge of social responsibility of the company and it helps to create a positive impact on brand image. However, there is no moderating effect of brand identification in the banking sector.

Gulati *et al.* (2020) have suggested a framework for the construction of an index for corporate governance in banks. The index comprises six different dimensions of corporate governance, namely, audit function, remuneration, risk management, board effectiveness, disclosure and transparency, and shareholders' rights and information. They have analysed 40 banks based on this framework and reported that it helps in ranking the banks based on their adherence to the regulations of governance.

The relationship between governance practices and the performance of the banking sector before the COVID-19 crisis has been positive. Alagathurai and Nimalathashan (2013) studied four aspects of corporate governance, namely, board diversity, board size, board meeting frequency, and outside board directors' percentage. The results show that out of these variables board size and outside board directors' percentages are positively related to the return on equity of both public and private sector banks, whereas board diversity and board meeting frequency are negatively related.

De Andres and Vallelado (2008) examined the dual role of the board of directors of a sample of large commercial banks and found an inverted U-shaped relationship between bank performance and board size and also a similar relationship between the proportion of non-executive directors in the banks and its performance.

Jizi *et al.* (2014) investigated the US banking industry following the subprime mortgage crisis from 2009 to 2011. The study seeks to investigate the influence of corporate governance on the quality of CSR disclosure in the annual reports of US-listed banks. They contend that board independence and board size are both positively associated to CSR disclosure. CEO duality has been shown to improve CSR disclosure.

2.1. *Role of corporate governance in the Indian banking industry*

Singh *et al.* (2020) have affirmed in their review that there is great consistency in corporate administration practices of Indian banks both out in the open and privately. Every one of the chosen banks has an optimal blend of boss-like authorities and free and non-official chiefs. There are legitimate courses of action for boards, and a few leaders' social affairs and cash-related issues are analysed by external monitors.

Panchasara and Bharadia (2013) proved that corporate governance practices have a positive relationship with the performance of the banking sector in India. Agnihotri and Gupta (2019) have investigated the impact of corporate governance on the performance of public and private sector banks in India. Their findings reveal that the higher ratio of block ownership and smaller board size have contributed mostly to the banks' performances. Dhar and Lama (2018) and Arora and Sharma (2016) found that larger boards have indicated higher intellectual knowledge and thereby enhanced decision-making and improved performance in Indian banking companies. Kanojia and Priya (2016) studied the key governance factors like CEO duality, the board size, number of independent directors, and capital adequacy ratio that can have a bearing on the performance of the banks. Their results reveal that in the Indian banking sector, the board size, non-CEO duality percentage of independent directors in the board, and capital risk adequacy ratio are governance attributes that are positively related to the performance.

Das and Ghosh (2004) have analysed the connection between CEO turnover and bank execution and tracked down that CEOs of inadequately performing banks face higher turnover when contrasted with the well-performing banks.

Corporate governance measures also have an impact on the credit risk exposure of the banks. Amos Layola *et al.* (2016) have explored this relationship and reported that good governance measures help the banks to maintain the optimum level of risk exposure and provide for adequate provision for loss in loans, thereby improving performance. Sharma and Dhaigude (2016) have analysed administration arrangements of a few banks, to be specific, HDFC Bank, Bank of Baroda, ICICI Bank, SBI, focussing on the way that banks are the foundation of any monetary framework, and to defeat any emergency they ought to guarantee straightforwardness, greatness, and amplify investors' esteem. Further, Swain (2009) endeavoured to dissect the corporate administration practices in the Indian financial area, zeroing in on practices followed by HDFC Bank, and the review reasoned that the corporate administration system and divulgence practices in India are great and on par with the practices adhered to around the world. In particular, the investigation discovered that the revelation standards of administration were awesome in HDFC.

2.2. *Experience from industry*

The Indian banking sector has been following corporate governance practices. The practices of some banks are discussed as follows:

ICICI Bank Limited: The board of the ICICI bank comprised 13 members as of 31 March 2021, out of which eight were independent directors, one, a government nominee, and four, executive directors. During the financial year, 12 board meetings were held. The diversity in the board members is maintained with their expertise varying from banking, finance, rural economy, agriculture, taxation, capital markets, and risk management among others. In terms of gender diversity, 23% of the board members are female. 54% of the board members are in the age group of 60 and 69, and 69% of the board members have worked for the ICICI Bank for between 2 and 4 years. The board committees of the bank include Audit Committee, Board Governance Remuneration & Nomination Committee, CSR Committee, Credit Committee, Customer Service Committee, Fraud Monitoring Committee, Information Technology Strategy Committee, Review Committee for Identification of Wilful Defaulters/Non-Cooperative Borrowers, Risk Committee, and Stakeholders Relationship Committee. The bank has also established an Environment and Social Governance framework, and it reviews all the new projects that may be having exposure in above the prescribed limit of polluting sectors. An active approach is considered by the banks towards risk management with various board committees and sub-committees performing regular independent monitoring, evaluation and reporting of risks. The Risk Management Group, Internal Audit Group, and Compliance Group are responsible for the evaluation of risks. The Remuneration Committee is responsible for recommending directors' remuneration, key performance indicators for the whole-time directors, and also the fee and commission payable to non-executive directors of the bank. Other policies help in managing a business responsibly, namely, whistle-blower policy, group compliance policy, cyber security and data privacy policy, customer service and redressal policy, and anti-bribery and anti-corruption policy. The bank undertakes a regular review of corporate governance practices to stay updated and be responsive towards the dynamic external environment.

Canara Bank Securities Limited: It is the wholly owned subsidiary of Canara Bank and it has reported a net profit of ₹14.92 crores for the financial year 2020–2021. The governance practices are followed by the bank as a whole and the committees responsible for governance are Audit Committee, CSR Committee, Nomination and Remuneration Committee, Management Committee, Risk Management Committee, Asset Liability Management Committee, and Stakeholders Relationship Committee. The board meetings are held by the bank after giving sufficient notice to the members and dissenting views presented in the meeting are recorded in minutes. The bank also has a group risk management policy, and a risk-based internal audit is also conducted wherein random checks on staff accounts are undertaken. The bank has eight board members, with expertise in the areas of business strategy, finance, technical skills, credit and risk management, etc. The board undertakes an annual evaluation of its members. The evaluation of the whole-time director is done as per the key performance indicators as defined under quantitative and qualitative parameters of the Department of Financial Services, Ministry of Finance, Government of India. The evaluation process ensures that there is independence and transparency in the performance of the board members. The bank has also drawn a whistle-blower policy.

IDBI Bank Limited: The bank has 14 board members at present and 16 meetings of the board were held during the financial year 2020–2021. The board members have skills and expertise in areas of finance, law, business management, economics, corporate governance, banking, and accounting. The board has 13 committees to follow governance practices, which are Audit Committee of the Board, Executive Committee, Stakeholders Relationship Committee, Frauds Monitoring Committee, Risk Management Committee, Corporate Social Responsibility Committee, Customer Service Committee, Information Technology Strategy Committee, Nomination and Remuneration Committee, HR Steering Committee, Recovery Review Committee, Non-Cooperative Borrowers' Review Committee, and Wilful Defaulters Review Committee. The risk assessment is periodically reviewed by the board members and mitigation measures are taken, with capital requirement maintained as per the Basel

III norms by the bank. The remuneration policy of the bank is transparent and all the payments made to board members are disclosed in annual reports.

Axis Bank Limited: Axis Bank has 12 members on the board of directors as per the annual report 2020–2021. The bank has ensured diversity in the board by having members with different expertise, ranging from finance, risk management, industry and technology, banking regulations, and others. The composition of the board is such that 50% of members are independent directors, 25% are non-executive directors, and 25% are executive directors. The board has a formal mechanism for the evaluation of board members and committees' members. The committees set up for governance are Committee of Directors, Audit Committee, Risk Management Committee, Stakeholders Relationship Committee, Nomination and Remuneration Committee, Special Committee of the Board of Directors for Monitoring of Large Value Frauds, Customer Service Committee, IT Strategy Committee, Corporate Social Responsibility Committee, Review Committee, Acquisition, Divestments, and Mergers Committee, and Committee of Whole-Time Director.

The bank has adopted a formal framework for conducting board meetings and committee meetings. The bank organises eight meetings in a financial year and has followed the rule of not exceeding 120 days between the dates of two meetings.

Yes Bank Limited: The bank, as per the annual report of 2020–2021, had eight board of directors that included one Managing Director and CEO, one non-executive Chairman, and two non-executive directors. The board members are from diverse fields, including law, technology, risk management, human resource management, insurance and investment, and economics, with experience in the banking business. The bank ensures to hold at least six board meetings in any financial year, and in the financial year 2020–2021, the bank conducted 20 board meetings. The bank has committees, namely, Audit Committee, Nomination and Remuneration Committee, Stakeholders Relationship Committee, Customer Service Committee, Risk Management Committee, Corporate Social Responsibility Committee, Board Credit Committee, IT Strategy Committee, Fraud, Wilful Defaulters and Non-Cooperative Borrowers Monitoring Committee,

Capital Raising Committee, and Meeting of the Independent Directors. As per regulation, the bank has a whistle-blower policy to implement a vigil mechanism. This vigil mechanism is periodically reviewed by the Audit Committee, and the bank encourages the reporting of genuine concerns.

IndusInd Bank Limited: The bank consists of 10 board members with different areas of skills, including accountancy, agriculture and rural economy, banking, cooperation, economics, finance, law, small-scale industry, information technology, and payment & settlement systems. In the year ending on 31st March 2021, the bank held 19 board meetings. The decisions regarding the appointment and re-appointment of the Managing Director and their compensation are made with the approval of RBI and shareholders of the bank. The various committees constituted by the board are Audit Committee, Committee of Directors, Compensation Committee, Customer Service Committee, Corporate Social Responsibility and Sustainability (CSR&S) Committee, Finance Committee, IT Strategy Committee, Nomination and Remuneration Committee, Risk Management Committee, Review Committee — Non-Cooperative Borrowers and Wilful Defaulters, Stakeholders Relationship Committee, Special Committee of the Board (for monitoring large value frauds), and Vigilance Committee. There is a whistle-blower policy in place whereby direct access to the chairman of the Audit Committee is provided. The bank also adopted the policy on steps to be taken in case of insider trading.

Jammu and Kashmir Bank Limited: There are nine board members in the bank with one Chairman & Managing Director, five non-executive Directors, and three independent directors. The board members have experience and expertise in risk management, corporate and retail banking, credit, finance, trade, agriculture, energy, human resource management, foreign exchange, and financial inclusion. The board held 16 meetings during the last financial year. The committees of the board responsible for governance procedures are Management Committee, Audit Committee, Integrated Risk Management Committee, Special Committee of Board on Frauds (SCBF), Customer Service Committee, Legal and Impaired Assets Resolution Committee, Information Technology Strategy Committee, Nomination and Remuneration Committee, Corporate Social Responsibility Committee, Stakeholders Relationship Committee, Human Resource

Development Committee, Investment Committee, and GST Steering Committee. The bank has formulated and adopted the board diversity policy, board evaluation policy, policy on the preservation of documents, and archival.

The South Indian Bank Limited: There are 10 board members of the bank, with experience in banking, business management, human resource, rural and agricultural economy and law, economics, accountancy risk, and treasury IT and payment systems. The board held 12 meetings during the last financial year. The committees in the bank are Management Committee, Audit Committee, Nomination and Remuneration Committee, Non-Performing Assets (NPA) Review Committee, Customer Service Committee, Stakeholders Relationship Committee, Special Committee for Monitoring and Follow-Up of Frauds, Premises Committee, Risk Management Committee, Information Technology Strategy Committee, Corporate Social Responsibility Committee, Capital Planning and Infusion Committee, and Committee of Independent Directors. The board also has an approved compensation policy to design just and fair packages for its staff.

Kotak Mahindra Bank Limited: The board size of Kotak Mahindra Bank comprises 10 members with five independent directors, one non-executive director, and four executive directors. The board members have expertise in agriculture, finance, rural economy and management, IT, and banking. The board held 14 meetings during the last financial year with advance notices of agenda and timings of them. The committees responsible for governance mechanism are Audit Committee, Stakeholders Relationship Committee, Nomination and Remuneration Committee, Share Transfer and Other Matters (STOM) Committee, Special Committee of the Board for Monitoring and Follow-Up of Frauds (earlier known as the Committee on Frauds), Customer Services Committee, Management Committee, Risk Management Committee, Employee Stock Ownership Plan (ESOP) Allotment Committee, Committee on Derivative Products, Review Committee for Classification and Declaration of Borrowers as Wilful Defaulters, and Group Risk Management Committee.

RBL Bank Limited: The bank has board members with proficiency in agriculture, finance, law, IT, payment mechanisms, leadership, human resources, and regulatory supervision. The performance of the board is evaluated as per the guidelines laid down in the Nomination and Remuneration Committee. The Corporate Governance committees of the bank are Risk Management Committee of the Board (RMCB), Audit Committee of the Board (ACB), Board Investment and Credit Committee (BICC), IT Strategy Committee of the Board (ITSC), Compliance Implementation Committee (CIC), Operational Risk Management Committee, Business Operations and Technology Committee (BOT), Retail Risk Management Committee, Product Approval Committee (PAC), and Information Security Steering Committee. The bank also has an Environment and Society Governance Committee, a vigilance mechanism along with the framework for prevention of insider trading, and an independent function for compliance management.

The Federal Bank Limited: The board members comprise 11 members with one Chairperson and non-independent director, seven non-executive independent directors, and three executive directors with diverse skills in the fields of agriculture, finance, governance, rural economy, payment and settlement, risk management, investment banking, retail lending, compliance, economics, etc. The board held 15 meetings during the financial year 2020–2021. The board meetings are conducted with structured agenda and periodically review the compliance procedures. The board committees include Audit Committee, Nomination, Remuneration, Ethics, and Compensation Committee, Credit Committee, Stakeholders Relationship Committee, Investment and Raising Capital Committee, Customer Service, Marketing Strategy, and Digital Banking Committee, Special Committee of the Board for Monitoring and Follow-Up of Cases of Frauds, Information Technology and Operations Committee, Corporate Social Responsibility Committee, and Review Committee of the Board for Wilful Defaulters.

Development Bank of Singapore Limited (DBS): One of Asia's top financial services groups is DBS Bank, with its headquarters in Singapore. The Development Bank of Singapore (DBS), founded in 1968, has evolved into a global bank with a significant presence in important markets like Singapore, Hong Kong, China, Taiwan, India, Indonesia, and others. DBS offers a wide range of banking and financial services to individuals, companies, and corporations through a network of offices, subsidiaries, and affiliates. With a long history of innovation and change, DBS has positioned itself as a leader in technology-driven solutions and digital banking. When it comes to utilising digital infrastructure to improve customer service and boost productivity, the bank has been at the forefront.

Bandhan Bank Limited: The bank has nine committees for compliance with governance practices. The committees are the Audit Committee, Nomination and Remuneration Committee, Risk Management Committee, IT Strategy Committee, Customer Service Committee, Corporate Social Responsibility Committee, Stakeholders Relationship Committee, Committee of Directors, and Special Committee for Monitoring High-Value Frauds. For risk management, the bank follows the framework of three levels, namely, Bank's Board, Risk Management Committee of the Board, and other risk-related committees at various levels such as Credit Risk Management Committee, Asset Liability Management Committee, and Operational Risk Management Committee.

Paytm Payments Bank Limited: The bank has four committees for governance mechanisms, namely, Audit Committee, Nomination and Remuneration Committee, CSR Committee, and Stakeholders Relationship Committee. The Stakeholders Relationship Committee was set up as the number of shareholders had crossed the 1,000 mark. The evaluation of board members is also undertaken based on peer evaluation. The annual evaluation of the board members and members of the committees also takes place. The number of board members is 13, and four meetings of board members were held in the year 2020–2021 with the gap between meetings not exceeding 120 days. The company has also adopted a whistle-blower policy to handle the instances of fraud or mismanagement if any. The risk management policy consists of different risk models that can help in identifying exposures, risks, and trends, and their impact on the company's performance. As per the rules, the bank has a policy on the appointment of directors, which includes qualification criteria determination, independence of a director, remuneration of directors, and relationships with other employees.

The Indian banks have been following good corporate governance policies. Apart from committees for risk management, credit management, audit, remuneration, CSR, etc., the banks have either committees or policies related to whistle blowers, prevention of insider trading, and prevention of sexual harassment.

2.3. *Risk mitigation strategies: To overcome future challenges*

The exposure to credit risk has to be more emphasised in the case of the banking sector. Credit risk arises from the banks' regular dealings with and lending of funds to the corporates, individuals, and other financial institutions. Singh (2015) has found a significant relationship between credit risk management depicted by non-performing assets and banks' performance in the public sector given by return on assets. The study further recommends that the public sector banks should make effective use of technology to overcome the challenges faced by the private sector. They should also provide training to employees in risk assessment. The role of technological advancement cannot be overemphasised, and banks need to upgrade their IT infrastructure to ensure better customer services and also take adequate measures for cybersecurity.

Tursoy (2018) has emphasised the application of the Basel norms in the internally operating banks as an effective method to healthier banks around the world. Safitri *et al.* (2020) have found a negative relationship between non-performing assets and banking performance. In addition, the study also concluded a negative relationship between capital adequacy ratio and return on equity and net interest margin, and no relationship was found between capital adequacy and return on assets. With the onset of COVID-19, many policy initiatives were taken to mitigate the impact of the outbreak. In their study, Patel *et al.* (2020) have outlined the measures taken by companies to function despite restrictions. They also outline the measures taken by companies, such as the building of technological infrastructure. The annual general meeting of the companies was allowed to be held in hybrid mode. The government also provided relief from compliance with certain regulations and started the "Companies Fresh Start Scheme". To overcome uncertain situations, corporate governance mechanisms must be strengthened by the banks.

3. Revolutions in Corporate Governance Shaping Future of Banking

In this new period, India will highlight economic expansion and sustainability for sustained growth and influence on the world stage. More than two years after the World Health Organisation declared

COVID-19 a pandemic, the world is still grappling with the virus's consequences. The pandemic's toll on healthcare systems has had the deepest and far-reaching consequences. Then there's the more constant and resounding economic toll.

With the advancement of digital technology, today's customers have become increasingly demanding of virtual experiences. The outbreak has only increased the need for convenient access to financial goods, services, and information, as well as the demand for stress-free access to banking products and services. Banking's future will be shaped by huge technology shifts and will undergo a dramatic transformation. Banking's future is "Digital". The COVID-19 epidemic has redesigned our life in terms of how we buy, work, and even bank, resulting in a substantial shift in customer behaviour.

Corporate governance has to be improved within the organisations, which seems like work in progress that does not often reach its realisation. In light of this, it is important to develop within the culture of the banking sector a mindset to adopt corporate governance and to initiate certain corporate social responsibilities.

As India's banking industry undergoes significant positive changes, the country's banks are changing as well. They are profitable in the long term with regard to digital technology to compete with the world's leading companies. The size of the board of commissioners, the proportion of independent commissioners, commissioner experience, and the size of the audit committee were all characteristics that encouraged banking executives to enhance their businesses' corporate governance compliance. This suggested that board monitoring is an effective technique for decreasing information asymmetry (Zulfikar *et al.*, 2020).

Good corporate governance and social responsibility will improve the financial performance of the banking industry. The implementation of excellent corporate governance is inextricably linked to a company's success in enhancing its financial performance. The results indicated a proposal for the Indonesian banking industry, which is required to strengthen corporate governance and, as a result, financial performance. Companies in the banking sector must pay attention and raise their social responsibility since it can boost their financial performance (Maryam Mangantar, 2019).

Risk management, ownership structure, motivation, and general manager's remuneration were the central elements of the corporate governance of banks that was found in the research paper. The

Table 1. Evolution of corporate governance in Indian banks.

Year	Name of act/committee report
1934	The Reserve Bank of India Act, 1934
1949	Banking Regulation Act, 1949
1969–1980	Nationalisation of Commercial Banks
1991	Globalisation of Banking Sector
1998	Narasimham Committee on Banking Sector Reform
2001	Ganguly Committee Report
2003	Verma Committee Report
2012	Banking Reform Bill, 2012
2014	Nayak Committee Report

results taken from the literature study on risk management suggested a continuous increase in the relevance of this topic. The research paper aimed to present the topic of corporate governance within banking institutions. One of the limitations of this study was the lack of analysis in the current context triggered by the COVID-19 pandemic. The pandemic has affected in terms of corporate governance, but also risk management as a whole (Isbaita, 2020).

The four dimensions of corporate governance studied were board size (BS), board diversity (BD), outside director's percentage (OSDP), and board meeting frequency (BMF). The measures used to evaluate a bank's performance were Return on Equity (ROE) and Return on Assets (ROA). The findings indicated that all corporate governance factors are strongly connected with ROE in both public and private banks, with the exception of BD and BMF. Other variables have a strong negative association with ROE, which is at a 5% level of significance (Alagathurai and Nimalathashan, 2013). Corporate governance has progressed over some time in the Indian banking sector. Table 1 demonstrates the evolution of corporate governance in the Indian banking sector over a period of time.

The impact of corporate governance on CSR disclosure practices of Indian corporations is examined. Board age, audit committee size, board meetings, CEO duality, board independence, employee CSR training, independent directors board meetings, sustainability committee, and women on board were all employed as corporate governance factors. The sample comprises 386 businesses from the BSE 500 index across 10 years from 2007 to 2016, and panel data regression is utilised for analysis (Fahad and Rahman, 2020). Previous studies on the influence of corporate governance on management decision-making did not sufficiently explore the role of satisfaction with profitability. The study demonstrated that the relationship between corporate governance and CSR dimensions is dependent on variations in decision-making latitude caused by relative company performance compared to peer businesses (Arora and Dharwadkar, 2011). Business performance and CSR activities links have been investigated in Ecuadorian banking. The first model used ROA and ROE as proxies for financial performance, whereas the second model included non-financial corporate performance constructs gathered through a self-designed online questionnaire (Prieto *et al.*, 2020).

CSR promotes overall business insights. Banks, for example, have a symbiotic connection with their external settings, and their interaction with the wider world dictates, to a considerable part, how well they do in terms of generating profits. Socially responsible business practices are indeed in the interest of the firm and oppose the imposition of hidden social taxes on firms by engaging in socially responsible business practices, which implies that issues hinge on how well the firm exists in harmony with its external environment, and how the exchange of inputs and outputs with the environment determines the quality of its operations.

4. Impact of COVID-19 on the Indian Economy and Financial Sectors

Before August 2020, the government's economic reaction was supply-focused with a substantial demand-side deficit. The package's emphasis on job creation and increasing aggregate demand was necessary given the severity of the short- and long-term employment losses. Considering the exceptional magnitude of the crisis, the lack of a liquid and efficient bond market, and the dependence of the Indian economy on banks, the banking sector must step up to provide the required credit to businesses and consumers. Otherwise, far too many businesses would fail, and there would be a significant increase in unemployment. The micro, small, and medium enterprises (MSME) loans backed by a 100% government guarantee are a significant part of the "fiscal package" (Sengupta and Vardhan, 2020). Due to the banking industry's risk aversion, the government must step in and take on part of the credit risk so that banks may focus on what they

Table 2. Descriptive statistics.

Variable	Mean	Median	Minimum	Maximum
Average Net Profit in INR Cr	1,865.8	185.9	–4,682.6	10,600
CSR-Prescribed Expenditure in INR Cr	39.869	11.44	–5.97	212.1
CSR Spent in INR Cr	30.296	7.28	0	200

do best — allocating money. A credit guarantee programme is a step in the right direction in this regard. Another benefit is that credit guarantees do not immediately affect the budget of the government.

In terms of social responsibility, big banks have historically had poor corporate governance. Financial organisations such as JPMorgan Chase, Citigroup, Wells Fargo, and Bank of America have repeatedly favoured fossil fuel growth over green initiatives, as well as corporations that contribute to the growing income gap and social injustices. In reality, in the five years after the Paris Climate Accords were signed by world governments in 2015, the world's 60 top banks have invested more than $3.8 trillion in fossil fuel projects (with Chase investing the most of any bank). Table 2 explains the descriptive statistics for 15 banks, including public and private sector banks, of their average net profit towards CSR-prescribed expenditure and CSR spent pre- and post-COVID-19 crisis. Using the gretl software, the mean calculated for the average net profit, CSR-prescribed expenditure, and CSR spent were 1,865.8, 39.869, and 30.296, respectively, whereas the median calculated for the average net profit, CSR-prescribed expenditure, and CSR spent shows the result as 185.9, 11.44, and 7.28.

The data extracted were further calculated and show the results obtained for standard deviation, coefficient of variation, skewness, and ex kurtosis. The average net profit, CSR-prescribed expenditure, and CSR spent by the public and private sector banks reveal standard deviation as 3,019.6, 57.789, and 49.154, respectively, whereas the highest coefficient of variation was shown in CSR spent by the banks (Table 3).

Null hypothesis: The selected variable follows a normal distribution.

Table 3. Results obtained by gretl software for standard deviation, coefficient of variation, skewness, and ex kurtosis.

Variable	Std. dev.	C.V.	Skewness	Ex. kurtosis
Average Net Profit in INR Cr	3,019.6	1.618	1.349	1.162
CSR-Prescribed Expenditure in INR Cr	57.789	1.449	1.506	1.178
CSR Spent in INR Cr	49.154	1.622	1.863	2.405

Table 4. Normality test.

Normality test	Statistic	*p*-value	Result
Doornik–Hansen Test	10.824	0.004	Not normal
Shapiro–Wilk W	0.945	0.003	Not normal
Lilliefors Test	0.088	0.04	Not normal
Jarque–Bera Test	6.413	0.04	Not normal

Alternative hypothesis: The selected variable does not follow a normal distribution.

The Doornik–Hansen test for multivariate normality (Doornik and Hansen, 2008) is based on the skewness and kurtosis of multivariate data that are transformed to ensure independence. It is more powerful than the Shapiro–Wilk test for most tested multivariate distributions. The results interpreted show a *p*-value of 0.004, which means the data are significant. The *p*-value for Shapiro–Wilk W, Lilliefors test, and Jarque–Bera test indicates evidence in the sample that the variable follows a normal distribution. The *p*-value is smaller than α in each test, so it can be concluded that the selected variable does not follow a normal distribution at a 5% significance level (Table 4).

Table 5 reveals the results obtained by applying Pooled OLS model and shows that the relation between average profit and CSR-prescribed expenditure is significant, whereas there is no relation found between average net profit and CSR spent.

Table 6 describes the fixed effect model using 105 observations. The result dictates that there is a significant relationship between

Table 5. Pooled OLS model, using 105 observations.

Included three cross-sectional units
Time-series length = 35
Dependent variable: Average net profit in INR Cr
Gretl software is used to estimate the parameters of the average net profit equation
Average Net Profit = $\beta_1 + \beta_2$ CSR-Prescribed $_i$ + β_3 CSR Spent $_i$+ e_i, $t = 1, 2, \ldots, n$

	Coefficient	Std. error	t-ratio	p-value
Constant	−167.015	71.418	−2.339	0.021***
CSR-Prescribed Expenditure in INR Cr	47.52	3.434	13.84	<0.0001***
CSR Spent in INR Cr	4.562	4.037	1.13	0.261
R-squared	0.961			
Adjusted R-squared	0.96			
$F(2, 102)$	1,278.653			
p-value (F)	0			

Note: ***indicate significance at 1% level.

Table 6. Fixed effect using 105 observations.

Included three cross-sectional units
Time-series length = 35
Dependent variable: Average net profit in INR Cr

	Coefficient	Std. error	t-ratio	p-value
Constant	−220.294	74.492	−2.957	0.003***
CSR-Prescribed Expenditure in INR Cr	47.901	3.484	13.75	<0.0001***
CSR Spent in INR Cr	5.819	4.113	1.415	0.16
LSDV R-squared	0.963			
LSDV $F(4, 100)$	659.625			
Within R-squared	0.952			
p-value (F)	0			

Note: ***indicate significance at 1% level.

average net profit and CSR-prescribed expenditure as the p-value is <0.0001. However, there is no relation between average net profit and CSR spent by the banks.

5. Opportunities, Risks, and Future Directions

"Banks would need to strengthen their corporate governance practices and risk management strategies to build resilience in an increasingly dynamic and uncertain economic environment," the RBI said in its report on "Trend and Progress of Banking in India 2020–2021".[1] The rising scale and complexity of the Indian financial system emphasise the importance of improving corporate governance standards in regulated firms. Following massive blows to the financial industry because of failing governance systems in various institutions, it was deemed necessary to reinforce the governance culture in banks. Table 7 explains the CSR initiatives taken by the banks in the financial year 2020–2021.

Table 7. CSR initiatives.

Bank	CSR initiatives in FY 2020–2021
ICICI Bank Limited	• Contribution to PM CARES Fund and other COVID-19 relief efforts undertaken directly and along with ICICI Foundation • Skill development, rural livelihood, and social & environmental projects • Disaster relief, promoting healthcare, education, or other activities under Schedule VII of Companies Act, 2013 • Support activities in areas like disaster relief, environmental and social awareness, promoting healthcare and sanitation, making drinking water available, empowering women, supporting the economically backward groups
Canara Bank Securities Limited	• Rural Educational & Agricultural Labour Society (REALS), Chittoor District, Andhra Pradesh Akshaya Kshetram, Tirupati, Andhra Pradesh • PASS — MANOVIKAS, Tirupati, Andhra Pradesh • Abhaya Kshethram, Tirupati, Andhra Pradesh • Contributed to support the activities at M/s Swamy Vivekananda Youth Movement, Mysuru, Karnataka by providing an ambulance for promoting health
IDBI Bank Limited	• Provided laptops to tribal students of Vanvasi Kalyan Ashram in the Kharghar district of Raigad • Financial support was provided via college fees to tribal students of Vanvasi Kalyan Ashram • Contributed medical equipment to NMMC Health Department in Navi Mumbai
Axis Bank Limited	• Axis DilSe in Manipur in partnership with the Sunbird Trust • Financial Literacy and Health Awareness Programmes in 22 States and one Union Territory
Yes Bank Limited	• Say YES to Sustainable MSMEs in India • *Zimmedari Se Tayyari* initiative
IndusInd Bank Limited	• School Academic Improvement Programmes • Mother and Child Care Programme • Distribution of 50,000 happiness boxes

(*Continued*)

[1]Article on "Banks need to strengthen corporate governance", says RBI report. https://www.business-standard.com/article/finance/banks-need-to-strengthen-corporate-governance-says-rbi-report-121122800870_1.html.

Table 7. *(Continued)*

Bank	CSR initiatives in FY 2020–2021
Jammu & Kashmir Bank Limited	• No information is available
The South Indian Bank Limited	• Contribution to: The Prime Minister's National Relief Fund or Prime Minister's Citizen Assistance and Relief in Emergency Situations Fund (PM-CARES Fund); Any other fund set up by the Central Government for socio-economic development, relief, and welfare of SC/ST/OBC, minorities, and women • Eradicating hunger, poverty, and malnutrition • Promoting healthcare including preventive healthcare and sanitation • Contribution to *Swachh Bharat Kosh* set up by the Central Government for the promotion of sanitation • Making available safe drinking water
Kotak Mahindra Bank Limited	• Education and livelihood • Healthcare • Environment and sustainable development • Relief and rehabilitation (COVID-19) • Sports
RBL Bank Limited	• *UMEED*-1000 Cyclothon • Hope project
The Federal Bank Limited	• Health, education • Women empowerment • Environment • Sustainability
DBS	• Stronger together
Bandhan Bank Limited	• Bandhan Health Programme • Employing the Unemployed Programme • Bandhan Education Programme • Targeting the Hard Core Poor Programme
Paytm Payments Bank Limited	• PMCARES
ERNST & YOUNG Merchant Banking Services Private Limited	• Reviewing and advising on policies and practices on issues as such • Diversity • Environmental responsibility • Ethics • Community involvement • Human resources • Global sourcing • Philanthropy and product safety

Source: https://www.joinatmos.com/blog/corporate-social-responsibility-of-banks. https://www.csr.gov.in/search_page.php?query=bank.

6. Concluding Observations

Implementing corporate governance policies in the proper spirit is critical for banks. The RBI should expedite the implementation of several committee recommendations by conducting a post-implementation review of the governance environment. This process is hampered by government ownership. Banks have yet to confront genuine competition.

Banks will undoubtedly confront a serious struggle once they are no longer protected by the state. The findings point to a challenging path ahead. The expansion of new savings channels, the potential expansion of the capital market, and capital account convertibility will place banks on a different platform, influencing their deposits and loans. Corporate governance in banks will require a shift in focus in the coming years. Because this study demonstrates a link between governance and performance, the latter may be strengthened (Pati, 2006).

Bank managers are advised to pay attention to adopting corporate governance and actively participate in the CSR policy of the bank. During a health crisis such as a pandemic (COVID-19), the banks should mobilise and create a positive attitude among their customers.

References

Adams, R. and Mehran, H. (2003). Is corporate governance different for bank holding companies. *Economic Policy Review*, 9(1), 123–142.

Agnihotri, A. and Gupta, S. (2019). Relationship of corporate governance and efficiency of selected public and private sector banks in India.

Alagathurai, A. and Nimalathashan, B. (2013). Corporate governance and banking performance: A comparative study between private and state banking sector in Sri Lanka. *European Journal of Business and Management*, 5(20), 92–100.

Amos Layola, M., Sophia, S. and Anita, M. (2016). Effect of corporate governance on loan loss provision in Indian public banks. *Amity Journal of Corporate Governance*, 1(1), 1–15.

Arora, A. and Sharma, C. (2016). Corporate governance and firm performance in developing countries: Evidence from India. *Corporate Governance*.

Arora, P. and Dharwadkar, R. (2011). Corporate governance and corporate social responsibility (CSR): The moderating roles of attainment discrepancy and organization slack. *Corporate Governance: An International Review*, 19(2), 136–152. https://doi.org/10.1111/j.1467-8683.2010.00843.x.

Das, A. and Ghosh, S. (2004). Corporate governance in banking system: An empirical investigation. *Economic and Political Weekly*, 1263–1266.

De Andres, P. and Vallelado, E. (2008). Corporate governance in banking: The role of the board of directors. *Journal of Banking & Finance*, 32(12), 2570–2580.

Dhar, S.K. and Lama, P. (2018). A study on corporate governance practices followed by selected PSU and private banks of India. *IUJ Journal of Management*, 6(1), 5–10.

Doornik, J.A. and Hansen, H. (2008). An omnibus test for univariate and multivariate normality. *Oxford Bulletin of Economics and Statistics*, 70, 927–939. https://doi.org/10.1111/j.1468-0084.2008.00537.x.

Fahad, P. and Rahman, P.M. (2020). Impact of corporate governance on CSR disclosure. *International Journal of Disclosure and Governance*, 17(2–3), 155–167. https://doi.org/10.1057/s41310-020-00082-1.

Ferreira, F.H., Sterck, O., Mahler, D. and Decerf, B. (2021). Death and destitution: The global distribution of welfare losses from the covid-19 pandemic. *Policy Research Working Papers 9673*.

Gelter, M. and Puaschunder, J.M. (2020). COVID-19 and comparative corporate governance. *The Journal of Corporation Law*, 46, 557–629.

Gulati, R., Kattumuri, R. and Kumar, S. (2020). A non-parametric index of corporate governance in the banking industry: An application to Indian data. *Socio-Economic Planning Sciences*, 70, 100702.

Hsu, Y.L. and Liao, L.K.C. (2021). Corporate governance and stock performance: The case of COVID-19 crisis. *Journal of Accounting and Public Policy*, 106920. https://doi.org/10.1016/j.jaccpubpol.2021.106920.

Isbaita, I. (2020). Corporate governance in banking institutions. *Manager Journal*, 31(1), 75–85. https://EconPapers.repec.org/RePEc:but:manage:v:31:y:2020:i:1:p:75-85.

Jebran, K. and Chen, S. (2021). Can we learn lessons from the past? COVID-19 crisis and corporate governance responses. *International Journal of Finance & Economics*, 1–9.

Jizi, M.I., Salama, A., Dixon, R. and Stratling, R. (2014). Corporate governance and corporate social responsibility disclosure: Evidence from the US banking sector. *Journal of Business Ethics*, 125(4), 601–615.

Kanojia, S. and Priya, S. (2016). Corporate governance in Indian banks post subprime crisis. *International Interdisciplinary Business Advancement Journal*, 1(2), 50–62.

Khatib, S.F. and Nour, A.N.I. (2021). The impact of corporate governance on firm performance during the COVID-19 pandemic: Evidence from Malaysia. *Journal of Asian Finance, Economics and Business*, 8(2), 943–952.

Ltifi, M. and Hichri, A. (2021). The effects of corporate governance on the customer's recommendations: A study of the banking sector at the time of COVID-19. *Journal of Knowledge Management.*

Maryam Mangantar (2019). The influence of corporate social responsibility and corporate governance on banking financial performance. *European Research Studies Journal*, XXII(3), 95–105.

May, D. and Mackin, C. (2020). Responding to the COVID-19 crisis: Public policy and corporate governance considerations. *Challenge*, 63(4), 234–238.

Miras-Rodríguez, M.M., Martínez-Martínez, D. and Escobar-Pérez, B. (2019). Which corporate governance mechanisms drive CSR disclosure practices in emerging countries? *Sustainability (Switzerland)*, 11(1), 61. https://doi.org/10.3390/su11010061.

Mishra, P., Mishra, N. and Sant, G. (2021). Impact of Covid-19 on business industry and management: Pandemic challenges and responses. *Prastuti: Journal of Management & Research*, 9(2), 1–8.

Patel, C.D., Patel, N.K. and Patel, N.K. (2020). COVID-19 and corporate governance (India): Practical issues, implications and new relief measures (September 11).

Pati, A.P. (2006). Does corporate governance matter in Indian banking? Policy implication on the performance. *Indian Institute of Capital Markets 9th Capital Markets Conference Paper.* Available at: SSRN: https://ssrn.com/abstract$=$877810;~http://dx.doi.org/10.2139/ssrn.877810.

Prieto, A.B.T., Shin, H.K., Lee, Y. and Lee, C.W. (2020). Relationship among CSR initiatives and financial and non-financial corporate performance in the Ecuadorian banking environment. *Sustainability (Switzerland)*, 12(4). https://doi.org/10.3390/su12041621.

Safitri, J., Suyanto, S., Taolin, M.L. and Prasilowati, S.L. (2020). Inclusion of interest rate risk in credit risk on bank performance: Evidence in Indonesia. *Jurnal Riset Akuntansi & Perpajakan (JRAP)*, 7(01), 13–26.

Sengupta, R. and Vardhan, H. (2020, June 4). The pandemic and the package. Ideas for India. https://www.ideasforindia.in/topics/macroeconomics/the-pandemic-and-the-package.html.

Sharma, R.K. and Dhaigude, R. (2016). Practices of corporate governance in IndusInd Bank. *International Journal of Research in Finance and Marketing (IJRFM)*, 6(11), 82–88.

Singh, A. (2015). Performance of credit risk management in Indian commercial banks. *International Journal of Management and Business Research*, 5(3), 169–188.

Singh, R., Bansal, R., Gupta, N. and Srivastava, S.K. (2020). Corporate governance in Indian banking sector: An analysis. *Journal of Xi'an University of Architecture & Technology*, 7(2), 476–493.

Swain, K.R. (2009). Corporate governance in India: The case of HDFC bank. *IUP Journal of Corporate Governance*, 8(3/4), 119–130.

Tursoy, T. (2018). Risk management process in banking industry. https://doi.org/10.1227/01.NEU.0000349921.14519.2A.

Zattoni, A. and Pugliese, A. (2021). Corporate governance research in the wake of a systemic crisis: Lessons and opportunities from the COVID-19 pandemic. *Journal of Management Studies*, 58(5), 1405–1410.

Zulfikar, R., Lukviarman, N., Suhardjanto, D., Ismail, T., Dwi Astuti, K. and Meutia, M. (2020). Corporate governance compliance in banking industry: The role of the board. *Journal of Open Innovation: Technology, Market, and Complexity*, 6(4), 137. https://doi.org/10.3390/joitmc6040137.

https://doi.org/10.1142/9781800614239_0005

Chapter 5

The Impact of COVID-19 Crisis on SMEs and Their Risk Management and Survival Strategies: Evidence from Nigeria

Ignatius Ekanem* **and Dolapo Lawrence†**

Middlesex University Business School, The Burroughs, London, UK

**i.ekanem@mdx.ac.uk*

†dolyhabbies66@gmail.com

Abstract

This study aims to examine the effect of COVID-19 on the small- and medium-sized enterprises (SMEs) in Nigeria and their corporate risk management after the pandemic. The study employed a quantitative methodology to gather information from the SMEs in Nigeria. The findings indicate that Nigerian SMEs experienced the severity of the COVID-19 epidemic, with the majority of the companies surveyed saying that the current coronavirus outbreak had some influence on their firm, such as a reduction in income and the number of employees since the beginning of the pandemic. The findings suggest that conceptualising risk management in SMEs after the COVID-19 crisis within the context of three theories — the Keynesian Theory of Business Cycle, the Social-Ecological Theory, and the Social-Cognitive Theory — holds promise as the theories serve as explanation frameworks.

1. Introduction

This study builds a framework to understand the impact of COVID-19 on small- and medium-sized enterprises (SMEs) and their risk management and survival strategies, drawing evidence from the Nigerian context. The study utilises three theories, namely the Keynesian Theory of Business Cycle, the Social-Ecological Theory, and the social-cognitive theory (SCT) as the theoretical frameworks.

COVID-19 is a term coined for the coronavirus pandemic that broke out in 2019, which is an infectious disease associated with respiratory illness. COVID-19 was first discovered in Wuhan, China, and spread globally (Moore, 2020; Bularafa and Adamu, 2021). The COVID-19 pandemic led to an alarming health crisis, leading to business closures and economic shocks (Bartik *et al.*, 2020), with risks which the entire world is working hard to manage. Undoubtedly, the impact of COVID-19 pandemic on the economies of the world has led to unemployment, loss of life, economic recession, starvation, poverty, fall in living standards, and many other crises related to the pandemic (KPMG, 2020). The COVID-19 pandemic is among the most notable topics in modern history. It has affected 216 countries and territories across the world, causing the worst economic slowdown since the Great Depression (WHO, 2021).

Nigeria, with a population of 200 million, is the most populous black nation located in Sub-Saharan Africa. As of 17th October 2021, the Nigerian Centre for Disease Control (NCDC) confirmed 209,158 cases of COVID-19, 179,089 discharged patients, and 2,804 deaths from COVID-19 with a total of 3,142,971 tests performed in Nigeria (NCDC, 2021). Nigeria has reached a critical juncture as a result of the COVID-19 pandemic with declining economic status, hyperinflation, and governance issues (IMF, 2021a). Regardless of size, no enterprise was likely to have planned for COVID-19. Public health research has now advised corporate leaders to prepare for this sort of emergency at all times, but in practice, only large corporations have formalised preparations (Rebmann *et al.*, 2013). According to a survey undertaken by KPMG, 94% of companies in Nigeria have been affected by COVID-19 (KPMG, 2020) and are now experiencing failures which raise concerns about risk management strategies adopted during the post-COVID-19 crisis. Thus, COVID-19 has had a major impact on national and global economies.

Various businesses are dealing with a variety of problems, including a drop in demand, supply chain delays, cancellation of export orders, raw material shortages, and logistics disruptions, many of which result in a level of failure. Examples of these include essential medical supplies, food and other key necessities, and the costs of less e-commerce fulfilment. Nonetheless, it is clear that the COVID-19 pandemic has had a huge effect on industries all over the world. This research argues that SMEs in Nigeria are the main victims of the COVID-19 outbreak because, in contrast to large enterprises, SMEs typically lack adequate resources, especially financial and managerial, and are unprepared for such crises that are likely to last longer than anticipated (Bartik *et al.*, 2020). However, due to their size and scale, it is also easier for them to turn around quickly. This is only possible through proper government support, willingness to do so, and innovative risk management capabilities.

SMEs play an important role in social integration, rural innovation, and the creation of local jobs (Auzzir *et al.*, 2018). They also lack business continuity plans; however, implementing a solid business continuity plan and risk management will help mitigate the detrimental effects on business during a pandemic (Turner & Akinremi, 2020). A solid business continuity plan means a swift response to both the immediate impacts of the pandemic and to prepare for what comes next. It also means a continuous cycle of risk mobilising, sensing, analysis, configuration, and operation will help to optimise results and mitigate risks. A business continuity plan requires businesses taking the right actions to navigate both the financial and operational challenges of crises like the COVID-19 while addressing customers' and suppliers' needs.

COVID-19 has posed significant obstacles to SMEs around the world. This is because during the pandemic there were series of restrictions in the forms of lockdowns, movement restrictions, market closure, and social distancing. These restrictions and controls on movement have particularly affected SMEs in Nigeria on a high level because of their vulnerability (Bularafa and Adamu, 2021). Cash flow issues, weaker demand for manufactured products and services, failure to reach distribution deadlines, and heightened risk aversion in capital markets are among the negative consequences of the pandemic.

According to the Organisation for Economic Co-operation and Development (OECD) (2020a), SMEs are critical to an economy's smooth operation because they ensure that supplies are distributed before and after public emergencies. COVID-19 has had disastrous consequences on the Nigerian economy, including a dramatic decrease in oil prices, borrowers' failure to repay debts, a collapse in sales, and investors' withdrawal of funds from the Nigerian Stock Market (Ozili, 2020). This is mainly because imposing the lockdown has affected the consumers' purchasing rate, which fell from 59.2% to 41.1% between January 2020 and June 2020, which in turn affects the SMEs in the manufacturing sector's productivity (CBN, 2020). According to National Bureau of Statistics (NBS), the unemployment rate in Nigeria has increased from 23% to 33.5% between 2019 and 2020 as a result of the COVID-19 pandemic. There are around 39.5 million unemployed people in Nigeria (National Bureau of Statistics, 2020). The lockdown imposed led to a rise in the poverty rate from 43.55% to 52.2%, which highlights that over 17 million people fell below the poverty line (Andam *et al.*, 2020).

Moreover, Segal and Gerstel (2020) found that the Nigerian economy's growth would decelerate in the pandemic and it might also enter a recession at some point. This prediction has so far been true in the case of Nigeria. In a similar vein, Seth *et al.* (2020) pointed out that SMEs are the most affected by this pandemic. As a result, governments throughout the world have responded by starting different economic responses to combat the negative economic effects of COVID-19. But it is fair to say that the damage might have been done already and the world will continue to face the socio-economic impacts of COVID-19 for the foreseeable future even after the virus is eradicated (Richard & Beatrice, 2020).

By the same token, Joseph (2020) suggests that there is a reduction in spending and consumption in the economy due to the loss in income and increased uncertainty. These economic situations severely affect the operation of SMEs since they are more likely to lay off workers as they are unable to pay the daily salaries of workers and meet all their daily objectives. Such negative impacts on SMEs could lead to adverse effects on financial institutions due to the reduction in confidence and credit accessibility by the SMEs (KPMG, 2020).

Although the general impact of the pandemic has been mentioned by scholars, the extent to which the pandemic has affected SMEs, their risk management, and the survival strategies have not yet been sufficiently discussed. Therefore, the research questions for this study are two-fold:

1. What are the effects of the COVID-19 pandemic on SMEs in Nigeria?
2. What are the risk management and survival strategies for the entrepreneurs to manage SMEs in Nigeria?

The rest of the chapter is structured as follows. First, there is a review of the theoretical frameworks. This is then followed by the research method. The findings are then presented and discussed and the implications are drawn out based on the research results.

2. The Theoretical Frameworks

2.1. *The Keynesian theory of business cycle*

There is no unique theory in any economic literature that can explain the impact and the global challenges faced by businesses and the different approaches adopted by different businesses to deal with the pandemic. This is due to the sheer diversity and the rapidly evolving nature of the pandemic.

By studying the economic depression of the 1930s, Keynes proposed a theory known as the Keynesian Theory of Business Cycle, to explain the economic crisis (Bortz, 2021). Economic and financial crises have been experienced by the world economy cyclically and this has served as a global challenge for all businesses especially SMEs in the global economy. The Keynesian theory can be explained using two concepts: marginal efficiency of capital and effective demand. The term 'marginal efficiency of capital' refers to the expected profits from new investments. Entrepreneurial activity depends upon profit expectations. In his business cycle theory, Keynes assigns the major role to expectations.

The theory defines business cycles as periodic fluctuations of employment, income, and output. According to Keynes, income and output depend upon the volume of employment. The volume of employment is determined by three variables: the marginal efficiency of capital, the rate of interest, and the propensity to consume (effective demand). In the short period, the rate of interest and the propensity to consume are more or less stable. Therefore, fluctuations in the volume of employment are caused by fluctuations in the marginal efficiency of capital.

According to the theory, the course of a business cycle runs as follows: during the period of expansion the marginal efficiency of capital is high. Businessmen are optimistic; investment goes on at a rapid pace; employment is high; and incomes are rising, each increment of investment causing a multiple increase of income. However, during a period of crisis, the high marginal efficiency of capital receives a setback from two directions:

(i) the cost of production of new capital assets increases as shortages and bottlenecks of materials and of labour arise; and
(ii) owing to the abundance of output, profits are lowered below expectation.

When this happens, business optimism gives way to scepticism and then to pessimism. The marginal efficiency of capital collapses with catastrophic suddenness. At this point, investments expected to yield 10% actually yield only 3%, which reduces incomes still further. The downward movement occurs cumulatively, because every decrement of investment causes a multiple decrement in income. The economy proceeds towards a crisis and depression. Recovery only begins when confidence is revived, that is, when the marginal efficiency of capital starts to increase.

The theory suggests that the economic downturn is due to a low effective demand, which leads to increased unemployment and low production because of stock accumulation in the economy. This is also linked to the shortage of financial liquidity among different investors in the economy. Since external shocks strongly affect SMEs, a global economic crisis challenges the production capacity and sustainability of SMEs as there is usually a dormant period during such economic times. This theory proposes government intervention to support the economy to increase the demand by using different fiscal and monetary policy instruments. Hence, this theory proposes an aggregate level explanation of the economic challenge, which serves to be a major global challenge for business entities, and policy intervention. Therefore, it seems that the application of the theory to manage the risks from the COVID-19 economic crisis holds promise as an explanatory framework.

However, the theory is not without weaknesses. The main weakness of the theory is that it is based only on internal causes of trade cycles and the multiplier principle. A complete explanation of a trade cycle must consider external causes of a trade cycle and the role of the accelerator in causing investment and income fluctuations, and this study attempts to fill this gap.

2.2. *The social-ecological theory*

The Social-Ecological theory has it origin in biological theories that explain how organisms adapt to their environments. The term 'ecology' can be defined as "the study of the living conditions of organisms in interaction with each other and with the surroundings" (Naess, 1989, p. 36). Sands (2001) posits that the ecological perspective uses ecological concepts from biology as a metaphor with which to describe the reciprocity between persons and their environments with the attention being on the goodness of fit between an individual or group and the places in which they live out their lives.

The social-ecological theory is embedded in social work discipline, but the discipline has expanded this perspective to explain that an individual is constantly creating, restructuring, and adapting to the environment as the environment is constantly affecting them (Sands, 2001). This expansion has added the social elements to the interactive process, breaking down the term 'environment' into social determinants with varied levels of power and influence, as deemed by individual need and level of connectedness.

Unlike most behavioural and psychological theories, the social-ecological theory focuses on interrelational transactions between systems, and stresses that all existing elements within an ecosystem play an equal role in maintaining balance of the whole. The application of a social-ecological perspective to the COVID-19 pandemic can be best understood as looking at the environmental conditions such as cultures, communities, trust, and policies to identify and intervene upon strengths and weaknesses in the transactional processes between these systems.

Bronfenbrenner (1979) suggests four levels of ecological components as a useful framework in understanding how systems/

processes are influenced by various levels of environmental systems in which they function. None of these components can stand and function without depending on others (Durkheim, 1984). These components of the social systems are *Microsystem*, *Mesosystem*, *Macrosystem*, and *Exosystem*. The *Microsystem* is the most basic system, referring to the most immediate environment. It refers to the small-sized social system such as individuals and couples. The *Mesosystem* is a more generalised system referring to the interactional processes between multiple microsystems, examples include groups and extended families. *Exosystem* refers to settings on a more generalised level which affect the system indirectly (e.g. the effects of security). The *Macrosystem* includes the most generalised forces, the functioning of the overall systems. It refers to large systems such as communities and organisations.

Each of these components stands as a unit of a whole with a different property that differentiates it from other systems (Friedman and Allen, 2011). Bularafa and Adamu (2021) refer to this as the system's boundary. Thus, COVID-19 is interpreted as an element that breaks the boundaries of well-being and social systems, which are normatively defined (Bularafa and Adamu, 2021).

The social-ecological theory provides an understanding of the behaviour and reactions of a person, interpersonal interactions, and organisational, community, and public policies concerning the formation of behaviour within the surrounding social environment (Bookchin, 1960). The theory helps in recognising issues affecting behaviour and also offers direction for developing successful programmes through social environments (Bularafa and Adamu, 2021). The theory accentuates four levels of the model and influences including individual, relationship, community, and society.

The philosophies of social-ecological theory are connected with SCT perceptions, which propose that providing an enabling environment that results in change is significant in making it easier to implement healthy behaviour.

2.3. *The social-cognitive theory*

The SCT was started by Albert Bandura and developed into a theory in 1986. It posits that learning occurs in a social context with a dynamic and reciprocal interaction among the person, environment, and behaviour. The unique feature of the theory is the emphasis on social influence and its impact on external and internal social reinforcement. The SCT describes the influence of individual experiences, the actions of others, and environmental factors on individual health-related behaviours. The theory provides opportunities for social support through instilling expectations, self-efficacy, and using observational learning and other reinforcements to achieve behavioural change.

The theory considers a person's past experiences, which factor into whether behavioural action will occur. These past experiences influence reinforcements and expectations, all of which shape whether a person will engage in a specific behaviour and the reasons why a person engages in that behaviour.

The theory can be applied as a theoretical framework in different settings and populations. It is frequently used to guide behaviour change interventions. It can be particularly useful in rural communities for examining how individuals interact with their surroundings. The theory can also be used to understand the influence of social determinants of health and a person's past experiences on behaviour change (Bandura, 2004). Bandura (2004) examines SCT in the context of health promotion and disease prevention. The study describes how health behaviours are influenced by the interaction of individual beliefs, environment, and behaviours.

However, according to Flamand (2017), there are several limitations of SCT, which should be considered when using this theory in public health. First, the theory assumes that changes in the environment will automatically lead to changes in the person, when this may not always be true. Second, the theory is loosely organised, based solely on the dynamic interplay between person, behaviour, and environment. The extent to which these factors impact actual behaviour is unclear, as is which is more influential than another. Third, the theory focuses heavily on processes of learning and in doing so disregards biological and hormonal predispositions that may influence behaviours, regardless of past experience and expectations. Fourth, the theory does not focus on emotion or motivation, other than through reference to past experience. Fifth, the theory can be broad-reaching, so can be difficult to operationalise in its entirety.

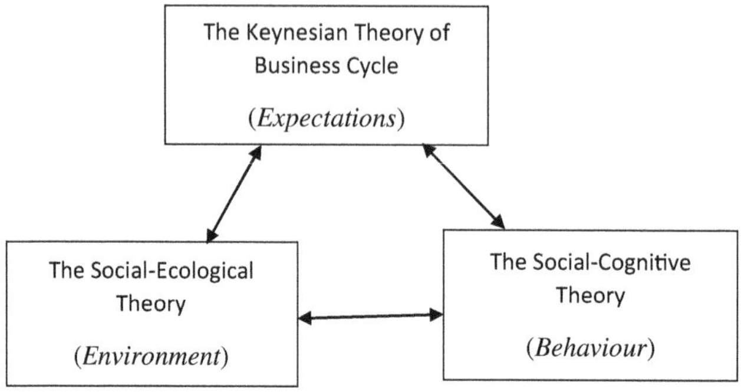

Figure 1. The theoretical relationship.

With the emergence of COVID-19, which separated Nigeria from other countries of the world, serious attention was required to shaping and adopting healthy behaviour such as sanitisation, social distancing, movement restriction, ban on worship, testing suspects, isolation, quarantining, and business closures. The relationship between the theory and this study is a detailed understanding of the reasons why people behave the way they do. Therefore, SMEs that can alter the way they do things during and after COVID-19 will survive and prosper (Figure 1).

3. Small- and Medium-Sized Enterprises

There is no widely accepted definition of SMEs in Nigeria although they form a major part of the economy of this country. However, one form of definition of SME in Nigeria is that it is an organisation with less than 100 employees (Etuk *et al.*, 2014). This is the definition adopted in this study.

SMEs are the primary motors of economic growth and job creation (Elimam, 2017). Small businesses are critical to the development of the local economy, especially in terms of job production, economic growth, and poverty reduction. SMEs are regarded as the backbone of every economy (Yoshino and Taghizadeh-Hesary, 2019). They have a major impact on a country's GDP, job production, and living standards (Abdul, 2018). According to Ifekwem and Adedamola (2016), SMEs contribute to the Nigerian economy in the following ways: mobilisation of local resources, job creation, equitable income distribution, raw material services, reduction of the rural–urban gap, foreign exchange development and sustainability, and business distribution. Despite the many challenges they face, SMEs contribute significantly to Nigeria's economic development. They have contributed 48% of Nigeria's GDP over the last 5 years, accounting for 96% of enterprises and 84% of jobs, with 41,543,028 businesses in 2017 (PWC, 2020).

4. COVID-19 Global Impact on SMEs

There have been several studies (such as, Bartik *et al.*, 2020; Beraha and Duricin, 2020; ITC, 2020) which observed the effects of the COVID-19 pandemic on SMEs of different countries. SMEs across the world have been found to be severely impacted by lockdowns during the COVID-19 pandemic and such lockdowns also served to give the affected people an economic shock. The lockdowns hindered the operations and trade of SMEs, which are a core component in their survivability and sustainability. The situation that is prevailing in the world right now has restricted SMEs to adopting and moving to online business and other marketing strategies to break even, operating during the pandemic and preparing to face the post-pandemic challenges (Acee-Eke and Ogonu, 2020).

The International Trade Centre conducted a study which revealed that the pandemic proved to be extremely challenging for the entire world, caused major health crises, and negatively impacted all major industries and different aspects of people's lives as to how they live, work, trade, and consume (ITC, 2020). According to this study, SMEs have suffered on the frontlines as the pandemic caused customers to stay home, and with the shutdown of supply chains, an extreme amount of stress was faced by countries where small-scale industries contribute 70% of work employment to people.

The key findings in Barti *et al.* (2020) on the impact of the COVID-19 pandemic on 5800 SMEs in the USA were as follows: (i) 43% of small-scale businesses and industries temporarily shut down since January 2020; (ii) all small businesses ran into financial crunches; (iii) many businesses aimed at seeking help through the Coronavirus Aid, Relief, and Economic Security (CARES) Act, but there were numerous barriers in accessing the aid; (iv) all businesses thought differently about the duration of the COVID-19 pandemic.

In Beraha and Duricin (2020), the key finding on the effects of the pandemic on the operation of different SMEs in Serbia was that the pandemic negatively impacted the daily operation of all SMEs in different ways such as, (i) 20% of the businesses entirely shifted online to allow workers to work from home; (ii) the change had led to a reduction in supply chain and the utilisation of business capacity; (iii) 30% of the businesses faced many issues due to reduction in working hours, lockdowns, resource scarcity, payment of workers' wages, inefficient production, and so on.

In Pakistan, the pandemic was found to have negatively impacted many SMEs and all of them suffered from financial, distributional, and multiple supply chain issues which had caused them to lose profits and sales (Shafi *et al.*, 2020).

Other research studies including Gustavsson and Larsson (2020) have also been conducted to observe ways to mitigate the effect of the pandemic by reducing losses. On the mitigation of effect of the pandemic on SMEs, Gustavsson and Larsson (2020) suggest that SMEs should employ different innovative marketing strategies incorporating different marketing mixes (price, product, and promotion) to deal with the crisis.

5. The COVID-19 Impact on SMEs in Nigeria

The greatest impact of COVID-19 on SMEs in Nigeria is the shortage of financial capital (Bularafa and Adamu, 2021). The impact of COVID-19 on Nigeria's economy and financial markets includes economic lockout of major cities (Abuja, Lagos, and Ogun State), resulting in economic losses, especially for daily wage earners from SMEs, investor withdrawal from the stock exchange market, and a drop in oil prices (Ozili, 2020).

The pandemic has brought cash flow disruptions for businesses in Nigeria. Cash flow management is seen as critical in planning and controlling the finances of a business (Jarvis *et al.*, 1996; Ekanem, 2002). Yet, a large proportion of small firms identify cash flow as their most important problem (Ekanem, 2002). The term 'cash' means coins, banknotes, and currency, while 'cash flow' refers to the flow of cash in and out of the business. Cash flow management, therefore, is the forecasting of the amount and timing of the future inflows and outflows of cash and can be prepared on a weekly, monthly, or quarterly basis. It is often presented by a schedule showing clearly when cash is to be received and paid out by a business and a closing balance at the end of each interval (Poutziouris *et al.*, 1999).

It is often assumed that the rationale for the use of cash flow management is to support growth. However, previous research has shown that only a relatively small proportion of small firm owner-managers adopt an explicit growth strategy (Storey, 1994; Ekanem, 2002). It is therefore argued that for small companies, cash flow management is used to assist them in their survival aims (Ekanem, 2002).

As companies have changed the levels of their operations due to lower demand, these disruptions have led to the average linear revenue of companies decreasing due to insufficient cash flow, higher absenteeism of workers, customers having been affected by the pandemic, and the demand going down, leading to declining sales, excessive stock, and overtrading (Andam *et al.*, 2020). Cash flow problems arise when a business is not in a position to pay its debts as and when due. Although cash flow problems can occur in a business due to other reasons, these were particularly acute during the pandemic. Cash flow problems can cause serious disruptions for SMEs. Therefore, it is important to understand, identify, and manage the causes before they occur.

In Nigeria, other consequences of COVID-19 on SMEs include missing important regulatory deadlines, staff working from home, an employee working outside their country due to the travel ban, limits on executives holding board meetings due to the travel ban, and supply chain shortages (KPMG, 2020). The current devaluation of the currency due to a drop in crude oil prices is also a negative impact of the COVID-19 in Nigeria.

The currency devaluation together with increased cost of transportation, shortage or lack of transportation mode, and traffic congestion were identified as the impacts of COVID-19 on transportation in Nigeria, which also led to the increase in the overall cost of living in the country as well as supply chain shortages (Akanni and Gabriel, 2020).

Before the COVID-19 pandemic, the supply chain was taken for granted. As a matter of fact, very little thought was given to the logistics industry as a whole. The full impact of this epidemic on businesses and supply chains is still unknown, with a full global recovery lagging, depending on how other geographies are ultimately affected by the virus. Supply chain disruptions also have cash flow implications across the extended supply chain that cannot be underestimated (Deloitte, 2021).

The traditional linear supply chain model is transforming into digital supply networks (DSNs), where functional silos are broken down and organisations become connected to their complete supply network to enable end-to-end visibility, collaboration, agility, and optimisation (Deloitte, 2021).

In Nigeria, the lockdown affected businesses and economic activities and supply networks (Craven *et al.*, 2020). The lockdown, movement restriction, market closure, and social distancing rules truncated many businesses and in turn affected the movement of goods and services which stand as the backbone and which the SMEs depend on for their smooth routine activities (Bularafa and Adamu, 2021). SMEs are an integral part of social and economic systems of day-to-day life in Nigeria. This important role played by SMEs is now facing threats from unmatched effects of COVID-19 as customers, as well as facilitators of SMEs, are under the threat of business bankruptcy as a result of the recession experienced in Nigeria (Bularafa and Adamu, 2021). Hence, as a result of the above reasons, Bularafa and Adamu (2021) suggest that serious action with well-determined programmes and donations are urgently required. Therefore, reliable micro and macro measures should be supported with effective controlling tools from the appropriate government agencies (Akanni and Gabriel, 2020). The major challenge in Nigeria is the sustenance of the widespread pandemic that could result in a lengthy recession (Bularafa and Adamu, 2021).

6. Governments Response to Curb the Impact of the Pandemic on SMEs

In response to the pandemic, governments of different nations locked down, stopped commercial operations, and handed over to staff and businesses what are called palliatives (OECD, 2020b). As the virus spread rapidly, policymakers across the world took extraordinary action to curb the rate of spreading. The interventions included travel bans, absolute country lockdowns, and curfews, which led to worldwide chaos in different ways (KPMG, 2020). Many companies, not least innovating start-ups, have suffered from the lockdown of major sections of society and the economy (Kuckertz *et al.*, 2020).

Nigeria has taken palliative measures to ensure economic stability, similar to many other countries around the world. The Central Bank of Nigeria (CBN), for example, unveiled multiple palliative measures on March 16, 2020, to ensure the economy's stabilisation.

Also, in Nigeria, SMEs are encouraged to switch to digital marketing and to cut down in certain areas. The cut down includes, smaller offices, office sharing, reducing employees, and investing in solar electricity to reduce rent rather than using turbines. Other measures include temporary wage cuts, rotating employees, restructurings of wages, and hazardous pay for employees who were unable to work from home (KPMG, 2020).

In March 2020, the Nigerian Government in collaboration with the Central Bank of Nigeria launched a new stimulus package of 50 billion Naira known as Target Credit Facility (TCF) to help SMEs and households who were affected by COVID-19 (CBN, 2020). The objectives of the stimulus package were to (i) help mitigate the effects of COVID-19 on SMEs and small households; (ii) support SMEs and households who suffered economically due to COVID-19; and (iii) assist SMEs by providing them with credit for the expansion of their productive capacity through upgrading equipment, research, and development.

The IMF responded well and speedily to the pandemic with huge financial assistance to many countries including Nigeria. The assistance was designed to protect the most vulnerable and to prepare for inclusive and sustainable recovery (IMF, 2021b). The organisation approved its largest COVID-19 emergency financing package of US$3.4 billion Rapid Financing Instrument (RFI) for Nigeria (IMF, 2020). This is because the country has been hard hit by the pandemic, mainly because of the associated plunge in the price of oil, which is Nigeria's top export commodity. The IMF's financial assistance to Nigeria has provided a critical support to bolster the country's healthcare sector and to protect jobs and businesses.

The government has also reduced the registration fee and introduced e-registration with the help of the National Agency for

Food and Drug Administration and Control (NAFDAC) and Automated Product Administration and Monitoring System (NAPAMS) for SMEs (NAFDAC, 2020). Credits have also been introduced at the state level, for instance, a 1 billion Naira SME development scheme was launched in June 2020 by the Oyo state government. This fund aims at stimulating the state's local economy and providing jobs for youth to mobilise the post-COVID-19 economic recovery process.

For microeconomic units such as the SMEs, Bularafa and Adamu (2021) suggest that a micro credits incentive is required through the micro-financial institutions with determining goals, but supervision and support should serve as the key to the financial institutions. Bularafa and Adamu (2021) also suggest that supporting businesses to maintain their employees is critical. Therefore, assistance in the form of grants for the payment of salaries and wages, training and development, product innovation, and new production processes can help to prevent organisation downsizing. Matt *et al.* (2020) suggests that internal assessment programs can assist businesses in understanding the internal environment and relate to production and business connections more effectively.

7. Methodology

The study employed a quantitative methodology which comprised a structured questionnaire with a few open-ended questions to gather information from small and medium-sized enterprises in Nigeria. Due to the COVID-19 outbreak and lockdowns in Nigeria, the data were collected via an online survey. The approach entailed obtaining numerical data and evaluating it using mathematical tools, such as SPSS, to understand the problem. To boost the response rate, potential businesses were contacted via a number of social media platforms, including Facebook, LinkedIn, and WhatsApp, as well as via e-mail. All respondents were guaranteed complete secrecy, which allowed a significant number of businesses to participate in the study.

The questionnaires were distributed to 150 SMEs in four locations of Lagos state, comprising Surulere, Yaba, Ikeja, and Lagos Island, and 122 responded, giving a response rate of 81%. The sample firms were selected from Nigeria's NBS, which keeps a database of SMEs in the country. To be included in the study, the firms must have 100 employees or less and must have been in existence for at least a year.

The locations were chosen because of their uniqueness in relation to SMEs in the state. For example, Surulere has a significant number of SMEs in Lagos state, while Yaba is one of the most popular areas in Lagos state that the federal government of Nigeria closed because of the COVID-19 epidemic. Based on the information gathered from the Corporate Affairs Commission (CAC), an institution saddled with the responsibility of registering companies, it was identified that Surulere, Yaba, Lagos Island, and Ikeja have the largest number of registered SMEs in Lagos state (CAC, 2021).

The survey asked about fundamental information about businesses and their features, the impact of the COVID-19 epidemic on business, sales, and profit declines, the survival phase, the business normalisation period, and any request to the government for relief. The participating firms were also asked about the market risk connected with COVID-19 and containment methods (such as lockdown). COVID-19 preventive procedures, shipping logistics, access to inputs/raw materials, salary payment, local and overseas demand for products/services, output of the firm, job rate, and awareness of government policies to support their business were all covered in the questions.

The descriptive analysis approach was used to analyse the data. As the name implies, the descriptive analysis focuses on the study of single-variable distributions. An index is created from raw data as part of a descriptive study. The descriptive analysis also involves the use of the Statistical Package for Social Sciences (SPSS) to analyse the data, including the determination of frequencies and proportions of the data (Tables 1 and 2).

Table 1. Summary profile of companies — Forms of incorporation.

Form of incorporation	%	Number of participants
Small proprietorship	49	60
Partnership	21	26
Limited liability	23	28
Unlimited liability	7	8
Total	100	122

Table 2. Summary profile of companies — Size by no. of employees.

No. of employees	%	Number of participants
0–9	29	35
10–49	57	70
50–100	14	17

8. Results

The study was to understand the impact of COVID-19 on SMEs and the risk management and survival strategies employed by these businesses. The findings indicate that Nigerian SMEs experienced the severity of the COVID-19 epidemic, with the majority of the companies surveyed saying that the recent coronavirus outbreak had some influence on their firm, such as a reduction in the number of employees since start of the pandemic, while only a minority of companies said it had no impact. The details of the impact of the COVID-19 on the participating SMEs includes the effect of the lockdown, impact on income and sales, risk management, government support for SMES, and survival potential.

8.1. *The effect of the lockdown*

The study firms were asked about the effect of the lockdown on their businesses. The responses suggest that the effect of the lockdown on the scale of their operation included reduction in the number of staffs since the start of pandemic. Notably, about 98% of those surveyed said that partial and complete lockdowns had a significant negative impact on their operations. This included partial lockdown (68%) and complete lockdown (30%), while only 2% of the participating companies had not experienced any effect of the lockdown during the COVID-19 crisis (see Table 3).

This finding shows the devastating effect of the lockdowns on SMEs in Nigeria and is consistent with the finding of other studies. According to a recent Harvard Business School research, many small companies are financially vulnerable because of the ongoing pandemic (Bartik *et al.*, 2020).

Table 3. The type of lockdown imposed on the location of the SME.

Type of lockdown	%	Number of participants
No lockdown	2	3
Partial lockdown	68	83
Full lockdown	30	37
Total	100	122

Table 4. Effect on both the income and sales of the small and medium enterprises due to the pandemic.

Effect on income and sales	%	Number of participants
None	1	1
Low	16	20
Moderate	49	60
Extreme	34	41
Total	100	122

8.2. *The effect on income and sales*

When questioned specifically about the impact of the pandemic on the income and savings of SMEs, 34% of those participating said it had a considerable (extreme) impact, nearly a half saying it had a significant but moderate impact (49%), while 16% of businesses said there was a low impact but estimated that their profits had dropped by more than 30% because of the COVID-19 outbreak (see Table 4). The findings are consistent with those from studies in other countries. For example, small businesses in other nations also encountered similar challenges and saw a drop in consumer demand, supply chain delays, and staff absenteeism (NSBA, 2020). Considering the severity of the pandemic, these numbers are not surprising. The one company that reported no effect was an e-commerce company which sold most of its merchandise online.

Moreover, when asked about the major problems faced by enterprises during the pandemic, the findings included reduced sales, income, and logistics and 0% cash flow. Almost 90% of the responses found that the SMEs witnessed low sales overall, which also resulted in no supply and limited profit.

8.3. *Risk management and survival strategies*

On the strategies designed to manage the risk of COVID-19, the participant firms indicated a variety of strategies to curb the business crisis. Particularly, only 11% of enterprises were ready to deal with the pandemic, while a majority (89%) responded that they were not ready to deal with the pandemic (Table 5).

However, when asked about the specific strategies or plans to manage the risk of the crisis, 40% of the participants reported that they had either taken a bank loan or planned to take a bank loan, while 31% of the businesses reported that they planned take a loan from friends and family. Eleven percent (11%) decided to use trade credits to deal with the crisis, 10% chose to sell off assets of the enterprise, while 8% had no coping strategy in this regard as demonstrated in Table 6.

Although some of the firms in the study thought they were not ready to deal with the pandemic, an overwhelming number of firms

Table 5. Enterprise readiness to COVID-19 pandemic.

Enterprise readiness	%	Number of participants
Yes	11	14
No	89	108
Total	100	122

Table 6. Risk Management strategies adapted by SMEs.

Risk management strategies	%	Number of participants
Bank loan	40	49
A loan from friends and family	31	38
Usage of business credit	11	13
Selling off assets of the enterprise	10	12
No coping strategy	8	10
Total	100	122

(92%) had some survival strategies in place in the form of bank loans, loan from friends and families, and use of trade credit, which has been established as a credible source of finance for small businesses.

8.4. *Government support for SMEs*

Other survival strategies included government support. When asked about the support from, and efforts made by, the local and provincial governments, 48% of the participating businesses reported that the efforts made by the government were poor, 18% described the efforts as terrible, that the government was yet to offer aid to SMEs in Nigeria, while 22% acknowledged that there has been some sort of effort from the government, describing it as average. Only 12% of the participants believed the government to have done extremely well in supporting SMEs, with 2% indicating that the support is excellent, while 10% thought it was good (see Table 7 for the breakdown).

This finding is an appalling indictment on the Nigerian government as far as their response to the pandemic is concerned. It suggests that the effort of the government is very limited in direct impact despite the claims by the Central Bank of Nigeria (CBN) that it has set out a number of measures to tackle the impact of the coronavirus. These measures include establishing a fund to support the country's economy (of 50 billion naira; i.e. EUR 121 million), targeted at households and micro and small enterprises. There are also claims by the CBN of cuts in interest rate, a moratorium on principal repayments, and tax measures designed to help businesses. From this finding, it seems that these measures are either not working or

Table 7. Efforts of the government in protecting SMEs.

Government support	%	Number of participants
Excellent	2	3
Good	10	12
Average	22	27
Poor	48	59
Terrible	18	22
Total	100	122

are insufficiently organised and consolidated to reach the intended targets.

9. Survival Potential

In terms of long-term survival following COVID-19, 93% of businesses indicated that they can survive in the future, while just 7% said they cannot (see Table 8). This finding is remarkably encouraging when compared with a recent survey study on the impact of COVID-19 on SMEs in the United States by Senz (2020) where 65% of small firms were apprehensive about surviving if the pandemic lasted another four months.

Included in the survey questionnaires was an open-ended question where the participants were invited to discuss their COVID-19 plans or risk management in detail. The answers to the question revealed that most businesses prefer to reduce the number of workers and cut employee wages. They suggested that SMEs should be given palliatives, loans should be provided, and intervention funds at low interests for SMEs should be initiated by the government. Furthermore, many of the respondents indicated that they intended to change to an online mode, working from home, while maintaining social distance. Given the severity of the outbreak, layoffs and the closure of numerous enterprises were also predicted.

10. Percentage Responses of the Questionnaire Variables

Table 9 indicates that the lockdowns during COVID-19 had a greater impact on SMEs' survival in the study region with a mean value of (2.27). Moreover, the greater mean values of (3.69) and (3.16) show that the government also could not make suitable efforts to

Table 8. SMEs' survival potentials.

Survival potential	%	Number of participants
Yes	93	114
No	7	8
Total	100	122

Table 9. Representation of the percentage responses over questionnaire variables (mean, standard deviation, variance).

Variables	Minimum	Maximum	Mean	Std. dev.	Variance	Count
Company size	1.00	5.00	1.94	0.81	0.66	122
Number of staff reduction	1.00	2.00	1.40	0.49	0.24	122
Lockdown on SMEs	1.00	3.00	2.27	0.51	0.26	122
Enterprise readiness	1.00	2.00	1.88	0.33	0.11	122
Business survival	1.00	2.00	1.07	0.25	0.06	122
Survival strategy of SME	1.00	5.00	2.15	1.27	1.62	122
Efforts of government	1.00	5.00	3.69	0.96	0.91	122
Time to recovery for SME	1.00	4.00	2.42	1.08	1.16	122
Incomes and savings	1.00	4.00	3.16	0.71	0.51	122

assist SMEs as COVID-19 affected both incomes and saving of SMEs. These variables reveal how much COVID-19 affected/impacted SMEs in the Lagos state of Nigeria.

11. Discussion

The evidence in this research shows that the pandemic, as well as government restrictions such as partial and full lockdowns, had substantial effects on SMEs in the Lagos Island, Ikeja, Surulere, and Yaba regions of Nigeria. A decrease in revenue was also evident among the participating SMEs because of the pandemic, indicating that COVID-19 had a typically negative impact on revenue. Furthermore, a drop in marketing activities and performance were found to be the result of a cessation of clientele or buyer traffic. These findings are consistent with the findings of research in the area. For example, in a recent Harvard Business School research, numerous SMEs were found to be economically vulnerable because of the pandemic (Bartik *et al.*, 2020). The findings are also consistent with another similar study in Yobe State in Nigeria which indicated that three variables had a significant positive effect on SMEs' performance, such as movement restriction, lockdowns, and market closure (Bularafa and Adamu, 2021).

The study reveals that COVID-19 had a noticeable impact on SMEs' economic activities, resulting in many firms reducing their employees' wages and salaries throughout the lockdown period. This is consistent with the finding in Bartik *et al.* (2020) in which many small firms were found to have at least temporarily closed their shutters and fired 40% of their staff since January 2020 (Bartik *et al.*, 2020).

On the other hand, the findings suggest that SMEs are generally resilient, generally agreeing to keep doing what they were doing, and opposed to stopping their business because of the pandemic. The evidence suggests that most of the participant businesses are fighting to stay stable in different ways. This finding is consistent with the study of Bularafa and Adamu (2021) who conducted a similar study in Yobe State in Nigeria and found that some SMEs were resilient, reorganising themselves to remain efficient and survive amidst COVID-19; although some businesses were also in a state of fear of losing all investments or being kicked out of business in light of this global pandemic in Nigeria.

Similarly, in a study by Senz (2020) on the impacts of COVID-19 on SMEs in the United States, 65% of small firms feared they would not be able to keep functioning if the current emergency continued four more months. This suggests that in the face of an extended lockdown, many Nigerian SMEs are more likely to fail to function effectively and go into debt or even out of operation. In addition, those firms that have very low cash reserves are vulnerable and may not survive during crises like the COVID-19. Therefore, it is extremely necessary to mitigate not only the ongoing crisis but also the long-term effects caused by COVID-19.

There are several instances of environmental catastrophes that have caused anarchy in the regional and international economies.

In a study of Fortune 500 businesses' active participation in healthcare systems, it was found that their interest in global health was low when compared with their participation in environmental concerns (Kim *et al.*, 2020). This demonstrates that most businesses throughout the world are unprepared to deal with a pandemic-related health catastrophe.

Therefore, for future pandemics or other natural calamities, advance planning and prevention are critical. To deal with a similar tragedy in the future, businesses need investment in developing an adequate risk management strategy (Gittell *et al.*, 2006; Prasad *et al.*, 2015).

Surprisingly, although the participants in the study indicated that the lockdown affected their operations, most respondents did not believe the government's lockdown and restriction measures were necessary, and they were unlikely to modify their business operations because of the outbreak. They were also mostly in agreement that the government had not done much to stop the COVID-19 pandemic. Consequently, the SMEs in the study chose a different variety of strategies to curb the business crisis. These strategies include taking bank loans, loans from friends and families, and business credit, and selling off business assets.

Thus, the findings suggest that government-imposed partial and full lockdowns were obstructing access to sources at marketplaces, making sourcing and importing merchandise difficult, and influencing financing. These findings are consistent with studies conducted in other developing economies such as by Seth *et al.* (2020). The study shows that inadequate coping mechanisms, income and savings losses, and lower investment are all direct impacts of the pandemic (Seth *et al.*, 2020). Low-interest loans, loan payment flexibility, and tax payments' relaxation were the most popular sorts of government aid requested by respondents to help mitigate the impact of the pandemic on their companies. As per this study's findings, loan repayment, salary/wage payment, and rent were the most pressing financial concerns for SMEs during the COVID-19 pandemic. External factors like industry, geography, staff count, and legal position were not found to have an influence on how COVID-19 affected SMEs.

12. Conclusion

The aim of the study has been to provide understanding of the impact of COVID-19 on SMEs in Nigeria and their risk management and survival strategies. The key theme emerging in the study is the challenges faced by SMEs in Nigeria due to COVID-19. This is one of the few studies conducted on the impact of COVID-19 on Nigeria's SMEs.

The implication of the study for policy encompasses employee protection, which is critical during crises like the COVID-19 pandemic because the virus is highly infectious and fatal. Furthermore, in times of high tension, the quality of information is critical for keeping stakeholders informed about the conditions and company operations. The Nigerian economy has seen an unexpected recession as a result of the pandemic; thus, the economy should be encouraged by encouraging sales to resume in order to enable small companies to sustain this crisis (Steiner & Gurría, 2020). Furthermore, as this research shows, most SMEs have been badly impacted in relation to income and employment; as a result, they must restructure their strategy to alleviate the financial strain. In this regard, businesses should be encouraged to adopt online or digital sales and services.

It should be emphasised that modern technologies can be applied in all organisational functions, but the depth of implementation varies depending on the functional tasks. The sales function is the most likely function for modern technologies, as these technologies were introduced even before the pandemic began. Therefore, in the study, the pandemic acted as an external stimulus, threatening the firm's survival and forcing the firm to respond quickly by adopting modern technologies. A fast-paced technological transformation enhances competitive advantage although with a high level of risk. Secondly, there is no certainty that the introduction of new technologies will continue to be beneficial in the future after the end of the pandemic.

It is also important for the government to partner with local financial service providers to ensure that firms can build back better by providing a comprehensive package of financial support for SMEs, including short-term low-interest bridge loans to meet immediate needs and adapt to changes in the longer term.

The implication includes communicating clearly on any future pandemic mitigation actions to be taken in a timely way, so that firms can be prepared and adapt. It also includes providing technical assistance to help SMEs adapt business models, reach consumers online, or adopt processing or packaging to extend products' storage or shelf life. Finally, although not the focus of this research, it can be suggested that considering the differences of women-owned firms when designing future interventions will be critical to ensure equality in opportunities and outcomes for these firms.

13. Contribution

This study contributes, from the SMEs dimension and the emerging economies context, to the debate on understanding how the risk management strategies of companies should be revised during the post-COVID-19 crisis to adapt to the changes initiated by the pandemic. It contributes to whether the strategy or business model of SMEs to deal with the pandemic can be useful for big firms. For example, big businesses can learn from the survival strategies of SMEs during the pandemic and change their business model or some part of it to an online business or hybrid business model. Hybrid businesses are those that use a mix of conventional and internet-based methods, which allow internet presence.

The study is also useful as most SMEs are in the supply chain of most big companies. It contributes to the debate that disruptions in the supply chain may result in both financial and non-financial losses for the companies involved as well as the big organisations in the supply chain. Therefore, managing the risk of disruptions and survival in SMEs as a supply chain may be beneficial for all the organisations in the supply chain and be achieved by adopting specific redesign of business models.

It also contributes by suggesting that policymakers or regulators should restructure the support system available to SMEs. Finally, it contributes to the debate that although the pandemic is a global issue and SMEs are oftentimes based locally, policymakers should encourage them to think globally, while responding locally, through the emergence of new market niches by producing tailored products and services, made possible by modern process technologies.

At the same time and in line with all empirical research, the study has some limitations that provide avenues for potential future research. First, the sample size was limited both in scope and context since it was limited to one region and thus it is not certain to what extent the impact of COVID-19 on SMEs in Lagos State represented the situation in the entire country. Although the current study has value as an indicative work, a large-scale study would help to demonstrate the wider application of the research results, particularly if Nigeria's informal sector is included, which is exclusively SMEs and accounts for one-third of GDP (Okolo, 2014). Second, since the study was quantitative, it was difficult to assess the emotional views of the business owners on the impact of COVID-19 on their businesses. Thus, we would suggest a future research that employs a qualitative research method which would capture the emotional state of the business owners.

References

Abdul, O.E. (2018). Entrepreneurial skills and growth of small and medium enterprise (SMEs): A comparative analysis of Nigerian entrepreneurs and Minority entrepreneurs in the UK. *International Journal of Academic Research in Business and Social Sciences*, 8(5), 27–46.

Acee-Eke, B.C. and Ogonu, G.C. (2020). Pandemic marketing strategies and customer patronage of SMEs. www.accexgate.com. Accessed 5 December 2021.

Akanni, L. and Gabriel, S. (2020). The implication of COVID19 on the Nigerian economy. https://cseaafrica.org/the-implication-of-covid19-on-the-nigerian-economy/. Accessed 2 November 2021).

Andam, K., Edeh, H., Oboh, V., Pauw, K. and Thurlow, J. (2020). Impacts of COVID-19 on food systems and poverty in Nigeria. *Advances in Food Security and Sustainability*, 5, 145.

Auzzir, Z., Haigh, R. and Amaratunga, D. (2018). Impacts of disaster to SMEs in Malaysia. *Procedia Engineering*, 212, 1131–1138.

Bandura, A. (2004). Health promotion by social cognitive means. *Health Education & Behavior*, 31(2), 143–164.

Bartik, A.W., Bertrand, M., Cullen, Z., Glaeser, E.L., Luca, M. and Stanton, C. (2020). The impact of COVID-19 on small business outcomes and expectations. *Proceedings of the National Academy of Sciences*, 117(30), 17656–17666.

Beraha, I. and Duricin, S. (2020). The impact of COVID-19 crisis on medium-sized enterprises in Serbia. *Economic Analysis*, 53(1), 14–27.

Bookchin, M. (1960). *Post-Scarcity Anarchy.* Montreal, Canada: Chadwyck-Healey.

Bortz, P.G. (2021). Keynes's theories of the business cycle: Revolution and contemporary relevance. Working Paper No. 986, Institute of High Social Studies, National University of San Martín.

Bularafa, B.A. and Adamu, U.G. (2021). Effect of COVID-19 pandemic on SME performance in Nigeria. *Advanced International Journal of Business, Entrepreneurship and SMEs*, 3(7), 75–92.

Bronfenbrenner, U. (1979). *The Ecology of Human Development.* Cambridge: Harvard University Press.

CAC (2021). A well-researched guide to the Corporate Affairs Commission. https://explain.com.ng/topic/a-well-researched-guide-to-the-corporate-affairs-commission-cac/. Accessed 5 December 2021.

Central Bank of Nigeria (2020). Contributions/donations to CBN-led COVID-19 relief fund account domiciled with the Central Bank of Nigeria. Central Bank of Nigeria, 8 April. Available at: https://www.cbn.gov.ng/Out/2020/CCD/covid%20contributions.pdf. Accessed 23 June 2021.

Craven, M., Liu, L., Mysore, M. and Wilson, M. (2020). *COVID-19: Implications for Business.* McKinsey & Company, https://www.parking-mobility.org/2020/04/06/mckinsey-company-covid-19-implications-for-business/. Accessed 4 December 2021.

Deloitte (2021). COVID-19: Managing supply chain risk an disruption. https://www2.deloitte.com/ca/en/pages/finance/articles/COVID-19-managing-supply-chain-risk-and-disruption.html.

Durkheim, E. (1984). *The Division of Labor in Society.* Basingstoke: Macmillan.

Ekanem, I. (2002). The investment decision-making process in small manufacturing enterprises: With particular reference to printing and clothing industries. PhD Thesis, Middlesex University, London.

Elimam, H. (2017). The role of small businesses (small scale economic projects) in alleviating the acuity of unemployment. *International Business Research*, 10(3), 120.

Etuk, R.U., Etuk, G.R. and Baghebo, M. (2014). Small and medium scale enterprises (SMEs) and Nigeria's economic development. *Mediterranean Journal of Social Sciences*, 5(7), 656–662.

Flamand, L. (2017). Limitations of social cognitive theory.https://www.theclassroom.com/limitations-of-social-cognitive-theory-12215528.html. Accessed 7 December 2021.

Friedman, B.D. and Allen, K.N. (2011). Systems theory. *Theory & Practice in Clinical Social Work*, 2(3), 3–20.

Gittell, J.H., Cameron, K., Lim, S. and Rivas, V. (2006). Relationships, layoffs, and organizational resilience: Airline industry responses to September 11. *The Journal of Applied Behavioral Science*, 42(3), 300–329.

Gustavavsson, S. and Larsson, S. (2020). https://www.semanticscholar.org/paper/Marketing-Innovation-for-SMEs-during-COVID-19-%3A-A-Gustavsson-Larsson/b3bc3bdf8cd54a6cc22741f2249a9ce2c2fbbd4c. Accessed 4 December 2021.

Ifekwem, N. and Adedamola, O. (2016). Survival strategies and sustainability of small and medium enterprises in the Oshodi-Isolo local government area of Lagos state. *Acta Universitatis Sapientiae, Economics and Business*, 4(1), 103–118.

IMF (2020). Nigeria's IMF financial assistance to support health care sector, protect jobs and businesses. https://www.imf.org/en/News/Articles/2020/04/29/na042920-nigerias-imf-financial-assistance- to–support-health-care-sector-protect. Accessed 11 May 2022.

IMF (2021a). Policy-responses-to-COVID-19. International Monetary Fund. Retrieved from https://www.imf.org. Accessed 5 December 2021.

IMF (2021b). The IMF's response to COVID-19. https://www.imf.org/en/About/FAQ/imf-response-to-COVID-19. Accessed 11 May 2022.

ITC (2020). SME competitiveness outlook 2020: COVID-19: The great lockdown and its impact on small business. International Trade Centre, Geneva.

Jarvis, R., Kitching, J., Curran, J. and Lightfoot, G. (1996). The financial management of small firms: An alternative perspective. ACCA Research Report No. 49.

Joseph, N. (2020). An overview of the economic impact of covid-19 pandemic on Nigeria. Retrieved from Business Day via www.businessday.ng.

Kim, J., Kim, J., Lee, S.K. and Tang, L.R. (2020). Effects of epidemic disease outbreaks on financial performance of restaurants: Event study method approach. *Journal of Hospitality and Tourism Management*, 43, 32–41.

KPMG (2020). Coronavirus: Global and domestic impact. KPMG International. Retrieved from www.KPMG/ng. Accessed 5 December 2021.

Kuckertz, A., Brändle, L., Gaudig, A., Hinderer, S., Reyes, C.A.M., Prochotta, A., Steinbrink, K.M. and Berger, E.S. (2020). Startups in times of crisis — A rapid response to the COVID-19 pandemic. *Journal of Business Venturing Insights*, 13, e00169.

Matt, C., Linda L. and Matt W. (2020, March). *COVID-19: Implications for Business.* McKinsey & Company, https://www.mckinsey.com/capabilities/risk-and-resilience/our-insights/covid-19-implications-for-business. Accessed 4 December 2021.

Moore, N. (2020). Chloroquine for COVID-19 infection: Springer. National Bureau of Statistics. Annual Statistics Report, Abuja, Nigeria.

Naess, A. (1989). *Ecology, Community and Lifestyle: Outline of an Ecosophy.* Cambridge: Cambridge University Press.

NAFDAC (2020). The new 80% discount on NAFDAC registration (2021 updated). https://samandwright.com/what-to-know-about-the-new-80-discount-on-nafdac-registration/. Accessed 5 December 2021.

National Bureau of Statistics (2020). Annual statistics report, Abuja, Nigeria.

NCDC (2021). COVID-19 Nigeria. https://covid19.ncdc.gov.ng/. Accessed 17 October 2021.

NSBA (2020). Small Business Impact poll. https://markets.businessinsider.com/news/stocks/new-poll-shows-widespread-small-business-impact-from-covid-19-1028999017. Accessed 4 December 2021.

OECD (2020a). COVID-19 and responsible business conduct. Tackling coronavirus (COVID-19). Contributing to a global effort. Retrieved from https://www.mneguidelines.oecd.org.

OECD (2020b). COVID-19: SME policy responses. OECD, Paris. Retrieved from https://www.oecd.dam-broadcast.com.

Okolo, P.O. (2014). NDDC, conflict, peace-building and community development, in the Niger Delta region. *Global Journal of Political Science and Administration,* 2(1), 36–54.

Ozili, P.K. (2020). COVID-19 pandemic and economic crisis: The Nigerian experience and structural causes. *Journal of Economic and Administrative Sciences,* 37(4), 401–418. DOI: 10.1108/JEAS-05-2020-0074.

Prasad, S., Su, H.C., Altay, N. and Tata, J. (2015). Building disaster-resilient micro enterprises in the developing world. *Disasters,* 39(3), 447–466.

Poutziouris, P., Chittenden, F. and Michaelas, N. (1999). The financial affairs of private companies: Research. MBS, University of Manchester, UK.

PWC (2020). PWC's MSME survey 2020 building to last. Nigeria report. https://www.pwc.com/ng/en/events/nigeria-sme-survey.html.

Rebmann, T., Wang, J., Swick, Z., Reddick, D. and delRosario Jr, J.L. (2013). Business continuity and pandemic preparedness: US health care versus non-health care agencies. *American Journal of Infection Control,* 41(4), e27–e33.

Richard, B. and Beatrice, W. (2020). Economies in the time of COVID-19. Centre for Economic Policy Research, London, UK.

Sands, R.G. (2001). *Clinical Social Work Practice in Behavioral Mental Health: A Postmodern Approach to Practice with Adults.* Needham Heights, MA: Allyn & Bacon.

Segal, S. and Gerstel, D. (2020). The global economic impacts of COVID-19, critical questions. Center for Strategic and International Studies (CSIS). https://www.csis.org/analysis. Accessed 5 December 2021.

Senz, K. (2020, April 13). Small businesses are worse off than we thought. Harvard Business School, Working Knowledge. https://hbswk.hbs.edu/item/small-businesses-are-worse-off-than-we-thought. Accessed 5 December 2021.

Seth N.J., Ganaie M.A. and Zafar F. (2020). Impact of COVID-19 (coronavirus) on small and medium enterprises (SMEs) in Pakistan. *Journal of Business Research*, 117, 280–283. DOI: 10.13140/RG.2.2.21236.09607.

Shafi, M., Liu, J. and Ren, W. (2020). Impact of COVID-19 pandemic on micro, small, and medium-sized enterprises operating in Pakistan. *Research in Globalization*, 2, 100018.

Steiner A. and Gurría A. (2020). How to avert the worst development crisis of this century. United Nations Development Program. https://www.undp.org/content/undp/en/home/blog/2020/how-to-avert-the-worst-development-crisis-of-this-century.html. Accessed 5 December 2021.

Storey, D. (1994). *Understanding the Small Business Sector.* London: Routledge.

Turner, J. and Akinremi, T. (2020). The business effects of pandemics — A rapid literature review. Enterprise Research Centre, Warwick Business School, Warwick, UK.

World Health Organization (2021). Timeline of WHO's response to COVID-19, 2021. Available at: https://www.who.Int/news-room/detail/29-06-2020-covidtimeline. Accessed 4 July 2021.

Yoshino, N. and Taghizadeh-Hesary, F. (2019). Optimal credit guarantee ratio for small and medium-sized enterprises' financing: Evidence from Asia. *Economic Analysis and Policy*, 62, 342–356.

https://doi.org/10.1142/9781800614239_0006

Chapter 6

Artificial Intelligence, T-Shaped Teams, and Risk Management Post COVID-19 and Beyond

Linh Tu Ho* **and Christopher Gan**†

Department of Financial and Business Systems,
Faculty of Agribusiness & Commerce,
Lincoln University,
Christchurch, New Zealand
**linh.ho@lincoln.ac.nz*
†*christopher.gan@lincoln.ac.nz*

Abstract

We explore the opportunity to apply Artificial Intelligence (AI) and T-Shaped Teams in risk management post the COVID-19 crisis and beyond. First, the study describes the three stages of AI adoption and the interest in AI before and during the COVID-19 pandemic. Second, the importance of AI in risk management is assessed based on the analysis of the performance of AI-implemented firms. Third, the roles of workforce, especially T-Shaped teams, in adopting AI at the firm level are highlighted. The new Technology, Innovation, and In-practice functions of the T-shaped teams are discussed along with the opportunities and challenges when building a T-shaped team and adopting AI in enterprises. Next, a guide for building T-Shaped Teams for risk management using AI is developed with the flexibility to implement in a wide range of corporates. The study concludes with future direction on risk management strategies to respond to new risks and make better business decisions to address shocks in the economy.

1. Introduction

Risk management is the norm in enterprises to identify, analyse, and evaluate risks and associated outcomes. To sustain in uncertain environments caused by different economic, financial, political, natural, and health-related events, risk management frameworks are developed and improved over time. The direct social-economic-health impacts of the COVID-19 pandemic on most businesses and individual activities over the world raise big concerns on how firms can manage risks and make management decisions quickly and effectively.

The development of science and technology, such as Artificial Intelligence (AI) in the form of robots, computers, and other machines, contributes to the success of firms in making better business decisions (FERMA, 2019). Enholm *et al.* (2021) contend that AI can be used in different business activities such as marketing, customer service, production, and enterprise management. For example, facial recognition technologies speed up the authentication process in business and daily life. Robots are used to process emails automatically. Chatbots can replace humans in doing repeated tasks such as answering simple questions, selling products, and resolving insurance claims. Lakshmi and Bahli (2020) show that deploying robots in businesses can enhance operating efficiency, increase profits, and improve firm performance.

Risk management plays a critical role in challenging environments. Managing risks caused by disasters, climate change, and other stressful events can help firms thrive for social, economic, and environmental (SEE) sustainability (O'Brien *et al.*, 2012). Aziz and Dowling (2019) explore the optimistic role of AI and machine learning in managing credit risk, market risk, operational risk, and compliance with risk management regulations. During the COVID-19 pandemic, AI adoption reduced the negative impacts of COVID-19 on firm revenues (Xu *et al.*, 2021), supported operating efficiency under the uncertain environments (Drydakis, 2022), and benefitted small and medium-sized enterprises (SMEs) in managing risks and predicting market trends (Drydakis, 2022). To combat risks caused by COVID-19, AI was adopted to maintain social distance, operate businesses remotely, and enhance customer deliverance. For example, the fingerprint and palm identification technique were replaced by the facial biometric recognition system to reduce the risk from COVID-19 (Kortli *et al.*, 2020).

Therefore, firms should consider the use of AI in risk management and factors that determine AI adoption in businesses. Alsheibani *et al.* (2018) propose the research framework of AI adoption that consists of technological readiness, environmental readiness, and organisational readiness. From the firm perspective, the organisational readiness for AI adoption is affected by top management support, employees, technologies, and firm size. Besides, human capital is identified as one of the most challenging tasks in AI adoption (CFA Institute, 2019, 2021) because the failure of adopting AI results from either focusing more on technology than skills (Alsheibani *et al.*, 2018) or a lack of required skillsets (Aziz and Dowling, 2019). To implement AI in corporations, T-shaped professionals (CFA Institute, 2019, 2021) are recognised as the important factor for AI and big data adoption in the investment industry.

According to the literature, to our best knowledge, no studies have addressed the opportunity to build T-shaped teams as the professional workforce for the success of AI adoption in risk management. Therefore, we explore why and how firms manage risks using advanced technology such as AI. This is important for businesses in terms of the AI adoption process, roles of AI in risk management, functions of T-shaped teams, and opportunities and challenges in building T-Shaped teams for AI risk management. This study contributes to the literature on risk management and how firms can be protected from uncertainty by building T-shaped teams and adopting AI. The practical implication of this study is support for firm leaders and stakeholders to identify their current position in the AI adoption process, make critical decisions on whether they should shift their businesses from traditional modes to the more tech-savvy modes, as well as to understand the challenges they face in uncertain environments. The applications of AI, T-shaped teams, and risk management are mapped to support the resilient and sustainable performance of enterprises post COVID-19 and beyond.

First, we investigate whether the development of AI follows a process with different AI adoption stages in firms, and how the world interest in AI changed before and during the COVID-19 period. Understanding the three stages of AI adoption (early, intermediate, and advanced) is necessary for corporations to successfully improve their performance in an uncertain world. We introduce the five streams of Leadershift, Strategy, Workforce, Process, and Resource to help firms identify each stage in the AI adoption process. The AI interest, data source availability, and attendance techniques in the before and during COVID-19 periods are presented and compared to explore the rapid increase in AI adoption worldwide.

Second, this is the first study that examines the performance of AI-implemented listed firms, which significantly supports the important roles of AI in enterprise risk management. Using the two AI market indices that include listed firms involved in the AI adoption activities from Bloomberg, our result showed that stocks of AI-adopted companies outperform in the stock markets from 2012 to 2021 regardless of different risk levels. More importantly, the higher the risk in the market, the better the performance of AI-implemented firms. Our finding suggests that AI plays a critical role in minimising the negative impacts of market risks. We expand the necessary roles of risk management using AI with the five values of workforce development, digital transformation, operational capability improvement, partnership development, and working towards a resilient and sustainable future. Among these, workforce is recognised as the most important factor in the AI adoption journey.

Third, we discuss why a T-shaped team needs to be developed for implementing AI in enterprises, and its functions, opportunities, and challenges post COVID-19 and beyond. The T-shaped teams with the new functions of Technology, Innovation, and In-practice are the key to building a professional workforce for the efficient applications of AI in risk management. Based on CFA Institute (2021), we define that the Technology function is executed by data science professionals and knowledge engineers. The In-practice function is accomplished by thought leaders and professional experts. The Innovation function connects the Technology and In-practice functions of T-shape teams to complete the letter T. With the focus on collaboration and digitalisation, we can conclude that Innovation staff are required to have the mixed skills of technology, professional expertise, communication, planning, leading, and organising.

Looking forward to rebuilding the economy post COVID-19 and beyond, firms are exposed to both opportunities and challenges in developing T-shaped teams and adopting AI. With the aim of a more sustainable performance, corporates have the opportunities to increase the workforce and business productivity, enhance technology innovation and industrial performance, and improve new business models as well as manage risk. However, firms should be aware of the six challenges of building a T-shaped team and adopting AI. The challenges are cost, talent, technology, leadership vision, time, and transparency and ethics (Aziz and Dowling, 2019; CFA Institute, 2019). The future is uncertain because risks are not limited to infectious disease outbreaks, natural disasters, social, economic, and political conflicts, and unpredictable events. To support firms to implement AI in risk management for a resilient and sustainability future, the guide on building T-shaped teams for AI-adopted risk management is prepared across the three functions of T-shaped teams.

The remainder of this study is organised as follows. Section 2 reviews the literature on AI, and the stages of AI adoption. Section 3 describes the methodology. Section 4 presents the results of the performance of AI-implemented firms using the AI market indices and explores the important values of implementing AI in risk management. Section 5 discusses the three new functions of T-shaped Teams that bring the opportunities and challenges to AI-adopted firms, and how to build a T-Shaped team for risk management using AI. Section 6 concludes the study with limitations and future research directions.

2. Literature Review

Artificial Intelligence or AI is a popular term not only in scientific fields of technology, investment, accounting, and finance, but also in daily life matters such as shopping, traffic controlling, communication, and health. Aziz and Dowling (2019) conclude that AI adoption diminishes the time-consuming and costly nature of risk management. How has the world interest in AI changed over time? We introduce three developing stages of AI adoption, namely, the early, intermediate, and advanced stages. Next, we describe the world's attention with regards to AI before and during the COVID-19 pandemic.

2.1. *Development of artificial intelligence*

Organisations adopt AI to improve the performance of their operations and manage risks. However, AI adoption in a firm depends on the firm's AI readiness. The research framework of AI adoption by Alsheibani *et al.* (2018) is decomposed into technological readiness, environmental readiness, and organisational readiness. If firms do not have adequate research capabilities, skilled workforce, big data, and the facilities, it will take a considerable amount of time to successfully implement AI in business. Therefore, the adoption of AI depends on the support of leaders, long-term strategies, suitable workforce, sustainable processes, and efficient resources.

We propose that the adoption of AI in corporations generally goes through three stages: early, intermediate, and advanced. To define the three stages, we introduce the five streams of Leadershift, Strategy, Workforce, Process, and Resource. Figure 1 summarises the three stages of AI adoption.

To endure in a dynamically changing world, roles of leaders change constantly. Thus, leadership should embrace a new set of leadershifts. The term "leadershift" was initially declared as the transformation efforts of CEOs to approach new dimensions of changes in the corporate world. Trahant *et al.* (1997) discuss 12 principles of leadershift in the context of the external environment, changing people's behaviour before changing culture, to be aware of false indicators of success. Maxwell (2019) refers to leadershift as the ability and willingness of changing leadership for positive organisation enhancement and personal growth. This includes 11 important leadershifts, or changes, that leaders should embrace such as Focus, Personal Development, Cost, Relational, Abundance, Reproduction, Communication, Improvement, Influence, Impact, and Passion Shifts.

Therefore, we use *Leadershift* as the first stream to define the AI adoption stages. Leadershift starts with the awareness of Maxwell's (2019) leadershifts, especially the Improvement Shift, in the early stage of AI adoption. In the intermediate stage, the commitment of leaders to making essential changes related to AI implementation is necessary. This leadershift commitment turns to the continuation practices in the advanced stage of AI adoption (see Figure 1).

The second stream to identify the AI adoption stage is *Strategy*. CFA Institute (2021) uses the term wholistic strategy to indicate the business and technology functions to enable AI and big data adoption at the financial institutions' level. We use the term Strategy instead of wholistic strategy for general organisations. Figure 1 shows that the development levels of Strategy are findability, alignment,

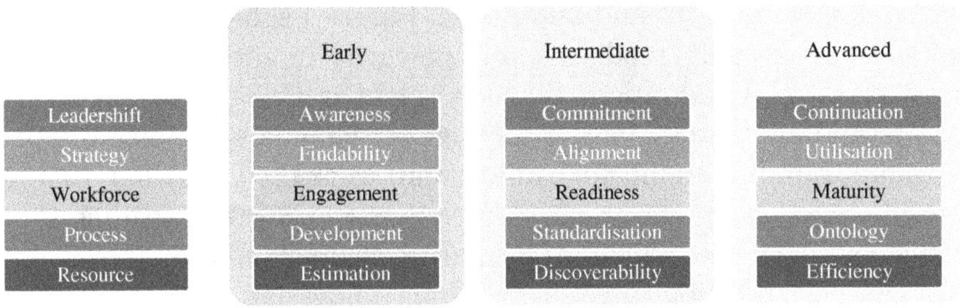

Figure 1. Three stages of artificial intelligence adoption.

and utilisation in the early, intermediate, and advanced stages of AI adoption, respectively.

AI adoption in financial institutions shows an engagement with big data. Bussmann *et al.* (2020) introduce an AI credit risk model to predict future behaviour of borrowers to manage risk in peer-to-peer (P2P) lending platforms. Using big data from 15,000 small and medium companies from Southern Europe in 2015, Bussmann *et al.* (2020) group the companies into two simple groups of risky and not risky borrowers based on financial characteristics from their balance sheets. The result shows that companies with different profiles (defaulted and non-defaulted on loans) have different important variables. The most important factors identified for defaulted companies are shareholders' funds plus noncurrent liabilities divided by fixed assets and profit before taxes plus interest paid divided by total assets and earnings before interest and taxes (EBIT) to interest paid for non-defaulted companies. Bussmann *et al.*'s study presents the Strategy stream at the findability level (the ability to identify important information) and the alignment level (the state of matching specific information with other aspects). However, at the utilisation level, further work is required before the models can be used effectively in practice.

Workforce is the third stream that we recognise in the AI adoption stages. To develop and grow sustainably, workforce is widely considered as the most important factor in traditional organisations. For high-tech companies, the vital roles of workforce remain and are highly critical to thriving in an uncertain world. When companies acquire new methods and technologies, it is essential to update their current employees' skills and knowledge, or hire new staff equipped with a new set of skills and knowledge. Figure 1 shows the Workforce flows of engagement, readiness, and maturity in adopting AI. In the early stage of AI adoption, the skill set of working with machines, understanding models, and applying mathematics, among others, is engaged to the mind-sets of current workforce. Moving to the intermediate stage, the work team needs to pose the readiness to implement AI in daily tasks. The mature team should feasibly maintain the best position in self-education, innovation, and interaction in the advanced stage of AI adoption.

Process is the fourth stream in the development of AI adoption. No organisations can operate without a designed process that is simple or complicated depending on the nature of businesses. In the context of implementing AI, the process has not been clearly defined. AI-adopted investment firms have not used the same process to discover and develop AI tools. The AI application in investment firms is still novel and we can identify this industry at the development level in the early stage of AI adoption. In terms of communication industry, facial recognition technology using AI has emerged and can be identified at the standardisation level in the next stage (see Figure 1). In the advanced stage of AI adoption, the process should not only be standardised but also required at the level of ontology to sustainably and adequately explain the contents, entities, and relationships.

Lastly, *Resource* cannot be overlooked in adopting AI. Besides human capital, time, cost, and tangible assets, virtual capital such as AI-powered intelligent automation technologies with virtual platforms and chatbots need to be integrated into the resource stream. The development level of resource is from estimation and discoverability, to efficiency in the early, intermediate, and advanced stages of AI adoption, respectively (see Figure 1).

2.2. *Artificial intelligence before and during the COVID-19 pandemic*

This section reviews the development of AI from three approaches such as the AI interest, attendance techniques, and data sources before and during the COVID-19 pandemic. Figure 2 shows the world interest in AI, Machine Learning (ML), and Deep Learning (DL) from 2004 to 2021. The world interest in AI reached the highest point (100) in 2021 when most countries were combating the COVID-19 virus.

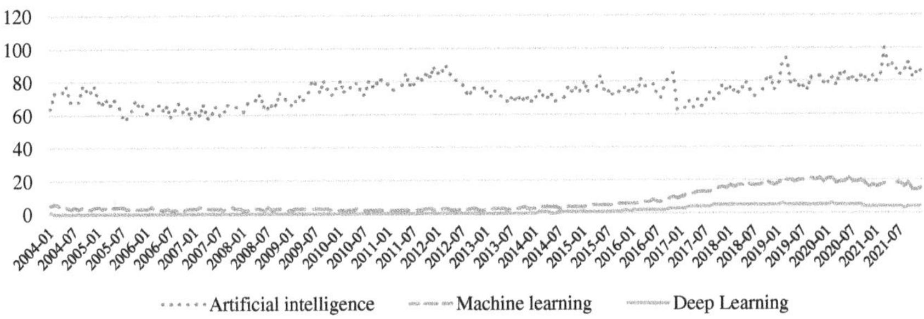

Figure 2. The world interest in artificial intelligence, machine learning, and deep learning.
Notes: The figure shows the world's interest in both Search Terms and Topics related to artificial intelligence, machine learning, and deep learning from 1/1/2004 to 15/12/2021. The numbers represent search interest relative to the highest point on the chart for the given time. A value of 100 is the peak popularity for the term. A value of 50 means that the term is half as popular. A score of 0 means there was not enough data for this term (Google Trends, 2021).
Source: Authors' calculation based on data from Google Trends as at 15/12/2021 at https://trends.google.com/trends/explore?date=all&q=%2Fm%2F0mkz,%2Fm%2F01hyh_,Deep%20Learning.

The interest in ML and DL rose rapidly between 2014 and 2021. The ML interest increased from 1 point in 2014 to 21 points in 2021 (see Figure 2).

Figure 3 shows changes in AI interest in 69 countries where data are available from Google Trends before and during the COVID-19 pandemic. Noticeably, both China and Vietnam recorded as the top two countries that were interested in AI topics before and during the COVID-19 pandemic. Although Croatia, Dominican Republic, and Nepal showed no records of searching activities pre-COVID-19 related to AI, these countries started to show interest in AI during the COVID-19 period. Italy, Iran, and Czechia showed the least interest in AI during the COVID-19 period. Among the 18 countries that experienced higher interest in AI during the COVID-19 period than the pre-COVID-19 period, the most dramatic changes have been recorded in Nepal (15 points increase) and South Korea (8 points increase).

The world's interest in AI-based techniques has been rapidly increasing ever since the COVID-19 pandemic. According to Statista (2021d), the revenue of the identity verification market worldwide

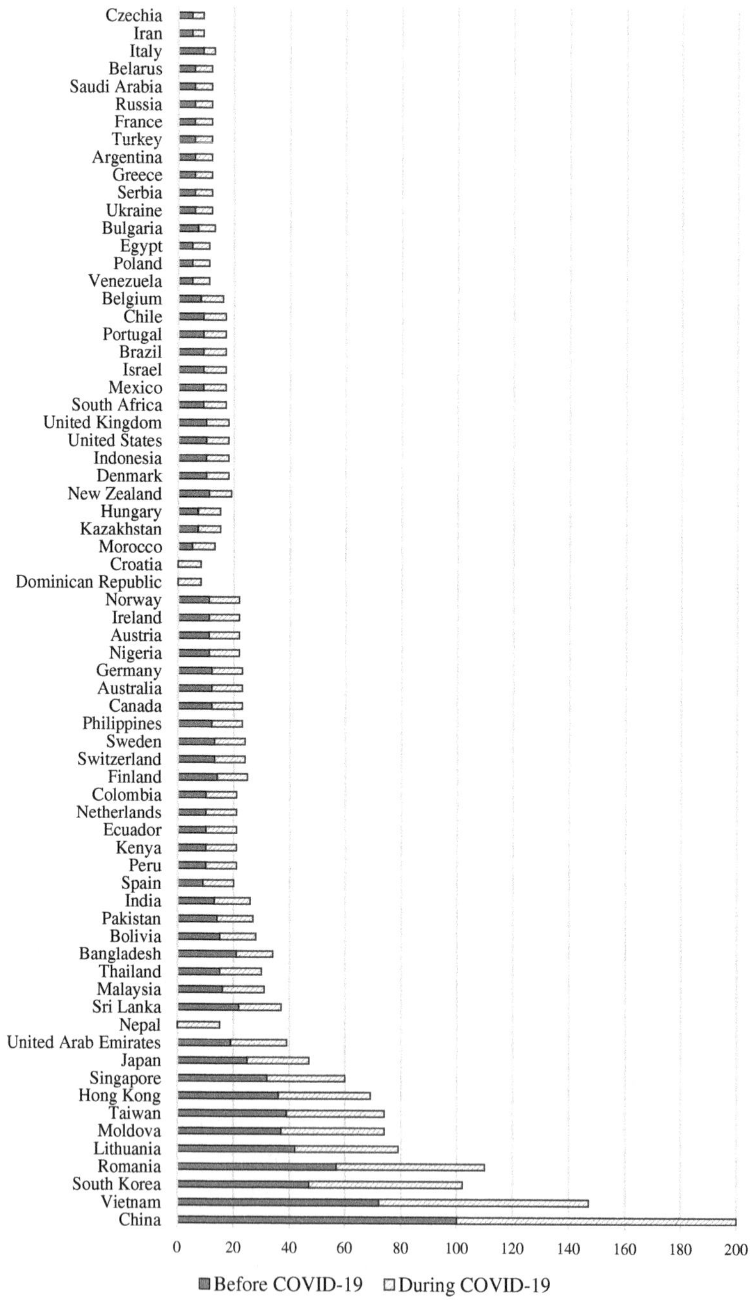
Czechia
Iran
Italy
Belarus
Saudi Arabia
Russia
France
Turkey
Argentina
Greece
Serbia
Ukraine
Bulgaria
Egypt
Poland
Venezuela
Belgium
Chile
Portugal
Brazil
Israel
Mexico
South Africa
United Kingdom
United States
Indonesia
Denmark
New Zealand
Hungary
Kazakhstan
Morocco
Croatia
Dominican Republic
Norway
Ireland
Austria
Nigeria
Germany
Australia
Canada
Philippines
Sweden
Switzerland
Finland
Colombia
Netherlands
Ecuador
Kenya
Peru
Spain
India
Pakistan
Bolivia
Bangladesh
Thailand
Malaysia
Sri Lanka
Nepal
United Arab Emirates
Japan
Singapore
Hong Kong
Taiwan
Moldova
Lithuania
Romania
South Korea
Vietnam
China
0
20
40
60
80
100
120
140
160
180
200
Before COVID-19
During COVID-19

Figure 3.

was 4.93 billion USD in 2017, and will reach the estimated value of 18 billion USD in 2027 (post the COVID-19 pandemic). Implementing biometric attendance technologies saves time and resources, and minimises human error. Therefore, the biometric market will explode with great applications in many industries such as healthcare, offices, education, manufacturing, retail, agency, banking, and travel and tourism.

According to THALES (2021), the most popular biometric techniques are fingerprints, face recognition, iris, palm, and DNA-based recognition. Before the COVID-19 pandemic, the fingerprint identification technique was known as the trusted and cost-effective biometric attendance system (Suharwardy, 2021). The single, dual, and multi finger options are available for this biometric technique. However, during the COVID-19 pandemic, the fingerprint and palm recognition systems, which require users to touch devices, proved to have a limited support in combatting the deadly virus.

As the pandemic emerged, the facial biometric techniques attracted more attention from governments, firms, and education institutions. According to Kortli *et al.* (2020), the face recognition system is one of the most important biometric authentication methods. Using a face detection technique and recognition framework, the facial biometric services have developed quickly from marking student attendance (Reddy *et al.*, 2020) to recognising individuals with faces partially covered by masks (Hernandez, 2020). However, two obstacles to adopting the facial biometric techniques are the disruption of hardware supply chain caused by the COVID-19 pandemic and the high-cost investment in new cameras and devices.

Figure 3. (*figure on facing page*) Artificial intelligence interest before and during the COVID-19 pandemic.

Notes: The figure shows the world interest in both Search Terms and Topics of Artificial Intelligence before the COVID-19 pandemic (1/1/2018–31/12/2019) and during the pandemic (1/1/2020–15/12/2021). According to Google Trends, the numbers represent search interest relative to the highest point on the figure for the given time. A value of 100 is the peak popularity for the term. A value of 50 means that the term is half as popular. A score of 0 means there were not enough data for this term (Google Trends, 2021).

Source: Authors' calculation based on data from Google Trends as at 15/12/2021 at https://trends.google.com/trends/explore?date=all&q=%2Fm%2F0mkz,%2Fm%2F01hyh_,Deep%20Learning.

Hence, instead of acquiring new hardware, it was recognised that a mobile app and desktop software would provide a great solution for adopting facial biometric techniques at low cost. This led to a new era of AI-based facial recognition system that can operate on any mobiles and systems without expensive hardware investments (Suharwardy, 2021). The software market has bloomed rapidly during the COVID-19 period. Statista (2021c) predicts that the facial recognition market worldwide will increase to 8.5 billion USD in 2025 from 3.8 billion USD in 2020. In term of software, the digital identity solution market revenue worldwide in 2026 is estimated at 49.6 billion USD, which is double the revenue in 2020 (23.3 billion USD) (Statista, 2021b).

Adopting AI means that big data are required for machines to learn from the past, test pilot samples, infer results, and predict the future. Therefore, as the data demand increases, it drives a quick rise in sources that provide data, software, and statistics. Table 1 summarises the number of big data sources that can be used for AI adoption from references in the last five years (2016–2021). The list of data sources by Marr (2016) has no dataset pre-processed for AI. In the updated list in 2018, Marr (2018) provides 30 new data sources, but only one source providing pre-processed data for ML (see Table 1). Lionbridge (2018) lists 50 free datasets for ML in general (see Table 1).

Stanford *et al.* (2020) present a list of 53 data sources, categorised into nine groups, in which five groups (39 sources) are specified as AI adoption (Machine Learning Datasets, Computer Vision Datasets, Sentiment Analysis Datasets, Natural Language Processing (NLP) Datasets, and Self-driving (Autonomous Driving) Datasets). Data providers and data buyers can meet their need on data marketplaces such as Datarade. As at 15/12/2021, Datarade Data Marketplace has more than 2,000 data providers worldwide grouped into 19 categories from Geospatial, Identity, Industry, to Political Data (see Table 1). In the Industry category, Datarade lists 51 providers of AI and ML training data.

Table 2 summarises the AI and ML training data providers on Datarade by country. Among the 51 providers, there are seven providers of Annotated Imagery Data, and 18 providers of Natural Language Processing (NLP) Data. The number of providers that are headquartered in the United States (US) is the highest with 20

Table 1. Data sources for artificial intelligence adoption.

Reference	Number of sources	Notes
Marr (2016)	33	Big Data: 33 brilliant and free data sources anyone can use dated February 12, 2016.
Marr (2018)	30	Big data and AI: 30 amazing (and free) public data sources dated February 26, 2018. • These sources differ from the 33 sources in Marr (2016). • Among 30 new entries, only one dataset is pre-processed for machine learning, that is UCI Machine Learning Repository with 588 datasets cited as Dua and Graff (2019).
Lionbridge (2018)	50	The 50 best free datasets for machine learning dated October 22, 2018.
Stanford *et al.* (2020)	53	Best public datasets for machine learning and data science dated August 8, 2020. • 6 sources of Dataset Finders; • 2 sources of General Datasets (Housing and Geographic); • 9 sources of Machine Learning Datasets; • 8 sources of Computer Vision Datasets; • 4 sources of Sentiment Analysis Datasets; • 9 sources of Natural Language Processing (NLP) Datasets; • 9 sources of Self-Driving (Autonomous Driving) Datasets; • 3 sources of Clinical Datasets; • 3 sources of Datasets for Recommender Systems.
Datarade (2021)	>2,000	Datarade Data Marketplace. Data providers worldwide grouped into 19 categories of geospatial, commerce, financial market, consumer, B2B, identity, transport and logistics, environmental, credit rating, real estate, web, mobile app, legal, healthcare, entertainment, energy, industry, political, and hospitality, travel, & tourism data.

Table 2. Datarade artificial intelligence and machine learning training data providers.

Country	Number of providers	Provider name	Service
US	20	DataPure	AI & ML training data
		DefinedCrowd	AI & ML training data
		h2o	AI & ML training data
		Lionbridge	AI & ML training data
		Brain Corp	AI & ML training and IoT data
		AppTek	AI & ML training and NLP data
		Cogito Tech	AI & ML training and NLP data
		Image DataSets	AI & ML training and NLP data
		PROME	AI & ML training and stock market data
		FactSquared	Automated voice and video transcription and analysis services
		TVEyes	Broadcast and radio transcripts
		ShAIp	Human-in-the-loop data platform and services
		Weather Source	Hyper-local weather and climate data
		CustomWeather	Industry-leading weather solutions
		People Data Labs	Innovative, trusted, data-driven products
		Crunchbase	Company, B2B contact, stock market data
		eSales Data	Sales leads, email/data appending, application development, and online marketing solutions
		Geospatial Insight	Satellite, AI & ML training, traffic, marine traffic data
		GWH Ventures	Stock market, alternative credit, and NLP data
		EPIC Translations	Translation
		Bitvore	Unstructured (text) data transformed into AI-driven intelligence for risk management

Table 2. (*Continued*)

Country	Number of providers	Provider name	Service
India	4	Ainnotate	Annotation services
		Automaton AI	End-to-end AI services on business transformation
		Knuckle Head	End-to-end services on AI Lifecycle
		ModFx Labs	In-store, shopper, location, app usage, and AI & ML training data
Canada	3	Globalme	AI & ML training data
		Bedrock AI	Algorithms to extract hard-to-find, problematic information from SEC filings, in real-time
		Agents Republic	Custom multilingual conversational AI training data via audio/voice
Israel	3	Endor	Demographic, consumer behaviour, consumer lifestyle, and AI & ML training data
		Cyabra	Effect of online conversations to uncover authenticity and measure impact
		Webhose.io	Structured web data
UK	3	Tessian	AI & ML training data
		Kieli	NLP techniques
		Geocento	Satellite, AI & ML training, map, and alternative data
China	2	ZhenXing	AI
		Datax	AI & ML training data
South Korea	2	Testworks	AI & ML training and annotated imagery data
		Deeply	Audio AI technology
Bulgaria	1	Humans in the Loop	AI & ML training data
Germany	1	TwentyBN	AI & ML training data
Hong Kong	1	AimMatic	AI & ML training data
Poland	1	Summa Linguae Technologies	AI & ML training and NLP data

(*Continued*)

Table 2. (*Continued*)

Country	Number of providers	Provider name	Service
Slovakia	1	KALM:IT	AI & ML training, annotated imagery, and car data
Russia	1	Qset	Cryptocurrency data and AI & ML
Spain	1	Danel Capital	Daily global AI score from 1 to 10 for each company based on the probability of outperforming the market in 30 days
Cyprus	1	InData Labs	Data science and AI-powered solutions
Finland	1	StageZero	Ground-breaking MicroTasks technology
Netherlands	1	TAUS	Language data network
Sweden	1	Sanctify Financial Technologies	ML software
Portugal	1	GBSN Research	Product Data, consumer analytics, data collection, and data processing solutions
Turkey	1	Mirage	Synthetic data

Notes: AI, Artificial Intelligence; ML, Machine Learning; NLP, Natural Language Processing.
Source: The authors' calculation from Datarade Data Marketplace as at 15/12/2021 at https://datarade.ai/data-categories/ai-ml-training-data.

providers, followed by India with 4 providers (see Table 2). The AI market revenues worldwide increased from 296.7 billion USD in 2020 to 341.8 billion USD in 2021, and are estimated to grow around 18.5% per year till 2024 (Statista, 2021a).

After obtaining data, users have a wide range of different AI software to choose from. The most common free and open-source AI software programs are TensorFlows, IBM Watson, Apache Mahout, OpenNN, Scikit-learn, Accord.NET, and Torch (Goodfirms, 2021). Noticeably, only IBM Watson provides Risk Mitigation as one of its key features. We identify Tensor Flow as the most user-friendly AI software because this software is designed to work on most platforms including Windows, Linux, macOS,

Android, iPhone, and iPad. However, if users prefer to use a Web-based platform, they can consider the other six AI software programs. For analysis, research, and decision-making, Quantumstat (https://index.quantumstat.com/) allows users to search for different topics and freely access paper titles, abstracts, authors, paper PDF files, Graphs, and Codes. However, AI Statistics sources are still limited and sometimes not free. For example, Statista has a great collection of statistics and facts on AI worldwide (https://www.statista.com/statistics/1229130/ai-investment-and-funding-worldwide/), but subscriptions are required to access source references and download data in PNG, PDF, and XLS formats.

In summary, the literature shows there is a higher demand for adopting AI, especially ever since the COVID-19 pandemic. This suggests that AI enables firms to manage risk in a volatile environment. However, no studies have investigated the performance of AI-adopted listed firms to verify the role of AI in risk management. More importantly, the stages of AI adoption suggest that firms should investigate how they manage risk using advanced technology and which factors affect the success of AI adoption. Among the organisational readiness factors, skilled workforce is identified as the most important task in enabling AI in businesses (Alsheibani *et al.*, 2018; Aziz and Dowling, 2019; CFA Institute, 2019, 2021). Therefore, to our best knowledge, this is the first study that attempts to address the opportunity to build a professional workforce such as the T-shaped teams for adopting AI for risk management.

3. Methodology

The important roles of AI adoption can be reflected in the performance of firms that implement AI in their operations. Few studies investigate the performance of AI-implemented firms because of data limitation. CFA Institute (2019) conducts a survey on applying technologies in the investment industry. The responses from the 230 portfolio managers indicate that the investment industry is at the early stage of AI adoption with only 10% of the respondents using AI or ML techniques in the investment process (CFA Institute, 2019). However, the performance of firms adopting AI or ML has not been widely investigated in the existing literature.

Table 3. Equity indices and definition.

Ticker	Index name	Members	Year
BAINTR Index	BlueStar Artificial Intelligence Index Net Total Return	107	2012
IBOTZN2 Index	Index Global Robotics & Artificial Intelligence Thematic v2 Index NTR	36	2021
SPX Index	S&P 500 Index	500	1957
RTY Index	Russell 2000 Index	2,000	1984
INDU Index	Dow Jones Industrial Average	30	1928
VIX Index	Chicago Board Options Exchange Volatility Index	—	1993

Notes: The "Ticker" column shows the Bloomberg index ticker. The "Index name" column presents the original full name of each index used in Bloomberg. The number of companies included in each index is shown in the "Members" column. The "Year" column shows the foundation year of each index.
Source: Bloomberg.

To examine the performance of AI-adopted firms, we use two AI market indices: the BlueStar Artificial Intelligence Index Net Total Return (BAINTR Index) and the Index Global Robotics & Artificial Intelligence Thematic v2 Index NTR (IBOTZN2 Index). The BAINTR Index includes 107 global companies that were involved in or benefitted from the adoption of AI, and focused on developing or implementing AI inference. The BAINTR Index has the earliest price date on 31/12/2012. Therefore, daily data were collected from Bloomberg from 31/12/2012 to 20/12/2021. Although the IBOTZN2 Index was introduced on 8/2/2021, during the COVID-19 period, this index is important to track the performance of 36 global companies that are expected to benefit from the increased adoption and utilisation of robotics and AI. We use the S&P 500 Index (SPX Index), Russell 2000 Index (RTY Index), Dow Jones Industrial Average Index (INDU Index), and the Chicago Board Options Exchange Volatility Index (VIX Index) as the benchmarks to evaluate the performance of the AI-adopted firms included in the BAINTR Index and IBOTZN2 Index. Table 3 summarises the equity indices used in this study.

The performance of AI market indices are used to explore the roles of AI in risk management. According to the Federation of European Risk Management Associations (FERMA) (2019), benefits in AI in enterprise risk management (ERM) are related to big data processing, efficiency improvement, real-time and faster predictive actions, and better business decision-making. Based on the FERMA benefits of AI in ERM and the three stages of AI adoption, the value of implementing AI in risk management will be explored, including factors that affect AI adoption in risk management.

4. Results

4.1. *Analysis of the performance of artificial intelligence-implemented firms*

Tables 4 and 5 summarise the members of the BAINTR Index and IBOTZN2 Index by country and industry as at 21/12/2021, respectively. Noticeably, the majority of members are from the US with the highest weights of 76.43% in the BAINTR Index and 41.62% in IBOTZN2 Index. The US, Japan, Switzerland, the UK, Canada,

Table 4. Members of the BlueStar Artificial Intelligence Index.

No.	Country	Weight (%)	Market cap (billion USD)	Members	Shares
1	United States	76.43	9,350.00	75	83,881.50
2	United Kingdom	5.10	25.78	3	15,081.61
3	Israel	2.99	29.05	4	6,424.52
4	Canada	2.89	177.80	4	3,610.82
5	China	2.87	329.62	5	69,072.34
6	Australia	2.49	94.54	4	14,325.45
7	Germany	1.92	172.98	3	5,566.08
8	France	1.34	82.21	2	2,093.87
9	Sweden	1.25	48.32	2	6,998.89
10	Japan	1.18	24.29	2	7,152.18
11	Austria	0.53	4.82	1	2,176.30
12	Switzerland	0.52	42.72	1	793.12
13	Norway	0.50	5.94	1	1,149.31
	Total	100	10,388.07	107	218,325.99

Source: Authors' calculation based on data from Bloomberg as at 21/12/2021.

Table 5. Members of the Index Global Robotics and Artificial Intelligence Thematic v2 Index.

No.	Name	Weight (%)	Market cap (billion USD)	Members	Shares
1	United States	41.62	854.52	15	32,164,910.82
2	Japan	38.15	287.35	14	24,543,393.20
3	Switzerland	12.46	81.97	2	13,256,823.02
4	United Kingdom	2.55	4.44	1	2,293,522.71
5	Canada	1.89	3.37	1	2,901,294.45
6	Israel	1.55	2.78	1	3,438,589.68
7	Finland	1.50	3.06	1	1,738,753.85
8	South Korea	0.30	0.30	1	843,392.23
	Total	100	1,237.79	36	81,180,679.96

Source: Authors' calculation based on data from Bloomberg as at 21/12/2021.

and Israel are the six countries that are included in both indices (see Tables 4 and 5).

Figures 4 and 5 illustrate the market capitalisation weight of the BAINTR Index and the IBOTZN2 Index by country, respectively. Among the 13 countries that are involved in or benefitted from the adoption of AI, and focused on developing or implementing AI inference in the BAINTR Index, the top three countries with the highest market capitalisation weights are the US, the UK, and Israel (see Figure 4). Noticeably, Japan and Switzerland are two countries that have a market capitalisation weight less than 2% in total in the BAINTR Index. However, these two countries and the United States are the top three countries with the highest market capitalisation weights (41.62% the US, 38.15% Japan, and 12.46% Switzerland) that benefitted from the increased adoption and utilisation of robotics and AI in the IBOPTZN2 Index (see Figure 5).

Both AI indices reveal that most of the listed firms implementing AI and utilising robotics are from developed economies. Although China is the only upper-middle-income country that appears in the BAINTR Index, it was the world's second largest economy in 2020 (World Development Indicators, 2022). This result implies that the listed firms in large economies have greater potential capabilities to adopt AI in businesses. This finding supports the framework of AI readiness introduced by Alsheibani *et al.* (2018) who emphasise the organisational readiness trait. The finding also suggests that firms

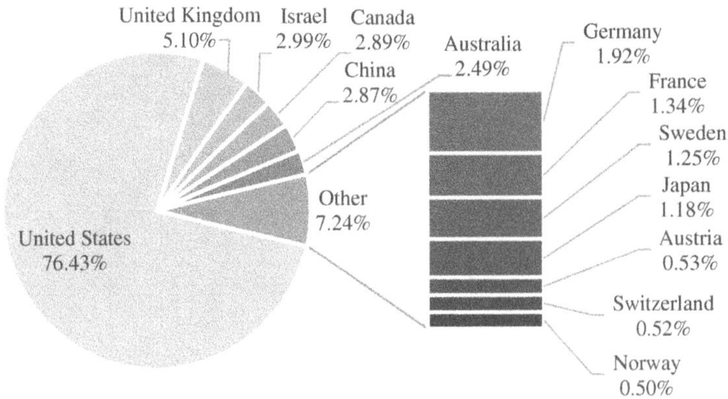

Figure 4. Market capitalisation weight of the BlueStar Artificial Intelligence Index by country.

Source: Authors' calculation based on data from Bloomberg as at 21/12/2021.

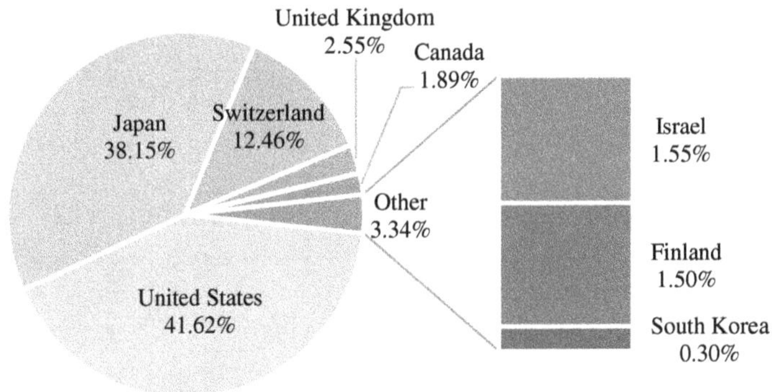

Figure 5. Market capitalisation weight of the Index Global Robotics and Artificial Intelligence Thematic v2 Index by country.

Source: Authors' calculation based on data from Bloomberg as at 21/12/2021.

should identify their current positions in the AI adoption process (early, intermediate, and advanced) to determine when they can implement advanced technology in their businesses.

Figure 6 shows the performance of the BAINTR Index compared with the benchmarks. The BAINTR Index outperformed the SPX, RTY, and INDU indices during and outside high volatility periods from 2012 to 2021. For example, in the pre-COVID-19 period from 5/2/2018 to 21/2/2020, the average premium between

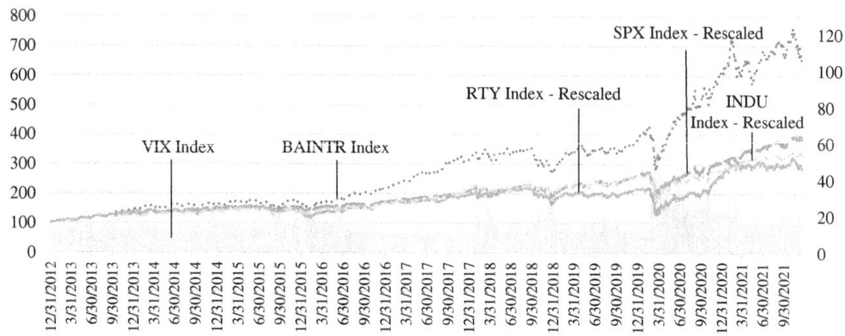

Figure 6. Performance of the BAINTR Index compared with the benchmarks.
Notes: The figure compares the performance of the BlueStar Artificial Intelligence Index Net Total Return (BAINTR Index) with the benchmarks including the S&P 500 Index (SPX Index), Russell 2000 Index (RTY Index), Dow Jones Industrial Average Index (INDU Index), and the Chicago Board Options Exchange Volatility Index (VIX Index). The BAINTR Index has the base of 100 on the first day of the study period on 31/12/2012. The SPX, RTY, and INDU indices were rescaled with the base of 100 on 31/12/2012 to return the index performance in a comparative basis.
Source: Authors' calculation based on data of Total Return Index (Net Dividends) from Bloomberg as at 21/12/2021.

the BAINTR Index and the SPX (the AI premium) was 113.03%. As the COVID-19 information started to spread on 24/2/2020, the VIX index increased rapidly from 17.08 on 21/2/2020 to the maximum value of 82.69 on 16/3/2020. Although all market indices were exposed to the COVID-19 shock, the BAINTR Index performance maintained the average AI premium with the SPX of 119.27% from 24/2/2020 to 1/4/2020, then increased to 271.37% on average from 2/4/2020 to 20/12/2021. Figure 6 shows that the AI premium between the BAINTR Index and the SPX, RTY, and INDU indices increased over time, especially during the COVID-19 period (24/2/2020–20/12/2021). The results show that stocks of companies with AI adoption and AI focus outperformed in the markets during both low and high volatility periods.

Figure 7 shows the performance of the BAINTR Index and IBOTZN2 Index from 8/2/2021 to 20/12/2021 (the second year of the COVID-19 pandemic). The gap between the two lines shows the return premium of the IBOTZN2 Index compared with the BAINTR Index. In general, the IBOTZN2 Index outperformed

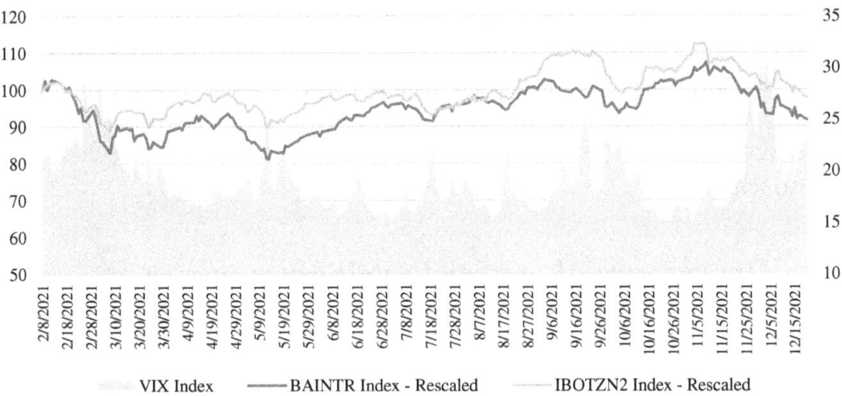

Figure 7. Performance of the BAINTR Index and IBOTZN2 Index.
Notes: BAINTR Index is the BlueStar Artificial Intelligence Index Net Total Return. IBOTZN2 Index is the Index Global Robotics and Artificial Intelligence Thematic v2 Index NTR.
Source: Authors' calculation based on data from Bloomberg as at 21/12/2021.

the BAINTR Index with the average premium of 5.05% (see Figure 7). The maximum and minimum return premium values are 11.19% and −1.54%, respectively. This means that stocks of companies that benefitted from the increased adoption and utilisation of robotics and AI in the IBOTZN2 Index generally outperformed stocks of companies with AI adoption and AI focus in the BAINTR Index. Furthermore, we observed that the higher the VIX index (higher risk), the higher the AI premium (see Figures 6 and 7). In conclusion, AI adoption plays an important role in enhancing the performance of listed firms, especially in the high volatility periods.

The results of the outperformance of AI market indices before and during the COVID-19 pandemic indicate the important role of AI in uncertain times. The finding emphasises the sustainable role of AI adoption in managing systematic and unsystematic risks in the securities market. Our results align with Aziz and Dowling's (2019) conclusion of the optimistic role of AI and machine learning in risk management. We found that AI adoption protects listed firms from the severe impacts of unexpected events such as the COVID-19 pandemic on firm performance. The finding sheds light on using AI as a tool to confront uncertainty in the business environment. In the context of sustainable performance, firms and policymakers can consider implementing or increasing the use of advanced technology such as AI, robotics, and other machines to gradually shift their businesses and operations from the traditional modes to more tech-savvy approaches.

4.2. *Importance of artificial intelligence in risk management*

Enterprises are exposed to systematic and unsystematic risks. The outperformed results of AI-adopted stock market indices during and outside uncertain times indicate the important roles of AI adoption as a shield to protect firms from risk exposure. The important value of AI in ERM is emphasised with key benefits related to big data processing, efficiency improvement, real-time and faster predictive actions, and better business decision-making (FERMA, 2019). In this study, we expand the value of implementing AI in risk management to the five pillars of workforce development, digital transformation, operational capability improvement, partnership development, and working towards a resilient and sustainable future (see Figure 8).

First, AI-adopted risk management plays an important role in *workforce development*. To implement AI in ERM, companies that have not had a digital team will form a new one. Risk managers will need to either develop their professional skills in data science or cooperate with data scientists. If companies have a digital team, they will aim to have a higher-skilled digital workforce. Using data from the International Data Corporation, Bhaskar (2020) discusses that 40% of organisations have a Digital Leadership team with a Single Digital Transformation Executive Lead, and 40% of the Digital Transformation initiatives are related to AI. In investments, CFA Institute (2019) lists talent as one of five difficulties (cost, talent, technology, leadership vision, and time) of AI applications. Therefore, building a good digital team is necessary for success in AI-adopted risk management, and enhances workforce development in enterprises.

Second, *digital transformation* is the next pillar in implementing AI in ERM. The development of digital workforce teams drives

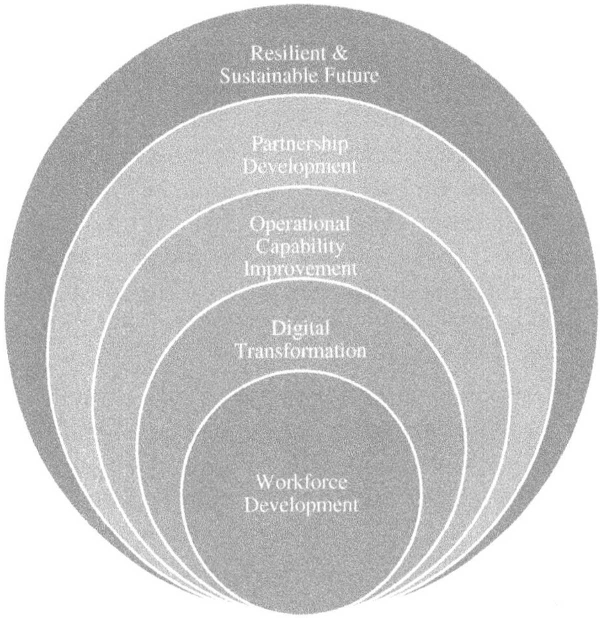

Figure 8. Important roles of artificial intelligence in enterprise risk management.

digital transformation in an AI-adopted enterprise. According to International Finance Corporation (IFC) (2021), AI applications are grouped into three types: basic, advanced, and autonomous AI. To implement AI in risk management, big data are essential. Therefore, any AI-adopted businesses need to start with acquiring and processing data. The basic AI applications such as chatbots and online matching establish an initial analytics solution in enterprises, enhance their business performance, and improve their digital platforms. This digital transformation role is enforced by the advanced AI. While the basic AI involves structured data in general, the advanced AI transforms basic digital applications to more human-mind platforms that focus on unstructured data analysis. Managing risk using the advanced AI is applied in fields such as medical diagnoses, security, and transportation using images, texts, and audios. The autonomous AI such as robotics drives digital transformation in enterprises to the next level of interaction with human beings. However, drawbacks of irregular and few data related to human beings limit the learning ability of machines and result in making biased decisions (IFC, 2021).

Third, adopting AI in risk management improves *operational capabilities*. Wu *et al.* (2010) introduce six operational capabilities, including operational improvement, operational innovation, operational customisation, operational cooperation, operational responsiveness, and operational reconfiguration. AI allows managers to identify regular and irregular risk early, reduce cost, increase successful trading rates, and facilitate real-time decision-making in uncertain environments. For example, BP Public Limited Company applied AI in 2010 to reduce oil spill risk to people and assets, then leveraged the AI management system to detect sand around well areas to manage risk to personnel and operations, and improve operational efficiencies (Matteson, 2021). Figure 8 shows that the great support from the digital workforce and digital transformation in the process of implementing AI in ERM improves the operational capabilities.

Fourth, AI adoption motivates *partnership development* in ERM. In the AI Action Guide for Risk Managers of FERMA (2019), besides own resources, AI can be implemented via partnerships as an alternative option. The rapid development of the AI industry (see Tables 1 and 2) enables business leaders and risk managers to partner with AI service providers, technology insurers, or third-party vendors such as Software as a Service (SaaS) providers, marketing companies, healthcare providers, telephone companies, consultants and advisors, and contractors. Although cybersecurity breaches and cyberattacks are common risks in using third-party vendors, FERMA (2019) discusses that selecting correct partnerships will bring greater cost–benefit effectiveness to host organisations.

Fifth, AI-based risk management drives a *resilient and sustainable future* (see Figure 8). O'Brien *et al.* (2012) emphasise the roles of risk management associated with disaster uncertainty, climate change, and other stressful events in SEE sustainability. In the light of epidemics and pandemics, especially the COVID-19 pandemic, risk management areas are broadened to heath events and the use of AI in enterprises to minimise the impacts of the deadly virus. Therefore, we expand the SEE sustainability of O'Brien *et al.* (2012) to the AI-based resilient and sustainable future as AI is used as a powerful tool in ERM.

5. Discussions

Our findings suggest that firms should adopt AI in risk management and understand the factors that determine the success of AI adoption in businesses. The results show that the professional workforce is the most important factor in the three stages of AI adoption (early, intermediate, and advanced) (see Figure 1) and in AI-adopted risk management (see Figure 8). In this section, we discuss why a T-shaped Team needs to be developed for AI adoption in enterprises, and its functions, opportunities, and challenges.

5.1. *New functions of T-shaped teams*

Bierema (2019) reviews the shape of professional teams in forms of I-shaped (deep specialisation in one area), Π (Pi)-shaped or H-shaped (deep specialisation in two areas), A-shaped or Y-shaped (deep specialisation in more than one area and bilingual), dash-shaped (breadth across areas but lack of depth), O-shaped (well-rounded), E-shaped (entrepreneurial), and T-shaped (deep specialisation and breadth across several areas). The term T-shaped was first introduced by Johnston (1978) and appeared in *The Independent* article titled "The hunt is on for the Renaissance Man of computing" in 17 September 1991. The vertical bar of the letter T means the depth of skills and knowledge in a single discipline, and the horizontal bar shows the ability to cooperate across disciplines.

With the rapid development of the AI industry, T-shaped professionals (TSP) are highly in demand and the definition of T-shaped team is extended. CFA Institute (2019) introduces the new concept of T-shaped investment teams with the three aspects of *Technology*, *Innovation*, and *Investment*. Building a T-shaped team with the new aspects is emphasised in the different stages of AI and big data adoption in the investment industry (CFA Institute, 2021).

In the light of adopting AI in common enterprises, we replace the third aspect of T-shaped teams (Investment) with a new aspect of *In-practice*. This replacement allows a diversification in implementing the functions of T-shaped teams in different industries rather than only in the investment field. The three new functions of T-shaped teams are *Technology*, *Innovation*, and *In-practice* (see Figure 9).

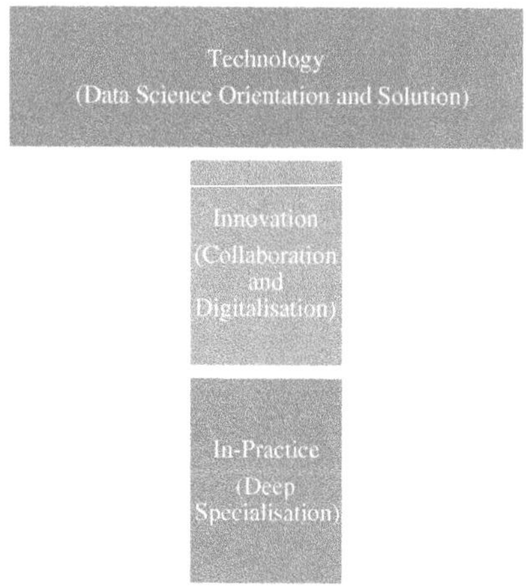

Figure 9. New functions of T-shaped teams in artificial intelligence adoption.
Source: Authors' compilation based on CFA Institute (2019, 2021).

5.1.1. *Technology function*

The role of data scientists in the digital workforce is very important for the adoption of AI in enterprises, which requires more knowledge and skills related to the Technology function of T-shaped teams. Fiore-Gartland and Tanweer (2016) coined the T, Γ, M, Π *network* that is a mix of T-shaped, Γ (Gamma)-shaped, M (Mu)-shaped, and Π-shaped data scientists in practicing data science, where specialisations of scientists increase from deep expertise in a single domain (T-shaped) to deep expertise in both a domain and methodological science (Π-shaped) (Fiore-Gartland and Tanweer, 2016). The specialisation of Γ-shaped and M-shaped data scientists are partially and relationally identified between the T-shaped and Π-shaped forms in the T, Γ, M, Π network.

Hiring a data scientist will be the first step in forming a T-shaped team and developing the digital workforce. Although it is not always easy to look for Π-shaped data scientists, enterprises should try to find talents among the T, Γ, M, Π network. These talents can help the enterprises to transform their business and operation systems to a more data science-oriented system and build a good fit solution for their specific objectives. Using third-party vendors is another option if firms cannot hire talents to fulfil the Technology function of their T-shaped teams. Although these third-party vendors cost more, the firms can eventually reach the T, Γ, M, Π network without spending a lot of time and effort in the recruitment process for data scientists.

The Technology function is on the horizontal bar of the letter T (see Figure 9). This means that the digital workforce with people holding degrees in Science, Technology, Engineering, and Mathematics (STEM) is not enough. Data scientists should have the ability to cooperate across disciplines to fulfil the Technology function on the letter T. Experience in previous relevant industries and connections with tech firms are important to transform pure data scientists to data science professionals. However, there is a shortage of these experienced professionals in the labour market (CFA Institute, 2021). Therefore, enterprises may not acquire an experienced professional instantly. Experiences and connections need time, cost, and effort. A solution is that firms should nurture potential data scientists, develop and train them using a learning-by-doing process.

The ability to cooperate across disciplines illustrated along the letter T's vertical bar also presents the ability of digital teams to acquire knowledge and learn new skills of other disciplines. Data scientists learn how to work with engineers to ensure that their models work in firms. This enables technology platforms and solutions developed by technology professionals to satisfy the needs of AI adoption in enterprises. The ability to learn new things can be applied to the current workforce of firms. If STEM professionals take finance and accounting courses, investment managers and data analysts can learn programming skills. Again, firms have an option of developing and training their employees to form a new Technology team rather than buy-in new resources, but this will take time and may not always be successful.

5.1.2. *Innovation function*

The Innovation function of the T-shaped teams is located in the vertical bar of the letter T and connects the Technology and In-practice functions (see Figure 9). According to CFA Institute (2021), the letter T now represents much more than depth in one area and breadth across areas. The digital and uncertain world shows that multidisciplinary knowledge and skills play an important role as firms are exposed to risks. An individual does not have skills in many areas, but a team with different individuals does. Based on the discussion on the Innovation function in the investment context by CFA

Institute (2021), we define the Innovation function of the T-shaped teams as the ability to connect the knowledge of technology professionals (data science professionals and knowledge engineers) and the in-practice stakeholders (thought leaders and professional expertise teams).

Adopting AI in enterprises requires the Innovation function of the T-shaped teams that focuses on collaborating and digitalising tasks related to the In-practice function using outcomes from the Technology function. The collaboration and digitalisation roles of the Innovation function are not very easy. Thus, AI-adopted firms face the most difficult task of looking for a right Innovation individual or team who can understand and communicate both languages of technology and professional expertise. The innovation roles are also extended to understand strategic plans of firms, align tasks of business and technical departments to help firms perform well in frequently changing environments.

The mixed roles of the Innovation team mean it is hard to look for an ideal candidate in the job market. Figure 10 illustrates the skills of the Innovation team in AI-adopted firms. The skills are technology, professional expertise, communication, planning, leading, and organising. These skills are not normally taught in one educational institution, but rather honed gradually from hands-on environments. The weights of the skills embedded in the Innovation team can be

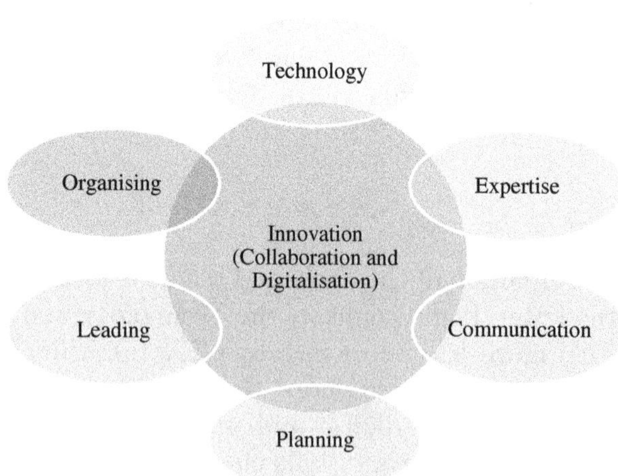

Figure 10. Skills in the Innovation function of T-shaped teams.

unequal. Each Innovation individual may have more or less experience in a specific skill, but effectively contributes to the success of the Innovation function of the T-shaped teams.

5.1.3. *In-practice function*

The In-practice function of the T-shaped teams is located in the second half of the vertical bar of the letter T (see Figure 9). The In-practice function is the root of enterprises where professional expertise works for the business survival. Different firms will specialise in different In-practice functions or disciplines such as investment, accounting, education, law, healthcare, engineering, and Internet of Things (IoT). The members of In-practice teams must have deep knowledge and skills in their area of expertise and be able to complete their commitments while working closely with the Innovation and Technology teams.

It is not a must for professional experts to learn programming and technical skills outside their fields. However, professional expertise is required to know how to apply AI and technologies to improve the performance. It will take less time and effort to introduce the applications of AI and technologies to users than require them to master any new programming and technical skills. Working in a T-shaped team means that different individuals specialise in different fields and they understand their important roles in the collaboration in the AI adoption journey.

When firms are interested in adopting AI in their operations, they should not undervalue their existing Human Intelligence (HI). Business leaders should know how to engage and develop their T-shaped teams to work in the AI and HI fashion. The professional experts with the HI and In-practice function gain new experiences and hone different skills day by day. They can be transformed from pure experts in one discipline into potential candidates with the skills of the Innovation function in the T-shaped teams (see Figure 9).

5.2. *T-shaped teams and artificial intelligence*

5.2.1. *Opportunities*

T-shaped teams with the Technology, Innovation, and In-practice functions bring many opportunities to AI-adopted firms. This section discusses three opportunities of the T-shaped Teams and AI: (i) increase the workforce and business productivity; (ii) enhance technology innovation and the performance of industrial applications; and (iii) support new business models and manage risk.

First, the functions of T-shaped teams improve the workforce and business productivity. When more skilled people are included in the T-shaped teams, the workforce productivity will potentially increase. The increase in labour productivity then boosts the business productivity, especially in AI-adopted businesses. According to Statista (2020), AI has the greatest positive impact on labour productivity in the developed economies. The estimated increases in labour productivity until 2035 in some selected developed economies are within a high range of 30–40% including Sweden (37%), the United States (35%), Japan (34%), and Austria (30%), and in a lower range from 20% to under 30% in countries such as Germany (29%), the UK (25%), and France (20%). In terms of the emerging countries, IFC (2021) emphasises the importance of AI in improving business productivity at low costs and with efficient investment in human capital with automation. The higher productivity growth due to AI is expected to take place in the emerging markets rather than in the developed markets. By 2030, while AI will contribute to an increase of 26% in GDP of China, the impact of AI on GDP of the US is only expected to be 14% (IFC, 2021).

Second, T-shaped teams and AI encourage technology innovation and improve the performance of industrial applications. IFC (2021) shows the opportunities of AI in specific sectors including power, transport, smart homes, agribusiness, financial services, manufacturing, healthcare, education, and gender equality. The role of digital transformation that the T-shaped workforce brings to AI firms becomes more evident. Some examples are a smart power sector with two-way communication between utilities and consumers; autonomous vehicles (AVs) or driverless vehicles with safety, reliability, predictability, efficiency, and sustainability; health technology or health-tech for consultation, prevention, efficiency, and effectiveness; and e-Learning with smart content, virtual assistants, and autonomous scoring systems.

Third, T-shaped teams and AI open a door to new business models and risk management. Across industries, new AI-adopted business models using big data are continuously improved (IFC, 2021).

For example, Datum blockchain-based marketplace allows users to share and sell data according to their specific terms (Haenni, 2019). NetObjex infrastructure platform connects devices to cloud-based systems using AI, blockchain, and IoT (NetObjex, 2022). Vytalyx healthcare professionals using AI give access to medical intelligence and enhanced data security (Vytalyx, 2022). Professional workforces such as T-shaped teams with the Technology, Innovation, and In-practice functions will enlarge the impact of AI in developing and implementing new business models, as well as managing risks in enterprises worldwide. Therefore, the T-shaped workforce will realise the success of the AI adoption journey in firms.

5.2.2. *Challenges*

Every journey faces challenges. The journeys of building T-shaped teams and adopting AI in enterprises are not free from challenges. CFA Institute (2019) discusses that cost, talent, technology, leadership vision, and time are the five challenges in adopting AI in financial institutions. We identify that transparency and ethics (Aziz and Dowling, 2019) form the sixth challenge of AI adoption, and all these six challenges exist in all industries. Firms hesitate to acquire big data and hire professional experts because of high costs. If firms have no concerns about the high costs, the task of finding suitable talent for AI adoption still remains a big problem. The shortage of talent equipped with any of the three functions of T-shaped teams slows down the progress of workforce development and AI adoption.

In addition, technology changes quickly. This makes firms worry about whether they are up to date and what if their professional workforce cannot stay ahead of the rapid development in technology. When technology changes, business models may need to be changed accordingly. Then, the availability of suitable big data used for the latest technology and models will be the big concern. The liability and accuracy of the new models and outcomes places more pressure on the T-shaped teams and firm leaders. The difficulties of high costs, talent shortage, and rapid changes in technology challenge the commitment of firm leaders in their AI-based business transformation. This will lengthen the Intermediate stage of AI adoption if the commitment level in the leadershift stream is weak (see Figure 1).

It may take years to accomplish the mission of building T-shaped teams and guiding firms through the Advanced (and final) stage of AI adoption.

Using big data poses the risk related to transparency and ethics in adopting AI in firms. Aziz and Dowling (2019) show that transparency is an issue that may occur on hidden layers between inputs (data) and outputs (decisions) used in the DL financial modelling. The more transparent the models, the less the risk the AI-adopted firms are exposed to. There are also ethical challenges in the use of data. Cyber security such as data breaches, malware, and insider threats are the ethical issues that AI-adopted firms need to plan for. If no risk management plans are prepared, costly tangible and intangible assets will not be protected from cyber security incidents.

5.3. *Building T-shaped teams for risk management using artificial intelligence*

In this section, we discuss a guide for building a T-shaped team for risk management using AI. To fulfil the five roles of AI in risk management (workforce development, digital transformation, operational capability improvement, partnership development, and preparing for a resilient and sustainable future), a T-shaped team must understand the applications of AI in the field of risk management (Aziz and Dowling, 2019), the barriers of AI adoption at the organisational level (Alsheibani *et al.*, 2019, 2020), AI-related risks (FERMA, 2019), and business risks. Table 6 summarises how to build a T-shaped team for AI risk management based on the functions of T-shaped teams.

First, T-shaped teams need to understand the applications of AI in at least one area of risk management. For example, according to Aziz and Dowling (2019), risk management has four different areas including credit risk, market risk, operational risk, and compliance risk. Table 6 shows that the in-practice or risk management professionals (the second half on the vertical bar of the letter T) need to know which risk management areas their firms should focus on. As for the innovation staff, they must also communicate the needs of adopting AI in the areas of risk management between the in-practice and technology professionals. The knowledge technology staff (the horizontal bar of the letter T) have to improve their knowledge and skills to implement AI in risk management in specific areas required

Table 6. Guide for building T-shaped teams for artificial intelligence risk management.

Roles of AI risk management	T-shaped team		
	In-practice	**Innovation**	**Technology**
Workforce development	Understand the applications of AI risk management	Understand and communicate the applications of AI risk management	Improve the knowledge and skills of applying AI in risk management
Digital transformation Operational capability improvement Partnership development	Identify and manage business and AI-related risks	Communicate, plan, lead, and organise digital projects for managing business and AI-related risks	Utilise AI models, technologies, or solutions for risk management
Resilient and sustainable future	Be aware of barriers of AI adoption at the organisational level	Understand and communicate barriers of AI adoption at the organisational level	Understand barriers of AI adoption at the organisational level

Sources: Authors compiled and developed the guide for building T-shaped teams for AI-adopted risk management based on Alsheibani *et al.* (2019, 2020), Aziz and Dowling (2019), and FERMA (2019).

from the innovation and in-practice teams. This is a recurrent learning process, which fills the first role of workforce development of AI-adopted risk management.

After learning the risk areas and the applications of AI in risk management, the next step for the risk management professionals is to identify business and AI-related risks. An existing Risk Management Framework (RMF) for business risks can be used as the initial risk management plan. The identified AI-related risks are added to the initial plan to develop the RMF for both business and AI-related risks. This developed plan will be communicated with the innovation and technology professionals to finalise possible identify–analyse–evaluate AI models, technologies, and solutions. The innovation staff plays critical roles in communicating, planning, leading, and organising digital projects with the technology professionals to utilise the optimal models, technologies, and solutions. In this critical and repeated process, the digital transformation, operational capability improvement, and partnership development roles of AI risk management are well presented (see Table 6).

To aim for a resilient and sustainable future based on AI-adopted risk management, the T-shaped teams should be aware of significant risks caused by disaster, climate change, and health events. Importantly, they need to be informed about the barriers of AI adoption at the organisational level (see Table 6). Using the Technology–Organization–Environment (TOE) framework and the Diffusion of Innovation (DOI) theory, Alsheibani *et al.* (2019, 2020) show that the most important barriers to AI adoption at the organisational level are the lack of in-house skills and leadership support, employee resistance to change, and uncertainty of government regulations. Without understanding and communicating these barriers among the in-practice, innovation, and technology professionals, the missions of a T-shaped team in AI-adopted risk management cannot be accomplished.

6. Conclusion

This study addresses the great opportunities and challenges of AI adoption and T-shaped teams in enterprise risk management. Combating future risks in an uncertain and volatile world requires more resources including artificial and human intelligence. Therefore, firms should plan for future direction on AI-adopted risk management strategies. For a resilient and sustainable performance post COVID-19 and beyond, the potential strategies are prioritised as follows.

First, firms need to identify whether they are in the early, intermediate, or advanced stages of AI adoption using the five streams of Leadershift, Strategy, Workforce, Process, and Resource. Besides, it is important to recognise the rapid rise in the world of interest in AI and data sources of AI, ML, and DL applications. The improvement in AI-based attendance techniques is the beginning of the evolution in multidiscipline technologies and applications.

Second, to perform better in an uncertain and volatile world, adopting AI is one of the most important strategies to obtain premium returns. Increasing AI adoption and robotics in business activities helps firms minimise the negative impacts of market risks, especially in highly volatile periods. If firms are not ready to implement AI in their specialisation areas, adopting AI in the field of risk management will fulfil the initial demands on workforce development, digital transformation, operational capability improvement, partnership development, and ensuring a resilient and sustainable future.

Third, building a professional workforce such as T-shaped teams essentially plays the most important role in any AI adoption journey. The new functions of T-shaped teams (Technology, Innovation, and In-practice) enable flexibility to be implemented in a wide range of corporates. Faced with the shortage of T-shaped professionals, firms can consider other options such as the use of learning-by-doing process to train their current workforce, buy-in resources, or third-party vendors.

Fourth, with the opportunities that AI and T-shaped teams bring to enterprises, it is clear that they also need to plan for the challenges. Building a T-shaped team and adopting AI is costly, takes time and effort, challenges leadership commitments, and potentially poses issues of transparency and ethics. Therefore, firms should prepare AI-adopted risk management frameworks or AI-RMF to maximise the opportunities and manage risks. While preparing the AI-RMF in each industry or individual firm, it is important to refer to the basic guide on building T-shaped teams for efficient AI-adopted risk management.

Last but not least, unpredictable risks and frequent changes in technologies are other constraints that firms face in adopting AI. Perhaps, the most potential risk related to technology is that AI will eventually become more intelligent than human beings. Thus, frameworks of risk management and governance regulations will have difficulties in keeping up with the rapid evolution of AI. To overcome these constraints, firms should bear in mind that the AI adoption process is a recurrent learning procedure with the three stages of early, intermediate, and advanced. When a new technology is initiated, the AI adoption process will turn back to the early stage, which requires firms to restart the first steps of leadershift awareness, strategy findability, workforce engagement, process development, and resource estimation.

This study did not examine the determinants of AI-adopted firm performance. Instead, we only focused on the AI organisational readiness or how to build a professional workforce such as T-shaped teams for AI risk management. Future research can investigate the determinants of AI stock returns at the industry and firm levels under different uncertain environments such as political crises, financial crises, supply chain disruptions, and natural disasters. To accomplish the three stages of AI adoption processes, other important factors such as AI technological and environmental readiness should be explored. Risk management strategies using AI should be studied to help firms and policymakers respond to new risks and make better decisions to address shocks in future economic crises.

References

Alsheibani, S.A., Cheung, Y.P., and Messom, C. H. (2018). Artificial intelligence adoption: AI-readiness at firm-level. In M. Tanabu, & D. Senoo (Eds.), *Proceedings of PACIS2018: Pacific Asia Conference in Information Systems (PACIS)* [37] Association for Information Systems. https://aisel.aisnet.org/pacis2018/37/.

Alsheibani, S.A., Cheung, Y.P., and Messom, C.H. (2019). Factors inhibiting the adoption of artificial intelligence at organizational-level: A preliminary investigation. Paper presented at the AMCIS. Retrieved from https://research.monash.edu/files/287736273/287674072_oa.pdf on 21/01/2022.

Alsheibani, S.A., Messom, C.H., and Cheung, Y.P. (2020). Re-thinking the competitive landscape of artificial intelligence. Paper presented at the HICSS. 10.24251/HICSS.2020.718.

Aziz, S. and Dowling, M.M. (2019). AI and machine learning for risk management (July 14, 2018). Published as: Aziz, S. and M. Dowling (2019). "Machine learning and AI for risk management", in T. Lynn, G. Mooney, P. Rosati, and M. Cummins (eds.), *Disrupting Finance: FinTech and Strategy in the 21st Century*, Palgrave, pp 33–50. Available at: https://ssrn.com/abstract=3201337 or http://dx.doi.org/10.2139/ssrn.3201337.

Bhaskar, S. (2020). Digital transformation & artificial intelligence: Is your organization ready? Retrieved from: https://www.digite.com/blog/digital-transformation-and-artificial-intelligence/ Accessed 13 January 2022.

Bierema, L.L. (2019). Enhancing employability through developing T-shaped professionals. *New Directions for Adult and Continuing Education*, 2019, 67–81. https://doi.org/10.1002/ace.20342.

Bussmann, N., Giudici, P., Marinelli, D. and Papenbrock, J. (2020). Explainable AI in Fintech risk management. *Frontiers in Artificial Intelligence*, 3, 26. DOI: 10.3389/frai.2020.00026.

CFA Institute (2019). AI pioneers in investment management. www.cfainstitute.org/-/media/documents/survey/AI-Pioneers-in-Investment-Management.ashx.

CFA Institute (2021). T-shaped teams organizing to adopt AI and big data at investment firms. https://www.cfainstitute.org/-/media/documents/article/industry-research/t-shaped-teams.pdf. Accessed 15 December 2021.

Datarade (2021). Datarade data marketplace. Retrieved from https://datarade.ai/. Accessed 15 December 2021.

Drydakis, N. (2022). Artificial intelligence and reduced SMEs' business risks. A dynamic capabilities analysis during the COVID-19 pandemic. *Information Systems Frontiers*, 24(2), 1–25. DOI: 10.1007/s10796-022-10249-6.

Dua, D. and Graff, C. (2019). UCI machine learning repository. Irvine, CA: University of California, School of Information and Computer Science. http://archive.ics.uci.edu/ml. Accessed 15 December 2021.

Enholm, I.M., Papagiannidis, E., Mikalef, P. and Krogstie, J. (2021). Artificial intelligence and business value: A literature review. *Information Systems Frontiers*, 24, 1709–1734. DOI: 10.1007/s10796-021-10186-w.

FERMA (2019). Artificial intelligence applied to risk management. Retrieved from https://www.ferma.eu/app/uploads/2019/11/FERMA-AI-applied-to-RM-FINAL.pdf. Accessed 20 December 2021.

Fiore-Gartland, B. and Tanweer, A. (2016, April 4). Community-level data science and its spheres of influence: Beyond novelty squared. Retrieved from https://escience.washington.edu/community-level-data-science-and-its-spheres-of-influence-beyond-novelty-squared/. Accessed 18 January 2022.

Goodfirms (2021). The best 7 free and open-source artificial intelligence software. Retrieved from https://www.goodfirms.co/blog/best-free-open-source-Artificial-Intelligence-software. Accessed 15 December 2021.

Google Trends (2021). Search engine by terms and topics of artificial intelligence, machine learning, and deep learning from 1/1/2004 to 15/12/2021. Retrieved from https://trends.google.com/trends/explore?date=all&q=%2Fm%2F0mkz,%2Fm%2F01hyh_,Deep%20Learning. Accessed 15 December 2021.

Haenni, R. (2019, May 25). What is datum? Retrieved from https://datumassist.freshdesk.com/support/solutions/articles/44001696006-what-is-datum-. Accessed 24 January 2022.

Hernandez, A. (2020). Facial recognition in times of pandemic. Retrieved fromhttps://www.mobbeel.com/en/blog/facial-recognition-in-times-of-pandemic/. Acesssed 17 December 2021.

IFC (2021). *Artificial Intelligence in Emerging Markets: Opportunities, Trends, and Emerging Business Models.* Second and Expanded Edition, March 2021. Retrieved from https://www.ifc.org/wps/wcm/connect/95a40480-27b5-4b99-8b4c-7768ae6a53a2/AI-Report_Web.pdf?MOD =AJPERES&CVID=nhLrsRc. Accessed 12 January 2022.

Johnston, D.L. (1978). Scientists Become Managers — The 'T'-shaped man. *IEEE Engineering Management Review*, 6, 67–68. DOI: 10.1109/EMR.1978.4306682.

Kortli, Y., Jridi, M., Falou, A.A. and Atri, M. (2020). Face recognition systems: A survey. *Sensors*, 20. DOI: 10.3390/s20020342.

Lakshmi, V. and Bahli, B. (2020). Understanding the robotization landscape transformation: A centering resonance analysis. *Journal of Innovation & Knowledge*, 5(1), 59–67. DOI: 10.1016/j.jik.2019.01.005.

Lionbridge (2018). The 50 best free datasets for machine learning. Retrieved from https://lionbridge.ai/datasets/the-50-best-free-datasets-for-machine-learning/. Accessed 15 December 2021.

Marr, B. (2016). Big data: 33 brilliant and free data sources anyone can use. Retrieved from https://www.forbes.com/sites/bernardmarr/2016/02/12/big-data-35-brilliant-and-free-data-sources-for-2016/?sh=7d399323b54d. Accessed 15 December 2021.

Marr, B. (2018). Big data and AI: 30 amazing (and free) public data sources. Retrieved from https://bernardmarr.com/big-data-and-ai-30-amazing-and-free-public-data-sources/. Accessed 15 December 2021.

Matteson, S. (2021). How AI is improving operational efficiencies across oil and gas, healthcare, and more. Retrieved from https://www.techrepublic.com/article/how-ai-is-improving-operational-efficiencies-across-oil-and-gas-healthcare-and-more/. Accessed 17 January 2022.

Maxwell, J.C. (2019). *Leadershift: The 11 Essential Changes Every Leader Must Embrace.* Summary published by arrangement with HarperCollins Leadership, an imprint of HarperCollins Focus LLC. 288 pages, ISNB 978-0-7180-9850-6. Retrieved from https://www.utep.edu/edge/_Files/documents/dil-11-essential-changes.pdf. Accessed 15 December 2021.

NetObjex (2022). About NetObjex. An intelligent automation platform. Retrieved from https://www.netobjex.com/about-netobjex. Accessed 24 January 2022.

O'Brien, K., Pelling, M., Patwardhan, A., Hallegatte, S., Maskrey, A., Oki, T., Oswald-Spring, U., Wilbanks, T. and Yanda, P.Z. (2012). Toward a sustainable and resilient future. In *Managing the Risks of Extreme Events and Disasters to Advance Climate Change Adaptation*, C.B. Field, V. Barros, T.F. Stocker, D. Qin, D.J. Dokken, K.L. Ebi, M.D. Mastrandrea, K.J. Mach, G.-K. Plattner, S.K. Allen, M. Tignor, and P.M. Midgley (Eds.). A Special Report of Working Groups I and II of the Intergovernmental Panel on Climate Change (IPCC). Cambridge, UK and New York: Cambridge University Press, pp. 437–486.

Reddy, K.P.N., Alekhya, T., Manjula, T., Sushma, Krishnappa, R. (2020). AI-based attendance monitoring system. *International Journal of Innovative Technology and Exploring Engineering*, 9. DOI: 10.35940/ijitee.B1057.1292S19.

Stanford, C., Iriondo, R., and Shukla, P. (2020). Best public datasets for machine learning and data science. Retrieved from https://pub.towardsai.net/best-datasets-for-machine-learning-data-science-computer-vision-nlp-ai-c9541058cf4f. Accessed 15 December 2021.

Statista (2020). Where AI is aiding productivity. Retrieved from https://www.statista.com/chart/23779/ai-productivity-increase/. Accessed 20 January 2022.

Statista (2021a). Artificial intelligence (AI) market revenues worldwide in 2020 and forecasts from 2021 to 2024. Retrieved from https://www.statista.com/statistics/694638/worldwide-cognitive-and-artificial-intelligence-revenues/. Accessed 27 December 2021.

Statista (2021b). Digital identity solution market revenue worldwide in 2020 and 2026. Retrieved from https://www.statista.com/statistics/1263580/worldwide-digital-identity-solution-market-revenue/. Accessed 17 December 2021.

Statista (2021c). Facial recognition market size worldwide in 2020 and 2025. Retrieved from https://www.statista.com/statistics/1153970/worldwide-facial-recognition-revenue/. Accessed 17 December 2021.

Statista (2021d). Identity verification market revenue worldwide from 2017 to 2027. Retrieved from https://www.statista.com/statistics/1036470/worldwide-identity-verification-market-revenue/. Accessed 17 December 2021.

Suharwardy, M. (2021). AI based attendance system on low computing device. Retrieved from https://www.thenews.com.pk/print/886647-ai-based-attendance-system-on-low-computing-device. Accessed 17 December 2021.

THALES (2021). What is biometrics? Retrieved from https://www.thalesgroup.com/en/markets/digital-identity-and-security/government/inspired/biometrics. Accessed 17 December 2021.

Trahant, B., Warner Burke, W. and Koonce, R. (1997). 12 principles of organizational transformation. *Management Review*, 86(8), 17–21. Retrieved from https://ezproxy.lincoln.ac.nz/login?url=https://www.proquest.com/scholarly-journals/12-principles-organizational-transformation/docview/206687868/se-2?accountid=27890. Accessed 15 December 2021.

Vytalyx (2022). Cognitive & decentralized healthcare technologies. Retrieved from https://vytalyx.io/. Accessed 24 January 2022.

World Development Indicators (2022). Gross domestic product GDP. Retrieved from https://databank.worldbank.org/source/world-development-indicators. Accessed 26 May 2022.

Wu, S.J., Melnyk, S.A., and Flynn, B.B. (2010). Operational capabilities: The secret ingredient. *Decision Sciences*, 41(4), 721–754. DOI: 10.1111/j.1540-5915.2010.00294.x.

Xu, D., Guo, Y. and Huang, M. (2021). Can Artificial Intelligence improve firms' competitiveness during the COVID-19 pandemic: International evidence. *Emerging Markets Finance and Trade*, 57(10), 2812–2825. DOI: 10.1080/1540496X.2021.1899911.

https://doi.org/10.1142/9781800614239_bmatter

Index

T

U

V

W

Y

Printed in the USA
CPSIA information can be obtained
at www.ICGtesting.com
JSHW062128071023
49613JS00003B/79

9 781800 614222